D1131640

Early Female Development

Current Psychoanalytic Views

Early Female Development

Current Psychoanalytic Views

Edited by

Dale Mendell, Ph.D.

Psychoanalytic Training Program
Post Graduate Center for Mental Health
& National Institute for the
Psychotherapies
N.Y., N.Y.

SP MEDICAL & SCIENTIFIC BOOKS
a division of Spectrum Publications, Inc.
New York • London

SPECTRUM PUBLICATIONS, INC.
175-20 Wexford Terrace, Jamaica, N.Y. 11432

Library of Congress Cataloging in Publication Data
Main entry under title:

Early female development.

   Includes index.
   1. Woman—Psychology—Addresses, essays,
lectures. I. Mendell, Dale.
HQ1206.E32   155.6'33   80-22398
ISBN 0-89335-135-0   AACR2

Contributors

DALE MENDELL, Ph.D.
Faculty and Associate Supervisor, Psychoanalytic Training Program, Postgraduate Center for Mental Health
Senior Faculty and Supervisor, National Institute for the Psychotherapies
Faculty, Senior Supervisor and Training Analyst, Training Institute for Mental Health Practitioners

ANNI BERGMAN
Faculty, Clinical Psychology Doctoral Program, and Director, Day Treatment Program for Psychotic Children and Their Families, City University of New York
Research Associate of Margaret S. Mahler, M.D.
Co-author of *The Psychological Birth of the Human Infant*

MARIA V. BERGMANN
Faculty, New York Freudian Society, Chair of the Theodore Reik Lectures

RUTH FORMANEK, Ph.D.
Professor of Education and Supervising Psychologist, Hofstra University
Staff Psychologist, Jewish Community Services of Long Island
Co-author of *Charting Intellectual Development: A Practical Guide to Piaget* and *Why? Children's Questions*

LAURICE W. GLOVER, M.S.S.W.
Assistant Clinical Professor of Psychiatry, Einstein College of Medicine
Faculty and Supervisor, Psychoanalytic Training Program, Postgraduate Center for Mental Health
Senior Faculty, National Institute for the Psychotherapies
Faculty, Senior Supervisor and Training Analyst, Training Institute for Mental Health Practitioners

JUDITH S. KESTENBERG, M.D.
Co-director, Center for Parents and Children
Clinical Professor of Psychiatry and Training Analyst, New York University and Downstate University
Pediatric Research Psychiatrist, Hillside-Long Island Jewish Hopital
Author of *Children and Parents: Psychoanalytic Studies in Development*

FRANK M. LACHMANN, Ph.D.
Faculty, Senior Supervisor and Training Analyst, Psychoanalytic Training Program, Postgraduate Center for Mental Health
Co-author of *Psychoanalysis of Developmental Arrests: Theory and Treatment* and *The Search for Oneness*

MARION M. OLINER, Ph.D.
Faculty, Psychoanalytic Training Institute, New York Freudian Society
Faculty, Institute for Psychoanalytic Training and Research

MARTIN A. SILVERMAN, M.D.
Clinical Associate Professor of Psychiatry, Training and Supervising Analyst, Research Chairman, and Secretary of the Child Analysis Section, The Psychoanalytic Institute at New York University Medical Center
Former Senior Research Psychiatrist, Child Development Center, New York
Associate Editor, *The Psychoanalytic Quarterly*

Contents

Introduction

The past fifteen years have seen a resurgence of interest in the psychology of female development, impelled by factors both intrinsic and external to psychoanalysis. Within psychoanalysis, increasingly sophisticated formulations regarding ego development and object relations have modified and elaborated drive-oriented conceptualizations of psychosexual development. In addition, the recent focus upon narcissistic and borderline adult pathologies has led to a closer examination of the earliest phases of life, with emphasis upon early mother-child interactions and the nature of early identifications, narcissistic development and the formation of gender identity. The social and cultural changes reflected in the women's movement resulted in widespread charges that Freudian doctrine concerning female development was denigrating and phallocentric; in responding to this challenge, psychoanalytic theorists were stimulated to reconsider established hypotheses that viewed femininity as a secondary, defensive formulation. In addition, new discoveries and reinterpretations relating to fetal development and the physiology of the female orgasm challenged traditional conceptions about the masculine nature of libido.

These various strands of developing knowledge and interest intersect in the area of early female development and make it a focal point from which to investigate and resolve major issues in psychoanalytic thinking. As inconsistencies and errors in the classical formulations about female psychosexual development are discovered, and reformulations made through closely detailed observations based on current theoretical assumptions, they in turn illuminate issues in ego psychology, object relations and narcissistic development, and enlarge the entire body of psychoanalytic theory. Such considerations provided the impetus for this book, which has a threefold purpose: to present significant new or ongoing conceptualizations of early feminine development; to compare these and other contemporary conceptualizations with traditional formulations; and to illuminate aspects of the development of identifications, narcissistic development and the separation-individuation process through their interface with female psychosexual development.

The following collection of papers, all solicited and written specifically for this volume, highlight important aspects of female development from birth through latency. While chapters are arranged chronologically, following the unfolding of successive phases of normative female development, the book does not attempt to give equal weight to each developmental period; in some instances more than one chapter covers the same chronological period, in order to present significant, but divergent, points of view. As might be anticipated in a field in which there are numerous unresolved theoretical issues, the contributors have somewhat differing points of view about the process of development; however, each writer attempts, to the extent possible, to integrate work in progress with other current findings in the field.

The psychosexual issues of infancy are intimately related to physiological and social factors. In her chapter, "On the Origins of Gender Identity," Ruth Formanek treats the continuing process of attaining gender identity as the result of a number of confluent factors, including the biological, social and psychological. She summarizes the biological factors which contribute to gender identity formation and reviews pertinent psychological infant research. Formanek offers a critique of psychoanalytic theories such as those of Stoller and Galenson and Roiphe, and then proposes a possible schema for the development of gender identity based on the cognitive psychology of Piaget, the developmental principles of Heinz Werner and the psychoanalytic conceptualizations of Pinchas Noy.

Marion Oliner highlights the importance of "The Anal Phase," emphasizing the girl's problem with integrating anality into later genital development, in large part because of difficulty in separating from her mother. Oliner points out that psychoanalysts "on this side of the Atlantic" tend to telescope the oral and the phallic phases, thereby minimizing the considerable influence that anal phase factors have on characterological and psychosexual expressions of feminity. She therefore gives considerable attention to the recent views presented by the French school of psychoanalysis (which is strongly influenced by the writings of Melanie Klein and Ernest Jones) which considers the anal phase struggle between mother and daughter the most important determinant of later psychosexual development. Oliner concludes by presenting a new and integrated view of female development during the anal phase, based upon traditional drive theory, current ego psychology views and the contributions of the French school.

Anni Bergman has been associated with Margaret Mahler as a primary observer-investigator of the separation-individuation phase of child development, one of the most important and fruitful new developments of our time, both in terms of its effect upon the theory of child development and the understanding of adult pathology. Her present paper, "Considerations on the Development of the Girl During the Separation-Individuation Process," is a contribution towards understanding the influence of the interaction between the separation-individuation process and psychosexual development on the development of female sexual identity. The method used is that of direct child observation, supplemented by parent reports, during the first three years of life, plus a follow up study during elementary school. With painstaking care and empathy Bergman details the interaction of a number of factors which influence the girl's experiences in regard to her feminine identity. These include the little girl's identifications and interactions with her mother, her discovery of the anatomical difference, her resolution of the rapprochement crisis and the mother's concerns and reactions to her own and her daughter's femininity.

Judith S. Kestenberg has done pioneering work in discovering and elaborating upon conceptualizations that have only recently gained general psychoanalytic acceptance. Over twenty years ago, undeterred by the then prevalent view that girls were unaware of their inner-genital space until puberty and that the wish for a baby was a substitute for the wish for a penis, Kestenberg combined findings from her analyses of children and adults and her observations of normal young children and postulated a phase of development occurring between the anal and phallic phases, which she calls the "early maternal" or "The Inner-Genital Phase." She believes this period occurs in both girls and boys, although for the purposes of this volume, it is only discussed as it pertains to girls. Kestenberg considers this phase to be the cradle of later maternal behavior as well as the model for the vaginal type of slow, spreading sensual excitation. In this chapter Kestenberg also summarizes her schema of the female life cycle, emphasizing the role of the inner-genital modality during each developmental phase. In addition, the pre-genital and phallic phases, which respectively precede and follow the inner-genital phase, are presented from a specifically feminine point of view, rooted in female anatomy and physiology.

Laurice Glover and Dale Mendell present their study, "A Suggested Developmental Sequence for a Preoedipal Genital Phase." According to data derived from adult analyses, during the period of the girl's advance into genital sexuality, her libidinal development, her object relations and her ego functions are directed toward the exploration of the boundaries and functions of her femininity. Glover and Mendell neither see phallic preoccupations as a major theme during this period nor view feminine development as defensive or reactive; therefore, they have substituted the term "preoedipal genital" for the inappropriate term "phallic" to describe the phase. Their data suggests that the preoedipal genital phase occurs between the anal and oedipal phases. In broad terms, it can be said to encompass both Kestenberg's inner-genital phase and Edgcumbe and Burgner's phallic-narcissistic phase, although the correspondence among them is far from exact. Glover and Mendell end their chapter with a reassessment of major issues pertaining to this developmental period, including fears of genital mutilation, reactions to the penis and identifications and object relations with each parent.

In surveying models of female development, Blum notes that "the contribution pre-Oedipal femininity makes to the onset and outcome of the Oedipal phase has not yet been sufficiently explored" (1976, p. 173). Maria V. Bergmann's chapter on "The Female Oedipus Complex: Its Antecedents and

Evolution'' is just such an exploration; Bergmann focuses upon the development of those pregenital and genital psychic precursors, including maternal identifications, the resolution of the rapprochement crisis, object relations and ego experiences, which influence and frequently distort the oedipal situation. The role of the preoedipal mother and her psychic representation is stressed in Bergmann's reassessment of traditional thinking about masochism and superego development. The chapter concludes with a profile of a contemporary type of female patient whose unresolved preoedipal problems, demonstrated by failures in identifications with both parents, result in an inability to deal with oedipal tasks.

Latency is well-known as a period when there is a great advance in the use of ego apparatus, both in the service of defense and of conflict-free reaching out for new skills and learnings. In "The Latency Period" Martin A. Silverman elaborates the various defenses most frequently utilized during this phase of development; he presents the latency girl as using her rapidly evolving ego apparatus, independence and reality testing to correct early distortions about deprivation and damage and to compensate her for oedipal loss. Silverman's far-ranging, imaginative discussion vividly portrays the intense, increasingly structured fantasy and interpersonal life of the latency girl and makes it clear that there is no respite from developmental struggles during the latency phase.

Frank M. Lachmann's chapter on "Narcissistic Development" explores the nature of the relationship between the development of narcissism and female psychosexual development. Lachmann summarizes and clarifies the various, contradictory theories of narcissism, including the seminal and controversial ideas of Heinz Kohut. He critically examines the classic view of narcissism as a normal feminine attribute, illustrates the intimate relationship of that viewpoint with the traditional understanding of women as masochistic, and utilizes recent conceptualizations in the area of structuralization and differentiation of self and object representations to revise traditional theory. "When narcissism is viewed from the standpoint of the function that . . . mental acts perform with respect to the maintenance (and) cohesion . . . of the self-representation, the psychosexual development can be seen as contributing to the development of separated, articulated self and object representations." In Lachmann's conceptualization, a synthesis of ego psychological views on self and object differentiation and the structure of the representational world is combined splendidly and naturally with Kohut's theory of narcissistic development to provide a model which is enriching to both.

The observations and conceptualizations regarding early feminine development presented by the contributors to this volume have been formulated against a background of new psychoanalytic knowledge regarding the nature of pre- and post-oedipal cognitive, libidinal, narcissistic and ego development. As a result it is now generally accepted that female development is primary and dominant. Areas of early development unique to the girl include a very early sense of female identity, the specific nature of early identifications, the early discovery of both internal and external genitalia, and the characteristic and separate meanings of the preoedipal attachment to each parent. Consonant with these findings, current schematizations of female sexual development differ markedly from the classic psychoanalytic model, which considers femininity to be a secondary, defensive formation.

One consequence of the recognition of the uniqueness of the girl's early development is the dissociation of the origins of femininity from the discovery of the sexual anatomical difference. As a result, penis envy, traditionally seen as the bedrock of female development, can now be considered as but one of a number of developmental phenomena. Each writer in this book has utilized the new freedom to deal with this issue by offering somewhat differing views as to importance, timing, intensity, phase-specificity, meaning and later impact. They present penis envy in the larger context of the ongoing narcissistic, cognitive, identificatory and object relational processes which make up the structuralization of the growing girl's development. Similarly, a number of other topics, notably the unique relationship of the girl to her mother, the concept of preoedipal genitality, the formation of gender identity and the development of narcissism are given new meanings in terms of the girl's evolving object relations, sexuality and ego development. To conclude, the articles in this book deal with a host of issues inherent in early feminine development in ways which push at the boundaries of current knowledge in the field.

I would like to thank James Fosshage, Stanley Lieberfreund, Phyllis Perera and, particularly, Jean Kemble for their assistance in discussing and amending portions of the manuscript. I am indebted to the authors who contributed their knowledge and efforts on behalf of this volume. I would also like to express my appreciation to my son, Aaron Cohen, and my mother, Clara Malmude, for their secretarial and editorial assistance.

Dale Mendell

Early Female Development

Current Psychoanalytic Views

1

On the Origins of Gender Identity

RUTH FORMANEK

I INTRODUCTION

Major questions of origin and development lie uncharted in the area between the physiological and the psychological: the origins of awareness and of self, the beginnings of structuring of the mind, the origin and development of gender identity. This paper concerns the development of feminine gender identity and assumes an epigenetic point of view. It proposes that gender identity, as other aspects of personality, does not arise fully formed at a given age as the result of given experiences. Rather, gender identity is the result of an integration by each individual of many confluent factors continuing well beyond childhood. These factors are originally physical — chromosomal, hormonal, anatomical. In the course of development, the importance of the physical factors in regard to gender identity formation recedes and is overridden by social and psychological factors. The latter are the more complex and have been the subject of extensive theorizing and controversy. We know something about how each factor contributes to the total picture, but how all are integrated to form a stable identity remains conjectural — perhaps forever.

In this section, I shall briefly outline the physical contributions as far as they are known. Early social influences are discussed in section II, which deals with infant research and studies on parental influences. Section III, on psychoanalytic views, briefly reviews Freud's ''conflict'' theory of the development of feminine identity, Stoller's ''non-conflictual'' revision, the observations of psychoanalytic infant researchers Mahler et al., and Galenson and Roiphe. Section IV postulates that the development of gender identity parallels and represents an aspect of the development of the sense of self. This process is conceptualized on two levels, following Noy (1979), by means of both primary and secondary process thought, and following the developmentalist principles of Piaget and Heinz Werner.

First some definitions:

The term *sex* has a biological meaning and refers to chromosomes, external and internal genitalia, hormonal states, etc. *Gender*, on the other hand, has psychological or social rather than biological connotations. "If the proper terms for sex are 'male' and 'female,' the corresponding terms for gender are 'masculine' and 'feminine.'" Gender terms may be independent of biological sex. Gender is the amount of masculinity or femininity found in a person, and obviously, while there are mixtures of both in many humans, the normal male has a preponderance of masculinity and the normal female a preponderance of femininity (Stoller, 1977).

Gender assignment is a special case of gender attribution which occurs at birth after the inspection of genitals categorizes the infant as either male or female.

Gender identity refers to the individual's own feelings, knowledge or awareness — conscious or unconscious — of whether he/she is man or woman. It is self-attribution of gender, and may differ from attributions made by others.

Core gender identity develops very early and, once it is established, at about eighteen to twenty-four months, cannot be changed any more. Little is known about this period in normal children and most information has come from cases in which the initial gender assignment was erroneous. Attempts therefore had to be made to "correct" it by reassigning the child and making the necessary hormonal and/or surgical changes.

Gender role includes a set of prescriptions and proscriptions for behavior — expectations about what behaviors are appropriate for a person holding a particular position within a particular social context. Prescribed and proscribed behavior for gender roles includes almost all areas of functioning: interests, activities, occupations, skills, dress, gestures, choice of sexual partner, etc. Terms such as "masculine" and "feminine" are used although their definitions vary with societal context as well as time period.

Long before gender identity develops, chromosomes accomplish the first sexual differentiation. They are the original determiners of sex: Mammals with two X chromosomes are female, and those with one X and one Y are male. The sex of the child depends on the sex of the sperm.

During the earliest stages of fetal development, only examination of the chromosomes can tell whether the embryo is male or female. With the growth of the fetus, the potential for both male and female internal sexual structures develops. When the gonad — testes or ovaries — first appears, it looks the same in both sexes, although it develops faster in the male. The intermediate steps between chromosomal determination and its subsequent effects on the embryo are not known. Between seven and eight weeks after fertilization, the male gonad is recognizable as a testis; not until two weeks later is the female gonad recognizable as an ovary. Nine weeks after fertilization, testosterone is secreted in the testes which causes the previously undifferentiated external genitalia to form a penis and scrotum. This formation is complete about thirteen weeks after fertilization. The testes also secrete a second hormone which causes atrophy of the structures that in females develop into the Fallopian tubes. In the absence of testosterone stimulation, the external genitalia develop about twelve weeks after fertilization into those of the female, without specific hormonal induction, and the potentially male structures atrophy. It seems to be generally true throughout sex differentiation that the female is the "basic" sex into which embryos develop if not stimulated to do otherwise.

While chromosomes seem to induce hormonal production, hormonal messages further differentiate the fetus: they cause the ovary to operate cyclicly, and the testis to operate non-cyclicly. While the messages come from the pituitary gland, they are initiated and controlled by the hypothalamus. This suggests that not only does the endocrine system have to be differentiated according to sex, but the hypothalamus does also, and that endocrine maleness is controlled by the hypothalamus and not by the testis or the pituitary.

Although critical periods for the action of hormones on the brain have been found in animals and are presumed to exist in human beings, none have been determined so far. In animals a second and higher brain center controlling types of mating behavior is also irreversibly differentiated, but there is no evidence for its existence in humans.

In addition to chromosomal, hormonal, and anatomical differences, the most important innate difference between male and female is in the rate of maturing. Halfway through the fetal period, the girl's skeleton is about three weeks more mature than the boy's. At birth, the skeletal difference corresponds to four to six weeks of maturation. Girls grow up faster than boys, enter puberty, and cease to grow at an earlier age than boys. In animals the degree of hormonal influence seems to depend on the time when hormones are administered during gestation and thus suggests a critical period (Tanner, 1978).

The most important determination of gender is neither chromosomal nor hormonal, *but social and psychological*, beginning with gender assignment. Studies by Money and Ehrhardt (1972), Stoller (1977), and others provide ample evidence of overriding social factors in infants born with genetic or hormonal sex ambiguities, so-called "errors of nature."

There are two main types of chromosomal errors: instead of *XX* or *XY* chromosomes, a fertilized ovum may have only a single *X* chromosome, or Turner's Syndrome. The infant will be a girl in external appearance, but with ovaries degenerating early in childhood and resulting in infertility. The other error—Klinefelter's Syndrome, or chromosomal type *XXY*—produces boys with long arms and legs, small testes, reduced fertility and, sometimes, slight mental retardation. There are other rare chromosomal abnormalities: *XXX*, *XXXY* and *XYY*. The latter produces particularly tall men.

There are hormonal "errors" owing to the administration of male hormone to the pregnant mother in order to prevent threatened abortion. Money and Ehrhardt interviewed twenty-five fetally androgenized genetic females and compared them to genetic females not androgenized, i.e., normal females. The androgenized girls ranged from four to sixteen years of age, had been receiving cortisone since birth, and/or had undergone surgical femininization early in life to give their genitals a more feminine appearance. The researchers suggest that genetic females androgenized in utero and reared as girls have a high chance of being tomboys in their behavior. For example, the androgenized girls showed more interest in masculine clothing and toys than did the control subjects. They had little interest in infant care and feminine pursuits, were considered tomboys by their mothers, and had a greater interest in careers than many girls their age, but not to the exclusion of "eventual romance, marriage and motherhood." "Tomboyish girls generally prefer slacks and shorts to frills and furbelows, though they do not have an aversion to dressing up for special occasions. Their preferred cosmetic is perfume." (Money, 1977, p. 69)

Several methodological faults cast doubt on the validity of these findings. The androgenized girls, as aware of their unique status as were their parents, were probably subject to different socialization experiences. These girls were also more familiar with the interviewers and the clinical setting than were the control subjects. Thus, the control group subjects may have been more anxious and may have responded in more stereotypically feminine ways to the interviewers' questions. The interviewers, moreover, knew which girls had been androgenized and which had not.

These studies precipitously bridge the hormone-behavior gap. Whether biologically based sex differences will cause differential behavioral predisposition is unclear. Social factors such as gender assignment and gender-specific rearing appear to obscure genetic and hormonal differences. Parents' attribution of gender to their infant is socially determined and occurs interpersonally. But the parents' psychological state determines their expectations: What is the conscious and unconscious meaning of becoming a parent? Did parents wish for a girl or a boy? What qualities do they project onto their infant? Such questions and many more have stimulated infant development research studies, to which we next turn.

II   INFANT RESEARCH

The recent profusion of research on infants has begun to recognize and clarify their capabilities. We now regard the infant as a "competent" organism. Almost immediately after birth, infants demonstrate that they can imitate tongue protrusions (Meltzoff and Moore, 1977) and follow a red toy with their eyes — as early as fifteen minutes after birth for some, and within four days after birth for most. In the early months, they prefer patterns, such as checkerboards and bullseye targets, to plain colors and show a special interest in patterns resembling the human face. Piaget (1952), one of the first researchers to note infants' capabilities, describes the reactions of his daughter at sixteen days of age as he held a lighted match about ten inches away from her face: "Only her expression changes at the sight of it and then she moves her head as though to find the light again. She does not succeed despite the dim light in the room. At twenty-four days, on the other hand, she follows the match perfectly under the same conditions. On subsequent days, her eyes follow the movements of my hand, a moving handkerchief, etc." (p. 63)

Until recently, many researchers perceived infants as immature in regard to their contact with their world, and most studies on their competence have been done only since the 1950s. Yet, at the same time, some writers — mostly psychoanalytical ones — considered infants capable of comprehending abstract phenomena: relationships among family members, especially of the parents to each other, the role of the father in conception, sexual differentiation as based on genital differences, and other notions. Present research suggests that infants' perceptual, motor, and cognitive apparatuses are more mature at birth and develop more rapidly in the first few years of life than had previously been supposed. However, despite these rapid developments, the accumulation of experience is a slow process — slower than had been supposed. Fleeting and repeating images must be stored, remembered and transformed into intuitive concepts, unstable and fragmentary at first and incompletely related to other similar concepts.

Infant research has its share of methodological problems:

1. The infant's state is important: A tired or hungry or colicky infant differs from a sleeping or peacefully alert one. And many infant behaviors lack stability. The more stable ones include sucking rate, formula consumption, and crying following the removal of a pacifier. When more stable behaviors were examined for sex differences, only one out of twelve studied was found to show one: Boys were able to lift their chins higher than girls when placed on their stomachs (Bell et al., 1971).

2. Observers of infant behavior usually know the babies' sex, and their own biases could affect their observations and ratings. In a study which explored the influence of observer bias, observers rated the same infant as displaying different emotions and different levels of emotional arousal when the infant was described as a girl than when it was described as a boy (Condry and Condry, 1976).

3. Sex differences often really reflect maturational differences. Since, on the average, girls are born more mature than boys, the "sex difference" may be a temporary maturational difference. In general, when there are significant sex differences, it is usually the girl who is more mature.

4. The anchoring of observation to theory is difficult. We only observe what is salient to us on the basis of knowledge of our theory; we focus on a particular phenomenon under scrutiny and overlook others not part of our theory.

On the one hand, we cannot do research without hypotheses derived from theory. On the other hand, we are tempted to omit the safeguards which might stand in the way of our supporting the hypotheses under study. We are critical of other researchers' sloppy methods, but take wildly intuitive leaps ourselves.

Psychological differences between boy and girl infants which may be precursors to later differences include the following:

1. Exploration, Aggression and Irritability

There is little evidence for early sex differences. Neither high activity levels nor aggression are characteristic of infant boys as they are later on in childhood. While infant boys appear to be more irritable, birth complications, which are more frequent with boys, have to be considered in addition to the boys' usually greater immaturity. One might speculate that early irritability interacts with parental expectations of greater aggressivity, independence, resistance, and negativism in boys.

The spontaneous behaviors in the newborn which occur in the absence of external or known visceral stimuli have been studied by Korner (1969). These behaviors consist of neonatal startles, smiles, erections, and reflex sucks. Korner related them to the state of the infant, sex, and individuality in thirty-two two– and three-day-old healthy neonates. She concluded that there is "a highly significant relation between state and the type and frequency of the spontaneous behaviors. The frequencies are highest during regular sleep when the infant is most deafferented and they diminish in direct proportion to the infant's closeness to wakefulness." Sex differences were found and "reflect a consistent trend that males startle more in all states and females engage more frequently in reflex smiles and bursts of rhythmical mouthing . . . females make up in smiles and reflex sucks what they lack in startles. The data also suggest that erections are spontaneous behaviors which occur over and above the other discharge behaviors." The function of the spontaneous behaviors may be to provide endogenous afferent stimulation under conditions of deafferentiation, during a period when such stimulation may be critical for the developing central nervous system, and may have significance for later development.

Korner also found that "the use of rhythmical mouthing bears no relation to the infant's gross mouthing, sucking or tonguing. . . . gross mouthing increases significantly with time since the last feeding, whereas rhythmical mouthing shows no relation to hunger." (p. 1046). She now leaps to fit this finding into theory: "The female's greater tendency in the direction of rhythmical mouthing may highlight that, congenitally, she may rely more heavily in her development on the oral mode, as was suggested by Erikson (1950)."

2. Play Behavior

"In the first year of life, boys and girls play with the same toys and do the same amount of banging and cuddling. In the second year, differences begin to appear in some, but not all, studies. By the beginning of the third year, boys spend more time with guns, blocks and trucks, girls with stuffed animals, dolls, puzzles, and pegboards. And by the end of the third year, sex differences in toy play are firmly established'' (Brooks-Gunn and Matthews, 1979).

3. Dependency and Attachment

Lewis and Kreitzberg (1979) followed 250 infants and their mothers over the first two years of life. The investigators found that one-year-old boys were more upset by their mother's preparation for departure, crying twice as often as the girls, and staying closer to their mothers. As though the mothers anticipated their sons' distress, they tended to prepare their sons for the departure, often giving them instructions as to what to do while mother was gone. However, while the mothers were gone, the girls began to cry sooner than the boys, perhaps because of the paucity of instruction given or perhaps for some other reason. When the mothers reappeared, the boys again cried more than the girls, with the mothers responding by holding their sons more.

Goldberg and Lewis (1969) and Brooks and Lewis (1975) found that, in free-play situations in which the mother was present, boys and girls engaged in similar activities. Girls spent more time near their mothers and looked at and babbled to their mothers more often than did boys. But these differences have not been found by all investigators. In the Lewis and Kreitzberg study, girls talked to, looked at, and smiled at the mother more than the boys did, while the boys fretted and cried more than the girls. Girls tended to sit right by the mother, while boys played a few feet away, but not across the room.

Girls sometimes exhibit wariness toward strangers earlier than boys, perhaps because of their earlier maturation (Beckwith, 1972; Robson, Pederson and Moss, 1969). But soon the boys seem to catch up with the girls.

4. Perception

John Watson (1969) found that fourteen-week-old boys were more responsive to visual information presented alone, girls to auditory and visual information presented together. While this finding has been cited as support for the belief that boys are attuned to sight, girls to sound, an alternative interpretation is that girls mature more quickly than boys. Since the auditory system develops later than the visual one, girls, with the greater maturity, have auditory capabilities earlier than boys.

Hoffman (1976) and others have studied the newborn's response to another baby's cry and have found that newborn girls cry longer than newborn boys when hearing a tape of another crying baby (Hoffman and Levine, 1976; Sagi and Hoffman, 1976). In some studies, girls seem to respond and interact more positively with their mothers and vocalize more to faces than to geometric forms. Yet other studies have failed to find sex differences in vocalization patterns. No sex differences in smiling have been reported.

5. Language

Michael Lewis and Roy Freedle (1973) found that mothers vocalized more to their three-month-old daughters than to their three-month-old sons, and daughters vocalized more in response to their mothers' vocalizations than did the sons, even though the boys and girls did not differ in their spontaneous babbling.

Maccoby and Jacklin (1974), on the basis of their summary of sex differences throughout childhood, consider the following differences to be *unfounded* beliefs: (1) that girls are more "social" than boys; (2) that girls are more "suggestible" than boys; (3) that girls have lower self-esteem; (4) that girls are better at rote learning and simple repetitive tasks, boys at tasks that require higher-level cognitive processing and the inhibition of previously learned responses; (5) that boys are more "analytic"; (6) that girls are more affected by heredity, boys by environment; (7) that girls lack achievement motivation; (8) that girls are auditory, boys visual.

They found the following sex differences *fairly well established*: (1) that girls have greater verbal ability than boys; (2) that boys excel in visual-spatial ability; (3) that boys excel in mathematical ability; and (4) that boys are more aggressive.

Too little evidence was obtained, or findings were ambiguous, on the following: tactile sensitivity, fear, timidity, and anxiety; activity level, competitiveness, dominance, compliance, nurturance and "maternal" behavior.

While the evidence is not overwhelming, some early sex differences appear to exist and result from a combination of factors: Lack of maturity causes the male infant to receive more attention; maturity combines with such factors as position among siblings and parental psychological make-up. Research is presently inadequate, especially in regard to the father's role, to which we next turn.

The Role of the Father

Schaffer (1977) has defined four essential components in the mother-infant relationship: (1) the provision of stimulation; (2) sensitivity to the infant's needs for the purpose of aiding his organizing processes; (3) the growth of an affectional bond between mother and infant; and (4) constancy in this relationship. The biological mother is not the only one to fill this role. Schaffer outlines psychological needs which may be provided by either mother or father. "The mother," says Schaffer, "can be a person of either sex." (See also Chodorow, 1978.)

The father's role in relation to the infant may be conceptualized in two ways: (1) directly interacting with his infant; and (2) indirectly, as a consequence of the father's interactions with the mother. Investigators have studied the father's role by comparing mothers and fathers in regard to their observed behaviors, or infants are observed relating to their parents.

In the past, the mother was considered the primary caretaker, and the infant's social competencies were inadequately understood; as a consequence, the role of the father was consistently neglected. Yet it is clear that even prior to direct interactions, fathers influence their infants by means of their relationship to the mother. Burlingham (1973) has stated that the father assists the process of individuation in the small child. Greenacre (1960), Mahler et al. (1975), and Abelin (1971) have stressed that the father's relationship to the mother affects the child indirectly.

Indirect father effects occur prenatally. For example, a wife's successful adaptation to pregnancy is associated with her husband's support (Shereshefsky and Yarrow, 1973). In a retrospective study, mothers who experienced postpartum depressions characterized their husbands as cold and distant (Kaplan and Blackman, 1969). Discrepant perceptions of the infant's behavior and temperament, which are most likely to occur when parents have few shared experiences with their baby, may influence the interactions of each parent with the infant (Pederson, Anderson and Cain, 1977).

The father's expectations and projections influence his perception of his infant. Rubin et al. (1974) investigated the reactions of parents to their newborn infants. Parents perceived male infants to be different in "personality" from female infants in the first twenty-four hours of the baby's life — despite the fact that doctors reported no significant objective differences in size, activity level, health, and so on. Both mothers and fathers agreed on the sex differences, disagreeing with each other on only one trait: Fathers thought the girls were more cuddly, and mothers thought the boys were more cuddly. Burlingham and Freud (1944) stated that "the infant's emotional relationship to its father . . . is an integral part of its emotional life and a necessary ingredient in the complex forces which work towards the formation of its character and personality."

Developmentally, a "critical period" may exist in the development of the father's attraction toward and interest in the child. Fathers who had no contact with their infants during the first few months may have difficulty showing affection for the child later on (Greenberg and Morris, 1974).

Studies of young children's behaviors toward mothers and fathers have been inconclusive. Some researchers have found differences at particular times, and others have found none. One- and two-year-old children interacting with mothers and fathers in structured playroom situations show few differences in behavior toward parents. Although some one-year-olds preferred mother for touching or staying near, by two years of age few differences were present (Lewis et al., 1973). In another study, infants showed little parent preference until twelve months of age. After that, about 55% of the children preferred the mother, 25% preferred the father and 20% preferred either parent over a stranger. Mothers and fathers elicited about equal amounts of separation protest when they left the room in a "strange situation" paradigm (Kotelchuk, 1972).

The sex of an infant, as well as birth order, appears to affect differences in parental response. Fathers touched and vocalized to their first-born sons more than to later-born sons or daughters of any birth order (Parke and O'Leary, 1975, in Lamb). Gewirtz and Gewirtz (1968) report that Israeli fathers remain longer in the children's house with their four-month-old sons than with a daughter.

That children know the word "daddy' before they know the word "mommy" has been observed by linguists (Jakobson, 1962) and researched by Brooks and Lewis (1975) with infants aged nine to thirty-six months. At fifteen months, 25% of the infants labeled pictures of their fathers correctly; no infants labeled pictures of their mothers. By eighteen months, all infants labeled pictures of their fathers correctly.

The present paucity of research data permits no definite conclusions. Yet, it seems clear that infants very early form close affectional ties with their fathers, that some infants react differently to the father than to the mother before the first year of life, and that there are both direct and indirect effects of the father on the infant. Too few studies have considered social class or sibling position effects. The absence of longitudinal studies prevents speculations on the beginnings of identification.

III PSYCHOANALYTIC VIEWS

Although Freud's views of female sexuality were based primarily on the memories and reconstructions of adults, he longed for more accurate information: "If you want to know more about femininity, you must interrogate your experience, or turn to the poets, or else wait until science can give you more profound and more coherent information" (Freud, 1933, quoted by Greenacre, p. 238).

Freud believed that the genital sexual life of children emerged in observable form about the third or fourth year of life, and that we knew more about the sexuality of little boys than of little girls. He stressed the importance of infantile masturbation, its associated fantasies, and the response of parents which contributes to castration anxiety. Masturbation in girls, according to Freud, involved at first only the clitoris. The vagina, less accessible and invisible to direct observation, was probably unknown to the little girl. Thus, he believed that all sexuality in both boys and girls through the phallic phase was a masculine one. Freud also believed that little girls masturbated less frequently and less energetically than little boys, and that masturbation is further removed from the nature of women than it is from that of men. The following was Freud's formula for the little girls' waning interest in masturbation: "Observation of anatomical difference → castration complex → penis envy → renunciation (in the phallic phase) of pleasure in clitoridal stimulation (masculine sexuality), feelings of inferiority—essential step in attainment of definitive feminity" (Kleeman, 1977, p. 8).

"The discovery that she is castrated is a turning-point in a girl's growth . . . the little girl has hitherto lived in a masculine way, has been able to get pleasure by the excitation of her clitoris . . . now, owing to the influence of her penis-envy, she loses her enjoyment in her phallic sexuality" (Freud, 1933, quoted by Kleeman, p. 8). The girl's recognition of the anatomical difference sets in motion her castration complex, her sense of inferiority and penis-envy. She turns to the father with the wish for a baby to compensate for her inferiority. "In girls, the Oedipus complex is a secondary formation. The operation of the castration complex precedes it and prepares for it . . . .Whereas in boys the Oedipus complex is destroyed by the castration complex, in girls it is made possible and led up to by the castration complex" (Freud, 1925, quoted by Kleeman, p. 9).

> A shift of the leading erotogenic zone from the clitoris to the vagina occurs as the girl turns into a woman and replaces childish masculinity with the assumption of the essence of femininity.

Freud's conception of women was challenged early by Horney (1926) and Klein (1932), among others. Horney stated that psychoanalytical thinking in regard to the development of women has been considered in masculine developmental terms. She suggests that, if we look at the present analytical picture of feminine development, we note that it does not differ "by a hair's breadth from the typical ideas that the boy has of the girl" (Miller 1973, p. 8). These typical ideas include: "Naive assumptions that girls as well as boys possess a penis; realization of the absence of the penis; idea that the girl is a castrated, mutilated boy; belief that the girl has suffered punishment that also threatens him; the girl is regarded as inferior, the boy is unable to imagine how the girl can ever get over this loss or envy; the boy dreads her envy" (Miller 1973, p. 9).

Recent writings have been influenced by direct observation of infants and children, by the work of Masters and Johnson (1966), Money and Ehrhardt (1972), studies on transsexuals, and show the influence of the women's movement which has systematically, and often bitterly, challenged Freud's views of the inferiority of women. There have been three main revisions of Freud's original position: one by Stoller (1977), which takes issue with the development of gender identity on the basis of conflict, e.g., penis envy, castration anxiety. Another view is that of Mahler et al. (1975) who chart the development of gender identity during the separation-individuation process. Galenson and Roiphe (1977) suggest that the developments leading to gender identity formation occur earlier in childhood than Freud assumed.

Stoller suggests that gender differentiations arise not only out of conflict, but out of an earlier conflict-free period during which a "core gender identity" is established. He asks, "Were it not for Freud's theorizing, would any one have doubted the existence of primary femininity?" (p. 68). According to Stoller, Freud's theory did not consider the many factors during the first months and years of life in regard to the origins of femininity: (1) biological factors such as the effect of circulating fetal sex hormones on the brain of the fetus; (2) sex assignment — the announcement at the time of birth to the parents that they have a boy or a girl; (3) parental attitudes — the effects of the sex assignment on parents and then reflected back onto the infant; (4) "biopsychic" phenomena — early postnatal effects caused by certain habitual patterns of handling the infant — conditioning, imprinting or other forms of nonconflictual learning; (5) developing body ego — sensations, especially from the genitals, that define the child's dimensions.

Stoller believes that the development of femininity may be divided into two phases, both of which lead to adult femininity, but each of which contributes in a different manner. The first, nonconflictual in origin, contributes a sense of femaleness and some of what allows for one's looking feminine; the second, the result of conflict, especially oedipal, "produces a richer and more complicated femininity, not merely one of appearance, but one enriched by desires to perform with the substance, rather than just the facade, of femininity" (p. 77).

Yet Stoller's disagreement with Freud's theory is only partial. He adds a preoedipal dimension where influences are not the result of conflicts in object relations but of simpler learning (e.g., conditioning, imprinting). He states that the production of "a richer and more complicated femininity" is the result of conflict, and leaves unclear the difference between "appearance," or facade, of femininity, and "substance of femininity." Stoller strays from Freud's original position, but not very far.

Mahler et al. (1975) have contributed infant observations. They speak of the "feeling of the mother about her child's body [which] may well have some early patterning influence . . . .Mothers often commented that the bodies of their girl babies felt different from those of the boys.''

''Whatever sexual differences may have pre-existed in the area of innate ego apparatuses and of early ego modes, they certainly were greatly complicated, and generally compounded, by the effects of the child's discovery of the anatomical sexual difference . . . sometimes during the sixteen- to seventeen-month period or even earlier, but more often in the twentieth or twenty-first months'' (p. 104).

''The boy's discovery of his own penis usually took place much earlier . . . but there is uncertainty as to its emotional impact. Around the twelfth to fourteenth month, however, we have observed that the upright position facilitates the visual and sensory-motor exploration of the penis . . . .It would seem that the little boy becomes aware of the involuntary movement of his penis at the same time that he develops mastery of his own body movement in the erect position.'' But Mahler et al. suggest that for boys and girls alike, ''in the very next month following the attainment of active, free locomotion, great strides were made toward asserting their individuality. This seems to be the first great step toward identity formation'' (p. 72).

''The girls' discovery of the penis confronted them with something that they themselves are lacking. This discovery brought on a range of behavior clearly indicating the girls' anxiety, anger and defiance. They wanted to undo the sexual difference. Therefore, it seemed to us that, in girls, masturbation took on a desperate and aggression-saturated quality more often than in boys and at an earlier age. . . .This discovery coincides with the emergence of the affect of envy; in some of our girls, early penis envy may have accounted for the persistent predominance of this affect'' (p. 105).

Mahler et al. are critical of their own research procedures, which they characterize as ''an appropriate balance between free-floating psychoanalytic observation and pre-fixed experimental design. They are further aware that they ''have not achieved freedom from bias, from halo, from evaluative considerations,'' in their assessment of evidence. While they describe their observations as ''frankly highly clinical and open-ended,'' they relied on ''repeated encounters with phenomena in a somewhat standardized situation, and subject to a fair degree of consensual validation'' (p. 18). Film data further aided the analysis of their observations.

Galenson and Roiphe (1977), on the other hand, seem less concerned with methodological rigor. They studied seventy children during nine years of research. Two mother-and-child pairs attended four two-hour sessions each week. Two observers gathered developmental information from the mother and observed the child's behavior, recording the data immediately after the observation session. Galenson and Roiphe speculate (as did Freud) that sexual drive organization exerts a special and exemplary role during the various psychosexual stages, but that drive organization is, in turn, consistently and extensively influenced by object relations. They believe that "very early genital zone experiences during the first sixteen months of life contribute to a vague sense of sexual identity, and undoubtedly exert an influence over many ego functions. Some genital sensations probably occur consistently in conjunction with feeding, as well as during many other interactions of the mother and her young infant" (p. 35). Between sixteen and nineteen months, the "genital zone emerges as a distinct and differentiated source of endogenous pleasure . . . exerting a new and crucial influence upon the sense of sexual identity, object relations, basic mood, and many aspects of ego functioning, such as the elaboration of fantasy and graphic representation in girls and the increased use of the motor apparatus in boys—the latter probably in the service of denial" (p. 54). Galenson and Roiphe differ with Freud in that they locate such developments in the preoedipal period. They believe that this "early genital phase" will inevitably shape oedipal phase developments.

The discovery of the sexual difference and the new genital sensations of the early genital phase are "unique, exemplary and of equal importance to the oral and anal aspects of psychosexual development which have preceded them . . . the little girl's reactions to the discovery of the sexual differences . . . include complex preoedipal castration reactions and penis envy, basic mood changes and the development of many defensive measures. There may, in addition, be a partial or complete renunciation of direct masturbation" (p. 54). Freud's original position, that penis envy and the feminine castration complex exert crucial influences on feminine development, is emphasized by Galenson and Roiphe. They believe, however, that these developments occur earlier than Freud had anticipated and that they are closely intertwined with fears of object and anal loss and the shape of an already developing, although vague, sense of femininity, stemming from early bodily and affective experiences with both parents. The castration reactions which vary in intensity from child to child, "profoundly influence ego development, in both enhancing and inhibiting directions." (p. 55).

While Galenson and Roiphe mention the importance of object relationships, they don't describe differences in the infants' relationships to their parents: whether parents encourage or discourage their children's genital play, whether they offer them the toys—especially pens, which the girls in their sample take only from their fathers—is left unclear. It is difficult to establish young children's toy preferences, and Galenson and Roiphe offer no data on how preferences were determined. It is unclear, for example, how they established that only girls reached for their fathers' pens. Did they observe it? Did they ask the parents? What were the questions? Did the boys reach for anything else? Did mothers have pens?

Equally unclear is the nature of the evidence on the interference with symbolic representations. One suspects that the researchers, at times, selected only certain types of evidence, while (perhaps unconsciously) omitting others. More research is needed to clarify the issues.

Observer bias may be involved in Galenson's and Roiphe's conclusions. In regard to masturbation, Kleeman (1977) has suggested that "the anatomy of the boy directs his sexuality outward and is more clearly visible, compared with the girl, so that *even the observer* [my italics—RF] of the girl's genital self-stimulation sees less" (p. 22).

Mischel (1973) has suggested that, in general, ratings may largely reflect the 'implicit' personality theory of the individual rather than the characteristics of the individual being rated.

Kleeman believes that genital play contributes to core gender identity although he does not consider it a major organizer of behavior, as Freud did. He describes a developmental line of genital activity beginning in the newborn period and emerging as genital-exploration play, probably more intense and vigorous in boys than in girls during the first year. An increase in genital sensation and genital awareness seems to occur sometime between fifteen and twenty-four months, which, however, may not be due to endogenous genital arousal, but may be derived from a confluence of factors. Such factors might include progressive body-image development and interaction with parents and others. According to Kleeman's observations, although their genitals are less visible and their genital and urinary anatomy less clearly understood by them, girls are also capable of intense and vigorous self-stimulation during the second half of the second year.

The genital line of development contributes to the establishment of gender identity although exactly when, or how, or to what extent, is as unclear as is the role of identification with parents. Both boy and girl initially identify with the mother, though the girl is permitted to retain her identification. The boy, on the other hand, must "dis-identify" with the mother and begins to identify with the father. He must renounce his wish to be like his mother while his mother must relinquish her hold upon her son bit by bit, with love for him and respect for his independence. (Greenson 1968). Since dis-identification is a complicated matter, it may be related to the greater incidence of gender-identity problems in men. Another view of dis-identification is that of Barglow and Schaefer (1977) who view it as a narcissistic trauma.

Crucial unanswered questions concern the issue of identification. The majority of children of single parents develop appropriate gender identities as adequately as children raised by two parents. The reasons for the lack of gender-identity problems in most children raised by single parents may include: (1) They identify not only with their parents, but with numerous others—relatives, teachers, friends; (2) mothers and fathers each may transmit gender identities which are neither totally feminine nor totally masculine, but rather are a mixture of "androgynous" traits; (3) children identify with their fantasy of the parent or of another person and not with their reality. Identifications are constructed by the child, not passively accepted or copied. The identification process is part of the process of the construction of reality in general. Such constructions probably are not accomplished once for all time during childhood, but continue over a long period of time. Cognitive capabilities, together with experiential factors, determine the development of each child's construction.

There are tacit assumptions in regard to cognitive achievements in the statements of Freud, Galenson and Roiphe, and Mahler et al.—specifically about the association between genital sensations and gender identity, penis envy, anger with the mother, and the role of the father.

1. How do genital sensations contribute to the establishment of gender identity? The infant is aware of sensations—pleasurable and unpleasurable—emanating from different parts of the body, but it is unlikely that such sensations are directly associated with gender. More likely, genital sensations and perhaps all sensations contribute to the establishment of a body image and aid in boundary formation. Genital sensations could only contribute to gender identity if infants had prior knowledge that boys' and girls' genitals differ. Genital sensations then would remind them of the difference. This attribution of causal thinking is unwarranted during the first few years of life. Causal thinking implies the ability to understand that one thing follows another because there is a connection between them which is not arbitrary but necessary and sufficient: If I have this or that genital, then I am of this or that gender. Such causal thinking is not characteristic of pre-schoolers.

2. Penis envy: The idea that the penis was once also possessed by the girl, the hope that it might be grown in the future or that a symbolic substitute will emerge, imply that the child has developed a sense of time, that she knows about both past and future—a rare occurrence before the age of four. Moreover, to attribute the cause of her deficiency to her mother, not her father or someone else, is unlikely in view of her inadequate causal thinking. In children's magical thinking, of course, the mother may be omnipotent, and if they are angry for not having been given their due, they are likely to blame the mother.

The girl's early awareness of genital differences may derive from the observation of the boy's urinary prowess. Thus, her envy may not be genital but urethral, aroused by the boy's capacity to direct his urine rather than let it flow uncontrolled. "Thus, she wants a penis as a tool for control rather than an organ for pleasure" (Kestenberg, 1975, p. 223). It seems adultomorphic to consider a little girl's attempts to urinate while standing as evidence of penis envy in a genital sense. To understand the genital function of the penis requires mature cognition, specifically the ability to make inferences, to know that an organ with an obvious function can also have a hidden one.

3. Turning to the father for a baby: Studies on children's concepts of the origin of babies (Bernstein and Cowan, 1975) suggest that the role of the father in conception is not understood until past school age. The more obvious, concrete but irrelevant household functions of the father are comprehended earlier, but not the hidden, procreative ones. That the father is an important person to the infant long before the phallic stage has been reliably established (see "The Role of the Father.")

IV GENDER IDENTITY AND THE SELF

I am suggesting that gender identity is an aspect of the self. A brief review of the literature indicates that the term "identity" is used differently by different authors, and usually has experiential, not metapsychological, status. "Identity" overlaps with such terms as self, personality, sense of individuality, and others. Stoller's "core gender identity" suggests that it is a primary given, an organizer for subsequent experiences, as yet incompletely understood.

Studies by Gallup (1979) and M. Lewis (1979) suggest that self-recognition in a mirror is perhaps the earliest evidence of a sense of self. It appears to be an emergent for both chimpanzees and human infants, but has not been found in phylogenetically lower animals. Some human infants appear to recognize themselves in mirrors, and to label pictures of themselves as early as fifteen months. The developmental line of self begins very early and progresses toward the establishment of the sense of self over the next few years — if not over the life span.

According to Lichtenberg (1975), early self-awareness is disconnected and fragmentary. With the emergence of "islands of functioning and islands of experience," (p. 454) and with increasing organization, body representations are established. Self-experience is not limited to consciousness, but also includes preconscious and unconscious sensing. "This total sensing is responsible for the quality of the sense of self — its cohesiveness, its continuity over time, and its retaining an essential sense of sameness in the midst of developmental changes." (p. 454).

Lichtenberg describes three component groups of self-images:

1. Self-images based on body experiences associated with instinctual-need satisfactions. They lead to experience of body boundaries, and include pleasure and unpleasure.

2. Self-images that emerge as entities having discrete differentiation from objects; the self is experienced as separate from an object.

3. Self-images that, by virtue of idealization, retain a sense of grandiosity and omnipotence shared with an idealized agent.

One might speculate that the first set of self-images probably originates at the beginning of the differentiation subphase with the awareness of body boundaries, pleasure and unpleasure. Soon it is followed by the second set: the differentiation of the self from objects. That is, separation from the symbiotic mother precedes or accompanies a primitive sense of self. While it is barely mentally represented, almost from the beginning it acquires content by means of externally supplied cues. Hearing the words "baby," "girl" (or "boy"), at first no more than meaningless sounds, soon aids organization of sensations, perceptions, feelings, and behavior. The "me" precedes the "I." The evidence is in the order of the acquisition of words relating to the self: infants refer to themselves as "baby," or by their given name, then by "me" long before they can conceptualize the "I." This "I," the subjective self, or the self as agent, is a late development. It lends a sense of consistency and continuity to the self over time, and permits a relationship to one's past—impossible before the existence of memory and a sense of time. With increasing age, a more cohesive, stabler inner world is eventually created out of the original undifferentiated awareness.

The sense of gender identity, a part of the sense of self, also is not established at one time, once for all time, but is a developmental phenomenon, subject to the influence of externally furnished organizers, the growth of cognitive structures, the differentiation of affect and, with increasing age, progressive internalization of experiences. Both gender identity and the sense of self arise epigenetically: they progressively differentiate on the basis of newly developing capabilities—maturing systems which enable the infant to accumulate experiences which, in turn, alter the systems. This process may be viewed as following Heinz Werner's (1948) developmental principles: (1) Development becomes increasingly more differentiated; (2) hierarchization and subordination are the corollary of differentiation; (3) behavior moves from syncretic to discrete, from diffuse to articulated, from indefinite to definite; from rigid to flexible, and from labile to stable.

The development of gender identity may further be conceptualized as a simultaneous development on two levels: primary and secondary process. In this respect, a reconceptualization of the two processes by Noy (1979) is relevant: Noy defines the two processes somewhat differently than Freud (1900), Rappaport (1960), and Holt (1967), in that he attributes development not only to secondary but also to primary process. To Noy, primary process refers to *self-centered* and secondary process to *reality-oriented* functioning. Primary process, as secondary process, continues to develop as part of the self-regulating functions. With increasing age, secondary process becomes more specialized in order to deal efficiently with reality—to perceive, represent, and understand reality, to solve problems and use language. Similarly, primary process becomes more and more specialized to deal efficiently with the expanding self. "[It] accommodates the self to an ever more demanding environment, and to maintain the integrity and cohesion of a self which is gradually beginning to differentiate into its dimensions.'' These dimensions include the actual self or the ''I,'' the social self or the ''me,'' and the ideal self (Noy, p. 176).

Primary and secondary processes form two developmental lines whose paths are determined by the same intrinsic maturational factors. Each new cognitive skill influences both processes, i.e., each process has the same ability to categorize, make mental representations, and operate in all other areas of cognitive functioning. The difference between the two processes in the realm of any of the cognitive functions remains always in the *mode of organization* only: self-centeredness for primary, and reality orientation for secondary process. Primary process categorizes objects according to the specific need they satisfy or the sense they stimulate. Secondary categories become organized in progressively more complex ways, by the addition of more subcategories as well as by the creation of supercategories and cross-categorizations. Secondary process further differs from primary process, which organizes experience, in that it organizes knowledge. The new secondary process categories transform primary process experiential categories.

The self-centered categories formed around a need, sense, wish, or emotional experience become disconnected from their relation to the self, assume an objective existence of their own. That is, they turn into generalized notions about particular objects, events or phenomena. Both primary and secondary processes are used as a means for organizing mental data. Secondary categories are not formed to replace primary ones, but are always added as another level.

I am suggesting, by extrapolating from Noy's scheme, that ''gender identity nuclei'' derive from amassing of sensorimotor experiences drawn from many sources, and include the attribution of gender to the infant at birth, the infant's learning sex stereotypes, identifications, observations of the anatomical difference, experiencing genital sensations, and so on. These repeated experiences—physiological needs and object-related events—which are at first chaotic, need organizing. Simple two-way categorizations, such as boy-girl, baby-adult, familiar-unfamiliar, organize the ''nuclei'' under the influence of maturing secondary process cognition, and construct the reality of gender identity. One might speculate that secondary process grows out of the mother's function as a ''container'' of the infant's disorganized and discarded early products, aiding the infant in organizing them into simple concepts (See Bion, 1967).

The development of primary process differs from the development of secondary process thinking in many important respects: With increasing age, secondary process thought progressively replaces earlier primary and secondary process thought, integrating earlier ideas into later ones. But earlier ideas do not exist discretely in later formulations. Primary process, on the other hand, despite developments, maintains a residue of primitive, self-centered ideas. In regard to gender identity, once it is learned that there are two sexes which differ on the basis of anatomical characteristics—that the cause for the attribution of gender is the anatomical difference—one cannot return to an earlier stage during which such causal connections were absent. Rather, the early stage is maintained as primary process, unconstrained by reality demands.

In the text below I sketch the presumed epigenetic development of gender identity on two simultaneous levels—primary and secondary process—using Piaget's, Heinz Werner's, and Noy's concepts. This separation into two levels may aid in categorizing findings from different theoretical orientations. In general, infant research has followed three theories: Psychoanalysts have dealt with either drive or object relations theory, and infant observations have focused in particular on genital behavior (Galenson and Roiphe) or on the struggle for the "consolidation of individuality" (Mahler et al.). Social learning theorists have studied sex role typing, modeling, the effects of parental warmth, etc., and cognitive-developmental theorists have concerned themselves with the development of the intellect and its contribution to identity formation.

1. The level of "core gender identity"—roughly the first two years of life. In regard to primary process modes, the infant is capable of perceiving parental attitudes and projections, yet remains unaware of their meanings. Behavior is no doubt shaped by identification with parental expectations, both conscious and unconscious. Pleasurable genital arousal exists from birth on and, again, its meaning in gender terms is not understood. On a secondary process level, time, space, causality, and the permanence of objects are initially absent, and they are slowly experienced and learned by means of actions. The beginning of independent locomotion and language both enhance feelings of competence. Early stereotypes are learned and categorizations appear (familiar-unfamiliar, baby-adult, boy-girl, bad-good, etc.), all of which act as organizers of primary process experiences.

2. During the next two years on a primary process level, the anatomical difference is discovered and absorbed in a self-centered manner, intuitions about parental sexuality may be present, identifications continue to be made, dis-identification in the case of boys. On the secondary process level, with causality still absent, the genital difference is noted but accepted as associated to gender identity. That is, it is not considered criterial, but merely as another attribute of the boy or girl. Fragments of accurate ideas are acquired, categorizations become more elaborate, and gender terms are used to organize behavior. Events such as pregnancy are understood as possible only for women. Neither the role of the father in procreation, nor the passage of time, nor causality is comprehended, and as such, interfere with an understanding of these complicated processes.

Gender identity, at this time, is obviously incomplete, intuitive, not causally related to anatomy. It is a simple and concrete idea, based on stereotypes, with unconscious and conscious contributions, with a particular sensitivity to the relationship with parents.

While we speak of the development of gender identity, we assume that its establishment as either feminine or masculine occurs once for all time. Perhaps we ought to speak of a series of feminine or masculine gender identities, implying change in the course of the life span, identities which progress in the direction of greater complexity, yet maintain the qualities associated with the development of the self—continuity over time, constancy, cohesiveness.

Many questions remain, despite recent advances. Although we know about some of the complexities, we don't know which developments are salient, during what periods of time, what is universal, culture-specific or idiosyncratic, the influence of drives, stereotype attribution, the role of cognition, affect, or the development of identification.

REFERENCES

Abelin, E.L. (1971). The role of the father in the separation-individuation process. In *Separation-Individuation*, ed. J.B. McDevitt and C.F. Settlage. New York: International Universities.

Barglow, P., and Schaefer, M. (1977). A new female psychology? *Female Sexuality. Contemporary Psychoanalytic Views*, ed. H.P. Blum. New York: International Universities Press, pp. 393–438.

Beckwith, L. (1972). Relationships between infants' social behavior and their mothers' behavior. *Child Development* 43, pp. 397–411.

Bell, R.Q., Weller, G.M., and Waldrop, M.F. (1979). Newborn and pre-schooler: organization of behavior and relations between periods. Monographs of the Society for Research in Child Development, 1971, 36 (Series no. 142) (in Brooks-Gunn, J. and Matthews, W.S.) *He and She: How Children Develop Their Sex-Role Identity*, Englewood Cliffs, N.J.: Prentice-Hall, 1979.

Bernstein, A., and Cowan, P. (1975). Children's concepts of how people get babies, *Child Dev.* 46:77–91.

Bion, W.W. (1967). *Second Thoughts*. London: Heinemann.

Brooks, J., and Lewis, M. Person perception and verbal labeling: the development of social labels. Paper presented at the meetings of the SRCD, 1975, and the Eastern Psychology Association, 1975.

Brooks-Gunn, J., and Matthews, W.S. (1979). *He and She: How Children Develop Their Sex-Role Identity*. Englewood Cliffs, N.J.: Prentice-Hall, 1979, p. 66.

Burlingham, D. (1973). The preoedipal infant-father relationship. *Psychoanalytic Study of the Child*, 28:23–47. New Haven: Yale University Press.

Chodorow, N. (1978). *The Reproduction of Mothering: Psychoanalysis and the Sociology of Gender*. Berkeley: Univ. of Cal. Press.

Condry, J., and Condry, S. (1976). Sex differences: a study of the eye of the beholder. *Child Development*, 47:812–819.

Erhardt, A.A., Epstein, R., and Money, J. (1968). Fetal androgens and female gender identity in the early-treated adrenogenital syndrome. *Johns Hopkins Medical Journal* 122:160–167.

Evers, K., and Money, J. (1968). Influence of androgen and some aspects of sexually dimorphic behavior in women with the late-treated adrenogenital syndrome. *Johns Hopkins Medical Journal* 123:115–122.

Erikson, E.H. (1950). *Childhood and Society*. New York: Norton.

Freud, S. (1900). *The Interpretation of Dreams Standard Edition* 4 and 5.

———(1905). Three essays on the theory of sexuality. *Standard Edition* 7:125–2431. London: Hogarth Press, 1953.

———(1912). Contributions to a discussion on masturbation. *Standard Edition* 12:239–254. London: Hogarth Press, 1958.

———(1925). Some psychical consequences of the anatomical distinction between the sexes. *Standard Edition* 19:241–258. London: Hogarth Press, 1969.

———(1931). Female sexuality. *Standard Edition* 21:221–243. London: Hogarth Press, 1961.

———(1933). Femininity. *Standard Edition* 21:112–135. London: Hogarth Press, 1964.

Galenson, E., and Roiphe, H. (1977). Some suggested revisions concerning early female development. *Female Sexuality. Contemporary Psychoanalytic Views*, ed. H.P. Blum. New York: International Universities Press, pp. 29–57.

Gallup, G.G. (1979). Self-recognition in chimpanzees and man: a developmental and comparative perspective. *The Child and Its Family*, ed. M. Lewis and L.A. Rosenblum. New York: Plenum, pp. 107–126.

Gewirtz, H.B. & Gewirtz, J.L. (1968). Visiting and caretaking patterns for Kibbutz infants: age and sex trends. *Am. J. Orthopsychiatry*, 38:427–443.

Goldberg, S., and Lewis, M. (1969). Play behavior in the year-old infant: early sex differences. *Child Development* 40:21–31.

Greenacre, P. (1952). *Trauma, Growth and Personality*. New York: Norton, p. 238.

———(1960). Considerations regarding the parent-infant relationship. *Internat. J. of Psychoanalysis* 41:571–584.

Greenberg, M., and Morris, N. (1974). Engrossment: The newborn's impact upon the father. *Am. J. Orthopsychiatry* 44:520–531.

Greenson, R.R. (1968). Dis-identifying from mother: its special importance for the boy. *Internat. J. Psychoanalysis* 49:370–374.

Hoffman, M.L., and Levine, L.E. (1976). Early sex differences in empathy. *Dev. Psych.* 12:557–558.

Holt, R.R. (1967). The development of the primary process. In *Motives and Thought*, ed. R.R. Holt. New York: Internat. Univ. Press. (Psychol. Issues 18/19:344–383).

Horney, K. (1926). The flight from womanhood: the masculinity complex in women as viewed by men and by women. *Internat. J. Psychoanalysis* 7:324–339. Reprinted in *Psychoanalysis and Women*, ed. J.B. Miller. New York: Brunner/Mazel, 1973.

Jakobson, R. (1962). Why "mama" and "papa?" In *Selected Writings of Roman Jakobson*. The Hague: Mouton (from M. Lewis (1976), The father's role in the child's social network, in M.E. Lamb, *The Role of the Father in Child Development*, pp. 157–184.

Kestenberg, J. (1975). *Children and Parents*. New York: Aronson.

Kleeman, J.A. (1977). Freud's views on early female sexuality in the light of direct child observation. *Female Sexuality. Contemporary Psychoanalytic Views*, ed. H.P. Blum. New York: International Universities Press, pp. 3–27.

Klein, M. (1960). Early stages of the oedipal conflict. In *The Psychoanalysis of Children*. New York: Grove, pp. 179–209.

Korner, A.F. (1969). Neonatal startles, smiles, erections, and reflex sucks as related to state, sex, and individuality. *Child Dev.* 40:1039–1053.

Korner, A.F. (1977). Sex differences in newborns. In *The Sexual and Gender Development of Young Children: The Role of the Educator*, eds. E.K. and J.D. Oremland. Cambridge, Mass: Ballinger, pp. 11–16.

Kotelchuck, M. (1972). The nature of the child's tie to his father. Unpublished doctoral dissertation, Harvard University.

——(1976). The infant's relationship to the father: experimental evidence. In *The Role of the Father in Child Development*, ed. M.E. Lamb. New York: Wiley.

Lewis, M., and Brooks, J. (1978). Self knowledge and emotional development. In *The Development of Affect*, ed. M. Lewis and L.A. Rosenblum. New York: Plenum, pp. 205–226.

——and Freedle, R. (1973). Mother-infant dyad: the cradle of meaning. In *Communication and Affect: Language and Thought*, eds. P. Pliner, L. Kramer, and T. Alloway. New York: Academic Press.

——and Kreitzberg, V. (work in progress). The effects of gender, birth order, and social class on social and cognitive development in the first two years of life. In Brooks-Gunn & Matthews. Educational Testing Service.

——and Weinraub, M. (1976). The father's role in the child's social network. In Lamb.

Lichtenberg, J.D. (1975). The development of the sense of self. *J. Amer. Psychoanal. Assn.* 23:453–484.

Maccoby, E.E., and Jacklin, C. (1974). *The Psychology of Sex Differences*. Stanford: Stanford University Press.

Mahler, M.S., Pine, F., and Bergman, A. (1975). *The Psychological Birth of the Human Infant*. New York: Basic Books.

Masters, W.H., and Johnson, V.E. (1966). *Human Sexual Response*. Boston: Little, Brown.

Meltzoff, A.N., and Moore, M.K. (1977). Imitation of facial and manual gestures by human neonates. *Science* 198:75–78.

Mischel, W. (1973). Toward a cognitive social learning reconceptualization of personality. *Psychology Review* 80:252–283.

Money, J. (1977). Human hermaphroditism. In *Human Sexuality in Four Perspectives*, ed. F.A. Beach. Baltimore: Johns Hopkins University Press, p. 69.

——and Ehrhardt, A.A. (1972). *Man and Woman; Boy and Girl*. Baltimore: The Johns Hopkins Press.

Mueller, J. (1932). A contribution to the problem of libidinal development of the genital phase of girls. *Internat. J. Psychoanalysis*, 13:361–368.

Noy, P.P. (1979). The psychonalytic theory of cognitive development. *Psychoanalytic Study of the Child* 34:169–216.

Parke, R.D., and O'Leary, S. (1975). Father-mother-infant interaction in the newborn period: Some findings, some observations, and some unresolved issues. In *The Developing Individual in a Changing World*, ed. K. Riegel and J. Meacham, *vol. 2, Social and Environmental Issues*. The Hague: Mouton.

Pedersen, F.A., et al. (1979). Conceptualization of father influences in the infancy period. In *The Child and Its Family*, ed. M. Lewis and L. Rosenblum. New York and London: Plenum Press, pp. 45–66.

Piaget, J. (1952). *The Origins of Intelligence in Children*. New York: International Universities Press, p. 63.

Rapaport, D. (1960). Psychoanalysis as a developmental psychology. In *The Collected Papers of David Rapaport*, ed. M.M. Gill. New York: Basic Books.

Robson, K.S., Pederson, F.A., and Moss, H.A. (1969). Developmental observations of dyadic gazing in relation to the fear of strangers and social approach behavior. *Child Development* 40:619–627.

Rubin, J.Z., Provensano, F.J., and Lurin, Z. (1974). The eye of the beholder: parents' views on sex of newborns. *Am. J. Orthopsychiatry* 44:512–519.

Sagi, A., and Hoffman, M.L. (1976). Empathetic distress in the newborn. *Dev. Psychology* 12:175–176.

Schaffer, H.R. (1977). *Mothering*. Cambridge, Mass.: Harvard University Press.

Shereshefsky, P.M., and Yarrow, L.J. (1973). *Psychological Aspects of a First Pregnancy and Early Postnatal Adaptation*. New York: Raven Press.

Stoller, R.J. (1977). Primary femininity. In *Female Sexuality. Contemporary Psychoanalytic Views*, ed. H.P. Blum. New York: International Universities Press, pp. 59–78.

Tanner, J.M. (1978). *Fetus Into Man, Physical Growth from Conception to Maturity*. Cambridge: Harvard University Press.

Watson, J.S. (1969). Operant conditioning of visual fixation in infants under visual and auditory reinforcement. Dev. Psychology 1:508–516.

Werner, H. (1948). *Comparative Psychology of Mental Development*. New York: International Universities Press.

2

The Anal Phase

MARION MICHEL OLINER

The anal phase sets itself apart from the oral phase preceding it by the fact that the child becomes aware of its ability to produce something; and it is around this product that many developmental steps are taken. Her love for her anal productivity brings the little girl into conflict with the mother, and the wish to control it involves mother and child in antagonistic aims which can only slowly be resolved. Therefore, the mutuality typical of the oral phase is seriously disrupted during this stage. Narcissistic wishes, as they pertain to the content of the body and its control, come into conflict with the wish to please the mother, and because of this contest of will, as well as the child's projection of her own aggression onto the mother, the mother is experienced as controlling and restrictive. Many compromises must be reached before this conflict is resolved in a way which gives the child a sense of mastery over herself and her environment and also enables her to comply with the requirements of socialization. This particular conflict is the prototype for all later problems concerning narcissistic and object-instinctual strivings, and the resolution of this dilemma creates for each individual the foundation for character, ego development and the further evolution of the psychosexual phases and their object choices.

This phase of development in the girl is not well explained in the psychoanalytic literature. Psychoanalysts who have specialized in childhood observation have approached this age group with a different emphasis in mind, and, therefore, while much has been written about related areas of development, bowel training as an organizer has been relatively neglected. Mahler (1963) says:

> We have seen how the oral phase enters into the process of separation-individuation. But we get only glimpses of the anal phase, even though we know it must contribute substantially to individuation in terms of the distinctions between inside and outside, animate and inanimate, I and Non-I. (p. 319.)

*All quotations of material which appears in the bibliography in French and German were translated by the author.

It is not difficult to speculate about the cause for the lack of data. In addition to unconscious factors related to disgust and other defense mechanisms, there is a lack of clarity concerning this phase, and the overlap between it and the preceding and following stages is such that there has been a tendency to allow it to recede into the background. This is truer of analysts working on this side of the Atlantic than in Europe, where there has been a renewed and vigorous interest in the influence of the anal drive component on all aspects of development. In the United States, on the other hand, this phase has been studied from the point of view of ego development and object relations; and where this is not the case, as, for example, with Fenichel, and more recently Roiphe and Galenson, oral and phallic interpretations seem to dominate clinical examples. In the current psychoanalytic literature originating in the English-speaking countries, the anal phase seems to have lost its place as an intermediary stage of libidinal development. The cause of this telescoping of the oral and phallic phases into one another may be twofold. One part of the cause is the shift of interest from drive development to ego and object relations during this time period, the other resides in the assumption that the period is not relevant for the fate of the libido, considering that it is so suffused with aggressive strivings. In this way, the dual instinct theory has actually done a disservice to the integration of the impact of each psychosexual phase on mature sexuality. Whether or not this reflects cultural differences in the patient populations or merely differences in the method of approach of the analysts can only lead to speculations, but the loss in terms of enrichment and integration of understanding by all concerned is considerable. Thus, there is a body of literature derived from adult analyses leading to theoretical formulations basing their understanding of the phenomena on anal drive components and the defenses against them which are largely unknown on this side of the Atlantic. And while there is general agreement among all theorists everywhere that the pregenital stages are not identical for both sexes, there has as yet not been a reformulation of the effect of the anal phase on the development of the girl specifically.

We are, therefore, still compelled to resort to literature which does not differentiate between the pregenital development of the sexes in order to tease out from it the impact on the growth of the female, and we shall observe that some of the early writers were quite aware of the importance of the anal phase as it relates specifically to feminine development, without revising the original position that the issue of the differences between the sexes does not arise until the phallic phase.

BACKGROUND

Historically the discovery of the anal development was closely linked with Freud's treatment of an obsessional male patient. Very early, in 1897, he knew the close connection between the interest in money and in feces, and he tied both to the neurosis based on what he called then the "perverse" impulses of anality. In his later descriptions of this phase, he either writes of it as anal-sadistic or as "sadism and anal eroticism" (1914, p. 108), and he stresses time and again that in that stage there is bipolarity between active and passive aims. He places less emphasis on the ambivalence caused by the conflict between the wish to expel and the wish to retain, and the subsequent literature shows that opinions among theorists seem to vary as to whether to consider the drive to retain an instinctual aim in its own right or whether to regard it as a libidinization of a defense, as Fenichel (1934, p. 308) does.

Freud (1908) is quite explicit about his view that the rebellion against the need to surrender the contents of the bowels and the wish to retain control over this bodily function by controlling its timing constitute the essence of the anal conflict. Therefore, he states that the retention serves two functions: to wrest control from the mother and to prolong the pleasure within the bowels. There are many references to the nature of this pleasure: "Since the column of faeces stimulates the erotogenic mucous membrane of the bowel, it plays the part of an active organ in regard to it; it behaves just as the penis does to the vaginal mucous membrane, and acts as it were as its forerunner during the cloacal epoch" (1914, p. 84). Also, "The essential novelty, as compared with the previous (oral) stage, is that the receptive passive function becomes disengaged from the oral zone and attached to the anal zone" (1914, p. 108). In women, these passive receptive longings, according to Freud, are eventually transferred to the wish for a baby, and the sadism is stunted as a result of the discovery of castration and the absence of a female phallus. Despite the temptation to link activity with masculinity and passivity with femininity, he knew that there were problems in these particular formulations, and he never allowed himself to theorize along these lines without warning that the analogy does not hold true.

> We are accustomed to say that every human being displays both male and female instinctual impulses, needs and attributes; but, though anatomy, it is true, can point out the characteristic of maleness and femaleness, psychology cannot. For psychology the contrast between the sexes fades away into one between activity and passivity, in which we far too readily identify activity with maleness and passivity with femaleness, a view which is by no means universally confirmed in the animal kingdom. The theory of bisexuality is still surrounded by many obscurities and we cannot but feel it is a serious impediment in psychoanalysis that it has not yet found any link with the theory of the instincts. (1929, p. 105.)

This particular problem gave Freud difficulties, and while he repeatedly stated the link between the vagina and the anal orifice, his clinical application of the derivation refers mostly to the psychology of men. Chasseguet-Smirgel (1976) rightly has pointed out, with reference to the wish for a baby as it appears in Freud's writings, that it seemed to be a primary wish in the case of the

Wolfman, whereas in his view of the psychology of women it is considered as a derivative of the wish for the penis. In the same way, it can be said that Freud studied the passive feminine attitude of the Wolfman without applying some of the same formulations — that is, the similarity between the vaginal and the anal orifices — to his women patients. The possibility that in the fantasy of a woman the vagina is not yet a sexual organ distinct from the anal orifice does not appear in his interpretations, even though he recognized it in theory. His formulations could not be clearer: ''The clear-cut distinction between anal and genital processes which is later insisted upon is contradicted by the close anatomical and functional analogies and relations which hold between them. The genital apparatus remains the neighbour of the cloaca, and actually (to quote Lou Andreas-Salome) 'in the case of women is only taken from it on lease''' (1905, p. 187). He states as late as in the New Introductory Lectures, ''interest in the vagina is also essentially of anal-erotic origin'' (1932, p. 101). It seems almost as if it were difficult for him to overcome the defense against this insight, and he seems to have needed to spare himself and his female patients the degradation he saw in such an analogy.

Freud was similarly uneasy when Abraham introduced the problem of an anal eroticism and sadism into the question of the dynamics of melancholia, and he wrote (1915, p. 211) that, while he was in full agreement, he thought that Abraham did not elaborate sufficiently the topographic aspects and the giving up of object cathexes. Abraham's (1924) formulation suggests that the object loss is experienced as an act of defecation and that the reintrojection of this fecal object is what constitutes the bad object in the case of melancholia. Thus, while Freud thinks of object loss in melancholia as an event taking place in external reality leading to guilt because of the ambivalent relationship to the object, Abraham suggests that the loss itself is experienced as the result of an act of expulsion, thereby giving the reintrojected object the quality of a bad introject. ''Thus when the obsessional neurotic is threatened with the loss of his object, and the melancholiac actually does lose his, it signifies to the unconscious mind of each an expulsion of that object in the sense of a physical expulsion of faeces'' (1924, p. 426). This is an important elaboration of the role of anal sadism which must be credited to Abraham. It allows for the conceptualization of an introjective process, coprophagia, which replaces the object into the digestive tract in an oral mode, but not as good food, therefore forming a bridge between the two phases. His views of the capacity to retain an object led Abraham to place the beginning of object love in the middle of the anal phase, when the object is being preserved instead of lost and destroyed. All later attempts at introjection are, according to Abraham, partial ones in which only a part of the object is appropriated while the object as such is spared. In a clinical example of a patient, he shows (1924, p. 484) the ambiguous nature of the object of this later type of introjection when he suggests that the patient wanted the father's ''Vermoegen,'' an expression literally denoting wealth but also, etymologically, potency. Here the aim is not total destruction since it spares the object, except for its castration, and yet the introjective mode is regressive since it does not yet aim at leaving the object outside, trying to rule it and to possess it, as is proper to the more advanced level of anal object relatedness. Abraham refines to a great extent Freud's formulations, and he has, in effect, interposed many gradations in the conceptualization which are extremely useful in refining the understanding of clinical phenomena. He traces the place of the object as it moves from being experienced as totally inside to totally outside. Unfortunately, these stages are not always easily identifiable, and the subsequent psychoanalytic literature often neglects some important aspects which Abraham discovered.

Prominent among those is the concept of anal introjection which Abraham mentions and Fenichel alludes to, but which was not taken up again until relatively recently when many of the psychoanalysts working in Paris found it a very useful explanatory device for certain phenomena ushering in the phallic phase as well as for structure formation. This will be taken up in great detail in the section dealing with the contributions of these analysts.

The legacy left by Abraham concerning the pivotal role of the anal phase is probably unsurpassed by any other theorist. He tries to separate the libidinal from the aggressive component and thinks of retaining and evacuating as libidinal pleasures, whereas he considers dominating and excreting or destroying as sadistic and therefore aggressive. And while this division does not solve some of the theoretical problems of libido and aggression in the anal complex, his further exposition on the role of conserving and controlling the object as against expelling and destroying it are very enlightening in the understanding of the importance of the anal phase for many important personality characteristics as well as for psychosexual fulfillment. In this context it might be relevant to show how Joyce McDougall (1974a) applies this theory to the study of psychosomatic illness and the deficiency in structure formation in patients suffering from these syndromes: "We enter here into the domain of retentions, clearly having its roots in the anal phase, and the inability to give libidinal meaning to the capacity to retain . . . one's thoughts, impulses, and inner objects" (p. 453).

Unfortunately, Abraham does not take his thinking in the direction of differentiating between the anal phase as it occurs in men and in women, and therefore he remains very much in the tradition of the notion that the phase is identical for both sexes.

Ferenczi is less inclined to do this. His concern is very much in the direction of studying the influence of the various psychosexual impulses on each other and on each sex. In his theory of amphimixis he delineates the influence of anal drive components on genitality, especially for women. "For the leading zone of genitality, in which in the male the emphasis is definitely upon the urethral, regresses again in the female chiefly to the anal" (1922, p. 24). He calls this influence of the anal on the feminine genital strivings "cavity erotism," and suggests the close relationship between vaginal receptivity and passive anal strivings, inferring that in regressive conditions the vagina could be experienced as the anus without there ever having to be a shift in the dominant zone. This, it seems to me, is one of the reasons that disturbances of female sexuality have been more difficult to study: The regression to the anal phase is less obvious than in male homosexuality and, therefore, can easily be confusing. As a further example of the admixture of erotisms relating to cavities, Ferenczi suggests the case of coprophagia: ". . .the obvious combination of anal with oral erotism, namely coprophagia, strives to atone for the pain of anal loss by the pleasure of oral incorporation" (1923, p. 14). This mechanism, already referred to by Abraham in his study of melancholia, has often been linked to female psychology and the reaction to losses, and will be reconsidered in the context of some of Jacobson's and Lewin's formulations.

As early as 1916, Lou Andreas-Salome makes apparent the increasing neglect of the study of the anal phase when she complains in an article on "Anal and Sexual" that anyone stressing an anal regression is treated by the Viennese school as if he were indulging in "family gossip" (p. 249). She points out that the revulsion against infantile sexuality was similar to that against dirt, and therefore directed at its anal derivative, not its sexual component per se. The article points to the fact that the anal period forces the child into a position against its own instincts, and she refers to the common origin of the vaginal and anal openings quoted by Freud. She stresses the turning away from the libidinization of the body as well as the individuation taking place during this stage, which she calls "hate-awakening."

Jones suggests that in normal female development the oral-sadistic phase is relatively weak, and the oral-sadistic fantasy of biting off the male penis is not highly developed. He considers the optimum development one in which there is a transition from the sucking to the anal stage.

> The two alimentary orifices thus constitute the receptive female organ. The anus is evidently identified with the vagina to begin with, and the differentiation of the two is an extremely obscure process, more so perhaps than any other in female development; I surmise, however, that it takes place in part at an earlier age than is generally supposed. A variable amount of sadism is always developed in connection with the anal stage and is revealed in the familiar phantasies of anal rape which may or may not pass over into beating phantasies. The Oedipus relationship is here in full activity; and the anal phantasies, . . . are already a compromise between libidinal and self-punishment tendencies. This mouth-anus-vagina stage, therefore, represents an identification with the mother. (1927, p.443.)

Clearly he considers the identification with a relatively passive mother and femininity as stemming from the anal period, based on cloacal erotism which other analysts have thought of as being interrupted by the phallic stage or some other kind of masculine identification process. Jones does not share this point of view. He seems to have equated the identification of the girl with the father as the underpinning for possible later pathology, and he states that "the repression of femininity springs more from . . . hatred and fear of . . . mother than from her own masculinity" (1935, p. 491). Why, in view of this, he does not give greater emphasis to the actively controlling mother as she is experienced by the girl in the anal phase is not clear, especially since, in another context, he refers to the girl's problems in relationship to her mother in the following way: "The anal-erotic conflict leads a girl to hate her mother — merely a little earlier and a little more cordially" (p. 557). If this statement is to be integrated with the previous ones, we may assume that he considers the identification with the mother's cavities as only one aspect of their relationship.

Jacobson's (1937) article on the female superego is extremely relevant to this study although Jacobson hardly refers to the influence of the anal stage and gives some of the observed phenomena the stamp of orality. This seems to me to be debatable. She points to the girl's fear of bodily harm as stemming from the preoedipal relationship to her mother and stresses that before the onset of the acceptance of castration there is a fantasy in which the missing penis has been displaced to the inside of the body: "The fantasized displacement of the body-part into the interior of the body changes castration anxiety again into the fear of the destruction of the internal genital" (p. 404). Considering that this particular development occurs well after the height of the oral phase, it seems justified to refer to this introjection as an anal one, or coprophagia, especially because of the sadistic component underlying these incorporative aims. She stresses that the greater the sadism the more complete the lack of erotization of the receptive organ. The evolution of the relationship to the father must help the girl to renounce gradually her aggressive-masculine craving, to come to terms with the lack of the organ, and to master her oral impulses to steal the penis and to convert them into vaginal wishes. This leads to an earlier and stronger impetus toward superego formation (the type which Grunberger (1974) later calls the early-superego and which he distinguishes qualitatively from the post-oedipal superego). This superego, according to Jacobson, inhibits oral and phallic strivings toward the mother and leads to an anal deprecation of the genital; it also causes the renunciation of the genital in favor of the object love to the father. Because of this development there is a tendency to project onto the father this particular superego, and thereby to convert what was at the outset internalized, into an external superego. This, in turn, manifests itself as social anxiety, and the observation of the particular form of externalization led Freud to think of the female superego as weaker. Jacobson thinks that with the advent of a feminine relation to the object there is a defense against the superego and a projective anaclesis of the superego onto the father, and as soon as there is a return to an identification with the mother due to oedipal rivalry, also onto the mother. This inhibits the formation of an independent superego and leads to the projection onto the man of the renounced ego ideal which is then loved in the object and reincorporated through love. She points to the prevalence of depression and melancholia in women to prove the presence of a strong and punitive superego in regressive conditions leading to the undoing of these protective mechanisms. Thus, according to Jacobson, the girl gives up her phallic narcissistic strivings and identifies with the mother whereas the boy retains those impulses but gives up his object. In normal development the wish to incorporate the penis evolves into the wish to obtain the penis genitally, and in the process some of the narcissistic valuation is projected onto the father along with the superego. It seems that the development as outlined by Jacobson is valid, perhaps to a greater or lesser degree regardless of the cultural milieu, and constitutes an important factor in the understanding of the dynamics of women, their depression and their difficulties in relating to men sexually. The unresolved issue does not lie in the validity of Jacobson's thesis but rather in whether she is justified in considering the formation of this early superego only as related to oral incorporative aims. It seems more likely that the introjection of controlling, inhibiting, and regulating factors is more a product of the anal phase, and therefore the early superego seems more related to the attempt to separate from the mother than part of the oral dependency on her. Regardless of these particular details, the importance of the article lies in its highlighting the existence of a rather strict superego in women even when this has been subsequently projected and, therefore, seems to be absent in those cases in which men seem to be setting the standards of value and conduct. Upon reaching the genital stages, these women relinquish a structure which they had gained previously.

The pathological aspects of this tendency were also studied carefully by Fenichel (1945) and Annie Reich (1940, 1953), both of whom refer to it as extreme submissiveness in women, which the former classifies as a perversion. Their formulations are similar to those of Jacobson, and Fenichel refers to an "oral fixation" in which the wish to be incorporated can be used against the drive toward active incorporation. "If the feeling of the union with the partner can be obtained without any action on the part of the subject, no violent way of establishing it is needed any more" (1945, p. 353). The maternal ego ideal is transferred without alteration onto the father, and if there is "insufficient acceptance of reality, the differentiation between ego and ego ideal may remain diffuse, and under certain conditions 'magic identification' with the glorified parent — megalomanic feelings — may replace the wish to be like him" (Reich,

1953, p. 188). In other words, the mechanism described avoids anality in favor of a regression to the oral phase. However, in *Trophy and Triumph*, Fenichel (1939) suggests that this submission to an object has aspects of a relationship to a trophy and can evolve from cannibalized introjects, through what he calls "castration," into possession, i.e., an anal derivative. While Fenichel tends to stress the oral, magical and fusional aspects of obtaining power, the anal-sadistic aspects are always in the background, as when he says, "for the masochist there is peaceful participation where once there was a sadistic wish to rob" (1930, p. 156).

It would be a logical step to continue from a consideration of these works highlighting female submissiveness or masochism to a careful analysis of Chasseguet-Smirgel's formulations. However, she bases her work on so many concepts which have to be mentioned before her position becomes fully understandable that this review of the literature becomes more comprehensible if the contributions by American theorists are summarized first before taking up those developments which have taken place in France and which have greatly enriched the literature on the anal phase.

An important contribution was made by Lewin (1930) in his study of menstruation, which he linked with feelings of loss and the need to reintroject through smearing or through eating. He considered this process of reintrojection copraphagia and suggests that women regard the menstrual flow as incontinence, as a failure of sphincter function, and as an anal castration which is compensated for by eating and smearing (reintrojection through the skin). It is related to the loss of the feces or their equivalents, and can be compensated for through coprophagia in the manner already described by Abraham. Lewin demonstrates this tendency in cases which he has treated and suggests furthermore that menstruation has the additional meaning of loss of the anal child. Like all other theoreticians, he too links the sense of incontinence and loss of body contents to the failure of the anal sphincter and not the urethral, assuming, therefore, that the urethral concerns fall into a later period and are not equated with the vagina in the same way as the anus is.

Roiphe (1968, 1977) and Galenson (1977), on the other hand, have observed the experience of the lack of the penis during the anal phase and have tended to attribute the girl's reaction of depression or lowered mood to the castration anxiety during this period, which they call an early genital phase. This is an illustration of the tendency toward telescoping which has been mentioned earlier and which tends to lead to an eclipse of interpretations using the dynamics of anal loss as explanatory terms. As E.A. Gargiulo (1977) writes in her discussion of a paper by Galenson:

> Castration "without oedipal resonance" may be more closely linked with
> anal loss than with the phallic phase . . . Galenson's three anxieties: castration

anxiety, fear of loss of the object, and fear of self-dissolution . . . could all be attributed, it seems to me, to the tasks and conflicts of the anal period (pp. 4–5.)

Gargiulo, using some of Jones' ideas, suggests that what Roiphe and Galenson interpret as an early genital phase is in reality an early manifestation of penis envy in the girl as a result of her disappointment in her anatomy as well as in her mother. But these experiences of deficiency take their place within the rest of the issues of the anal phase and do not justify the use of explanatory terms belonging to the anxieties of the phallic and oedipal periods. On the contrary, they suggest the earlier awareness of the difference between the sexes generating anxieties related to object loss and body integrity, that is, the heightening of anxieties of an anal nature in girls.

The passive, receptive aspects of femininity and its proximity to its antecedent have been mentioned by Fenichel (1945) and Greenacre (1950), but they have not received from anyone else the amount of attention that Kestenberg (1975) has given them for a number of years now. Her concern with the inner genital phase, which will occupy a chapter in this volume, highlights so many problems involving the anal phase that her work must be cited in this context even at the risk of repetition. Her focus concerns the inside of the girl's body, the inner genital, and she stresses the relationship between the vaginal sensations and the digestive tract. She considers the sensations coming from each as merged with each other, and that the cathexis of the cloacal sphere intensifies vaginal sensations. And most important for the anal phase: "Retention of feces and of urine can already serve for stimulation of alleviation of the sensation of inner swelling which seems to stem from the vagina" (1975, p. 11).

> The difficulty in localization as well as the enigmatic quality and multilocality of fleeting vaginal sensations create a confusion in her, which she tries to solve in two ways. In one type of solution she fuses vaginal tensions with others, coming from inside of her body, and displaces their common bulk to orifices with which she has become familiar, such as the mouth, the anus, and the urethral opening. A similar mechanism connects the genital to the nose. Such fusions and displacements are facilitated by the simultaneous occurrence of various sensations. The second, most important way, by which the girl tries to overcome her confusion about vaginal impulses, is to externalize them, at first to a baby and later, in the phallic phase, to a penis. Both are solid outer objects rather than parts of her own body. Fusions and externalizations do not give permanent relief and are, therefore, abandoned over and over again throughout the girl's development, thus creating a psychological readiness for the adult feminine cycles. (1975, p. 45.)

The problem of being able to control the vaginal sensations leads the girl back to the inside of her body, and, therefore, is close to the issues of the anal phase. Where the mastery is not possible on an inner genital it might be attempted through the anal cavity. Therefore, as Kestenberg mentioned, there is also the fear that the doll, which, according to her, is the externalization of the inner genital, might resemble an anal baby. To illustrate this point she cites the case of a girl who became disturbed by the brown color of a doll. By contrast, the boy achieves mastery of his genital more easily and is, therefore, less prone to anal regressions at this stage of development. Kestenberg's writings support the belief that the proximity and reciprocal pressures make the genital and anal factors more related in the girl than in the boy. The phallic phase ushers in the decathexis of the inner genital, but clearly for the girl this can only be a way station to a recathexis and a reawakening of the issues described in these studies. "Transitory and reversible in the girl, a tendency to desexualize inner genitality becomes a permanent characteristic of male integration" (1975, p. 321). Boys become aware of their genitals earlier since the dominant interest in the anal-abdominal area absorbs much of the girl's genital excitation. The girl's main fear is that something has happened to the inside of her body, that its contents have fallen out, and therefore, according to Kestenberg, the maintenance of a certain level of excitation is necessary to counteract this fear. From these writings the interrelationship between anal fears and genital ones becomes obvious; what concerns Kestenberg less are the implications of the sadism which is turned toward the inside of the body. The genuine inner genital phase is supposed to occur at a time when some of the aggression has been channeled into areas of possession, dominance, and sublimated activities, in keeping with Freud's theory of the transformation of instinct (1917); therefore, the vaginal cavity does not have the aggressive cathexis which the anus has. The more closely the two stages resemble each other, the more the inner genital phase will be influenced by the unresolved aggression stemming from the anal phase, and the more the inner genital will lack differentiation from the anal sphere and be regarded as more destructive.

This is in effect the main concern of Chasseguet-Smirgel, who approaches the problems of female sexuality from a different angle and with a different point of view. For her, the problem of sadism directed against an object or projected onto an object, which is then feared and experienced as persecutory, is one of the main issues in assessing the influence of the anal phase on female development.

Her theoretical formulations are anteceded and paralleled by the work of Grunberger (1960, 1971), whose studies on the fate of the anal sadistic drive are perhaps the most inclusive of any so far. He emphasizes the sadistic element of the anal drive, and, according to him, the anal phase adds the energizing factor between subject and object, which means that the expenditure of physical energy is added to the interaction between subject and object. This dimension lifts the individual out of the realm of fusion and psychosis into the world of reality and limits. The role of the energizing relationship to the object has many ramifications which pertain to the fate of aggression in basically libidinal object choices. It also plays a part in the pathological character structures in which, as Grunberger says, the patient "no longer cathects the object of his desire but his energizing relationship to it" (1960, p. 104). In this sense, the anal component leads to a structured and hierarchical view of the world in which people are assigned an identifiable place. This, contrary to the obstinacy and non-conformism which we associated with anality, is an aspect which craves order and stratification, and which derives from this energizing relationship in which distances between people are carefully measured by all the yardsticks such as income, social class, ladder of authority, and possibly, male and female (if one is held inherently to be superior over the other). Since the anal phase adds the dimension of organization to relationships, it is socializing, and therefore a support of organized society, despite the underlying aggressive component.

In this type of "anal object relation," as he calls it, there is a superego forerunner which he calls the early superego (1974) and which is based essentially on the submissive relationship of the individual to a structure into which his own aggression has been placed and which can easily be projected onto some object in the external world. The nature of this superego is that it is more punitive, but also more socialized, containing societal values rather than the more individualized ones of the more mature post-oedipal superego. It is this forerunner which forms the basis for many social orders and is, of course, reminiscent of the principle on which many groups function. The author does not mention whether or not this particular structure formation is more prevalent in one sex than in the other, but since elsewhere (1964) he suggests that women are essentially more narcissistic and tend to project this early superego on their love object, it is likely that what he describes is, in fact, more prevalent among men. Here we are assuming that narcissism works against socialization and that the conformism attributed to women is of a more personalized order than that based on principles of social stratification and hierarchization.

At the center of Grunberger's theory of psychosexual development and narcissistic completeness is a concept which has been alluded to but to which he gave full meaning: the anal castration of the father by children of both sexes. Here the notion of the passive receptive strivings of the anal cavity are described purely in their sadistic aspects which preceded them and are perhaps forever associated with them to some degree. According to Grunberger, this is a step necessary for both girls and boys, as well as part of the analytic process in which it takes the form of the anal castration of the analyst. On the one hand, the process described by Grunberger involves the fantasy of a true introjection of a genuine organ. On the other hand, it is apparent that this anatomical penis has the status of a phallus, which, according to Grunberger, has a modified form of the narcissistic and idealized qualities of which the phallic mother was the original possessor. These qualities evolve from the infantile grandiose type; they are labeled "energetic penis" and form the underpinning of narcissistic completeness and the right to be what one is by virtue of biological equipment. About this process McDougall (1974-b) says the following:

> The fantasy of absorbing into one's body, the highly valued penis, is typical of the anal stage of libidinal development. During this phase, the possession of phallic power is represented, in the imagination of children of both sexes, as an anal incorporation of the father's penis. . . .His fantasy incorporation of the father's penis will depend to a large extent on the unconscious attitudes of his parents and his relation to them. The wish may be felt as permitted, in which case it will become integrated within the ego and its identificatory system, thus opening the way to secondary identification and genital sexuality. But such wishes may also be regarded as dangerous, forbidden, and fraught with the risk of castration — castration of the father, of the mother, or of the child himself. (p. 297.)

Grunberger based a good part of his theory of narcissism on the sense of completeness which is derived from the anal introjection of the father's penis. This identification with the father which ushers in the phallic phase can, of course, misfire in that in women it could lead to excessive guilt or to a masculine identification which does not allow for the subsequent passive receptive attitude toward the penis; or, the introjection of a devalued penis could lead to a sense of uncertainty or worthlessness and a tendency to recathect an older idealized phallic mother imago. In his view, the ability to integrate all the component instincts of the anal phase and to cathect them narcissistically (the impulses as well as their objects) are the foundation of healthy narcissism. Defenses against this integration lead to regressions to fusion, immateriality, idealization and magical thinking. Grunberger is unique among the theorists on narcissism in attributing such a pivotal position to the anal phase, but he is very much in the tradition of Abraham, who set the demarcation line between psychosis and neurosis in the middle of the anal phase. A summary of his interesting views can be found in Oliner (1978), and the English translation of his book, *Le Narcissisme*, is now available.

Despite the narcissistic gain in this introjection, Grunberger considers it mainly as an act of aggression which leads to fantasies of damage to the object. As such, it generates considerable guilt and can be the fundamental motive for a masochistic attitude in both sexes. The interplay between object instinctual and narcissistic components is best illustrated by Grunberger himself when he says: "The phallus — while keeping its original penile form — can lose its purely instinctual qualities and take on narcissistic meanings exclusively. At that level the sexual distinction disappears, and having a phallus does not mean being a man or a woman, but instead means existing fully or wholly in the narcissistic sense" (1971, p. 212). Since it involves both the anal orifice and the anal sadistic drive, it complements the traditional theory of anal drive derivatives and suggests the identification with a part-object.

Fain and Marty, in an article which has become a classic in French psychoanalytic writings, speak about the structuring aspects of the homosexual cathexis in the psychoanalytic process. Referring to the internalization of the "being watched" in the analytic process, they say:

> We have insisted on the fact that this whole process unfolds during the anal stage and have demonstrated how much this type of relation was strongly relived during psychoanalytic treatment, the analyst watching the subject act and fantasize and giving interpretations about this. The subject relives then intensely all the conflicts concerning his wish to obtain something by invidious means from the analyst, mixed with the wish that the analyst could force something to penetrate into him. The homosexual impulse appears, therefore, tightly bound up with the patient's wish to acquire. (1959, p. 610.)

Since these authors consider this position of the patient as the equivalent of the child vis-à-vis the phallic omnipotent parent, they do not differentiate between men and women and consider what they describe as homosexual for both sexes. But, as is also apparent, it is a homosexuality so suffused with anal strivings and parents who are as yet sexually undifferentiated that it seems to belong to that phase, as well as to a passive sadistic striving which foreshadows femininity. It seems, therefore, that the authors describe a process which is firmly rooted in the pregenital phase, but also imply that the sadism of the anal phase has been overcome enough so that there is a predominance of libido. This implied transition makes the developmental time sequence of their formulations somewhat questionable since they seem to describe a process taking place somewhat later than the one described by Grunberger, yet consider it homosexual with regard to both sexes. Despite some of the difficulties in their conceptualization, however, they have made important contributions to psychoanalytic treatment and have added greater clarity to the difficulties inherent in the passive receptive aspect of the anal phase, especially as it manifests itself in analysis. They suggest that "whatever the sex of the person, passive-receptive tendencies are the most difficult to accept . . . [and] the projection of the subject's aggression on the object confers upon the latter such destructive potentialities that the temptation to yield to passive wishes, that is, to yield to the object's activity, must be fought" (1958, p. 613). The restructuring of the ego in treatment cannot take place until the patient accepts both the passive receptive satisfactions as well as his or her desire for the anal acquisition described earlier which distinguishes itself from the oral ones by the fact that it is more differentiated, localized, elective, and aims at the qualities of the object, its way of being. In their opinion, overt manifestations of oral cupidity often hide the anal greed, and the "I want everything" disguises the "I want this." In the course of development the aggressive aims of these incorporative wishes diminish and a more genuine passive receptive phase takes their place. It seems to me that what Fain and Marty are describing could rightly be called a feminine phase in both sexes and corresponds in some degree to the inner genital phase postulated by Kestenberg.

While basing many of her theoretical formulations of female sexuality on the assumptions of the previous authors cited, Chasseguet-Smirgel more than anyone else has studied the impact of conflicts concerning the anal sadistic drive component on the subsequent evolution of feminine sexuality. She has highlighted repeatedly the struggle of the growing girl against the mother who is experienced as omnipotent, and in a series of writings, some of which are not available in English, she describes in great detail, using many clinical illustrations, how the process of becoming free from the omnipotent mother entails not only the mastery over the mother but also the acquisition of mastery over the body. She gives examples of cases in which this development has not taken place owing to the inhibition of aggression, which, in cases where the mother is too frustrating or too powerful, becomes excessive and must therefore be curtailed. In one of her studies (1962), Chasseguet-Smirgel links the experiences of depersonalization with the failure in the integration of the anal sadistic derivatives with the rest of the ego. Bergler and Eidelberg (1935) previously established a link between depersonalization and an anal derivative, but in their cases the impulse under consideration was anal exhibitionism. However, both studies are in agreement concerning the role of the anal phase in the achievement of adequate representation of somatic and other body experiences in the ego. In the same article, Chasseguet-Smirgel stresses an important distinction: that between the mastery of the object which constitutes impulse gratification and the mastery of the impulse which is a defense mechanism. As she has shown, mastery of the object also leads to mastery of the body and the ability to "own it," whereas mastery of the impulse ushers in self-control. (In this context it might be stated that there is a third option, which is the turning of the impulse against the self, i.e., masochism, which may or may not be accompanied by the inhibition of sadism.) In her way of thinking, then, the taking possession of the body itself comes as a result of a successful resolution of the anal sadistic phase.

In the same article, she clarifies a concept which occurs frequently in present-day French psychoanalysis: the equation made between the anal penis and the anal introjection of the penis as well as the mastery over the paternal phallus:

> 1. Every introjection which has the characteristics of mastery and possession, and which permits the manipulation of the introjected object, is the equivalent of anal introjection, regardless of the anatomical site of this process (be it for instance the hand, the head, the eye, the vagina or even the mouth).
> 2. Every object on which the subject manipulates actually or virtually, contains for the unconscious a fecal component.
> 3. It is valid to think that at the anal stage the child makes new introjections on the anal mode or remakes introjections which have already taken place on another mode . . . This modifies fundamentally the vague and imprecise oral mode which preceded it.
> 4. To master, to manipulate, and to possess an object is a way of introjecting it. In order to master, one must enclose oneself over it, that is, to interiorize anally (etymologically possess equals to sit on (Freud). Mastery is accomplished through introjection. (p. 21.)

The definitions leave no doubt as to the anal nature of this process of introjection. Since, like all introjective processes, it contains a danger to the object, considerable guilt can become attached to the wish. In view of this, Chasseguet-Smirgel demonstrates that the fantasy of being trapped or the impulse to jump into a void stems from the reversal of the introjective impulse; it is, in fact, an introjection directed against one's own body. Instead of entrapping, in this case, the father's penis, there is ideation relating to one's own body being propelled into a destructive container. It is a reversal between container and contained, and in women seems to be a frequent defense against an identification with the mother's vagina which is fantasized as being castrating and destructive. It is clear from this that the more the passive receptive vaginal strivings contain in the way of anal–sadistic derivatives, and the vagina is still experienced as if it were the equivalent of the anus, the greater will be the conflict around genitality and the ability to tolerate penetration without guilt concerning the destruction of the penis in the process. An extension of the problems of anal introjection is the faulty introjection of the paternal phallus which, according to Chasseguet-Smirgel, leads to a sense of lack of genuineness, especially in the area of creativity. In a number of interesting articles, she traces the sense of falseness as it is experienced by artists or as it appears in the content of a work of art to the fear of the anal derivation of the production and the concommitant need to resort to artificiality and glitter in order to dissimulate the relationship between the product and the feared anal processes underlying it. She has shown repeatedly that the regression to anality is caused by the fear of the reality of the differences between the sexes and the generations, and, therefore, there is a defensive attitude which attempts to idealize pregenitality, but the tendency to idealize this regressive mode leaves the individual with the problem of a defensive evasion of castration anxiety or its female equivalent and with the uncertainty as to the validity of their productions because of the regression to anality (1966, 1971, 1974).

In her study of paranoia, Chasseguet-Smirgel delineates the importance of the first part of the anal phase for another aspect of structure formation and secondary narcissism. Her thinking is similar to that of authors like Abraham, Van Ophuisen, Reich, etc. who considered projection to be based on an anal expulsion of the object, followed by the strict avoidance of introjective aims. She points out convincingly that the expulsion does not have an oral character, as Freud would have it, since it is "a concerted process, which takes place in a precise time and place, therefore falls into the spatial-temporal domain" proper to the anal phase as contrasted to the more undefined and vague oral universe. In the process there also takes place the formation of a specific ego (which may be too narrow in its limits because of the projection but is, nevertheless, specific and structured). Because of the pathology of the process, the stress in the paranoiac is on autonomy and separateness, and therefore, there is a deficiency of give-and-take which would be proper to normal development. It seems to me that this particular theory has considerable implications for normal development as well, and it will be taken up again when the little girl's attempt to separate from a mother who has a greater tendency to identify with her than with her male child is discussed. "The acquisitions resulting from sphincter training are entirely put into the service of a narcissistic withdrawal, the object being expelled, controlled, mastered, the ego boundaries severely guarded" (1966, p. 59). In the normal development of girls, as Chasseguet-Smirgel sees it, the turning from the powerful mother to a possibly idealized father is extremely difficult, and she suggests that the struggle against the mother can lead to a split in cathexis during which the aggression is directed toward her, whereas there is a tendency to idealize the father. When this is not resolved the wish to incorporate the father's penis is fraught with excessive guilt because of the need for maintaining his position as an idealized object, and, therefore, there is an inhibition to reintegrate the cathexes in such a way that the father can become the object of both aggression and idealization. "As Freud said, the girl turns to the father to acquire the penis, but her fears, owing to the temporary split between her libidinal and aggressive cathexes at the time of the change of object, are tied to the mother, the guilt to the father" (Chasseguet-Smirgel, 1964, p. 117).

Chasseguet-Smirgel has made a careful analysis of the distinction between the anal wish to incorporate the father's penis and penis envy:

> Realization that possession of the penis presents the possibility of healing the narcissistic wound imposed by the omnipotent mother helps to explain some of the unconscious significance of the penis, whether it is that of a

treasure of strength, integrity, magic power, or autonomy. In the idea connected with this organ we find condensed all the primitive ideas of power. This power then becomes the prerogative of the man, who by attracting the mother destroyed her power. Since women lack this power they come to envy the one who possesses the penis. Thus woman's envy has its source in her conflict with her mother and must seek satisfaction through aggression (that is, what she considers to be aggression) toward her love object, the father. Any achievement which provides her with narcissistic pleasure will be felt as an encroachment on the father's power, thereby leading to many inhibitions, as already mentioned. In fact there is often an unfortunate connnection between violent penis envy and the inhibition or fear of satisfying this envy. The connection arises because penis envy derives from conflict with the mother, giving rise to idealization of the father, which must be maintained thereafter. (1964, p. 116.)

If penis envy is caused by the desire to liberate oneself from the mother, as I propose . . . the girl will simultaneously be envious of the penis and turn to her father, powerfully aided by a basic feminine wish to free herself from the mother. Thus, penis envy and the erotic desire for a penis are not opposed to each other but complementary, and if symbolic satisfaction of the former is achieved this becomes a step forward toward integration of the latter . . . Women do not wish to become men, but want to detach themselves from the mother and become complete, autonomous women. (1964, p. 118.)

And, as Luquet-Parat (1964) suggests, the fear of being penetrated stems from the lack of resolution of the anal-sadistic phase and a projection of the aggression on the object, which then becomes persecutory, making penetration a threat to integrity. Chasseguet-Smirgel makes an interesting differentiation between the identification which is part of normal female development and seems to correspond to the negative oedipal phase and that identification which concerns the autonomous phallus. The latter leads to impenetrability, pathological secondary narcissism, and the wish to be desired as an end in itself, and corresponds to the condition described by Freud when he speaks of narcissistic women. However, the woman who fantasizes being the woman-penis has the wish to complement and complete the man to whom she is closely attached. It is an identification with a part-object and has restitutional qualities stemming from the fear of being identified with a mother seen as anally aggressive and castrating. This pattern too inhibits the full deployment of object relation since libidinal elements come into conflict with a poorly resolved remnant of the aggression against the mother, and

Certain aspects of female masochism seem to be related to this position. One of the main aspects of the masochistic character is the role of being 'the other person's thing.' 'I am your thing. Do whatever you want with me,' says the masochist to his partner. In other words, I am your fecal stool and you can deal with me as you wish. One explanation of female masochism is to be found in its link with the guilt of incorporating the penis in a sadistic anal way, as though women, in order to achieve this incorporation, had to pretend to offer themselves entirely, in place of the stolen penis, proposing that the partner do to her body, to her ego, to herself, what she had, in fantasy, done to his penis. (1964, p. 131.)

The rule of the object is then her law, as was also described by Jacobson, Fenichel and Reich. In addition, however, it might be of interest to recall that Jacobson (1937), who was aware of the pathological consequences stemming from the fantasy of the incorporation of the father's penis, also suggested that, since the fantasy renews the interest in the inside of the body, it can have a favorable effect on the evolution of female sexuality.

As can be seen from the preceding view, the anal phase has a pivotal role in the subsequent psychosexual development of the woman as well as her narcissistic well-being. It was interesting to find that a number of analysts of the Paris Psychoanalytic Society have reanalyzed Freud's case of Dora, with the result that they have drawn attention to the neglect of the anal phase component. In a series of articles in the *Revue française de psychanalyse*, the various omissions are highlighted, and it becomes apparent that Freud's theoretical thinking in that area outdistanced his application of those insights when it came to understanding the relationship between mother and daughter during the anal phase. The articles support the idea that Freud tended to view hysteria as a telescoping of oral and phallic impulses but did not stress sufficiently that this constitutes a failure to integrate the anal strivings into the relationship to the object and that, as Wilhelm Reich (1949) says, "In the hysterical character, mouth as well as anus always represent the female genital while in other character forms these zones retain their original pregenital function" (p. 191). Claude Hollande (1973) highlights the vicarious nature of the hysterical "identification." According to him, it does not lead to a wish to replace the object but rather to enable the subject to participate in the gratifications without, however, doing what the object does. It can be said, on the contrary, that Dora's genuine but unconscious identification tends in the direction of the devalued mother who cleans house but who does not have sexual contact with the father, and not in that of Mrs. K, as Freud suggested. Evelyn Ville (1973) points to the premature character of Dora's oedipal development and the fact that this was achieved by a flight from the aggression against her mother and her inability to master her relationship with her mother so that the mother could become for her a dependable object. "The impossibility to manipulate the other was at the bottom of this incapacity to have a desire of her own. For does not the wish for the other have as its corollary the mastery of the other?" (1973, p. 331). The author suggests, furthermore, that in the case of Dora what is repressed is sexuality in all the aspects that are reminiscent of anality, and this leads to the patient's inability to reveal herself except very indirectly. At the core, however, is the unresolved anal rivalry with the mother, in which this obsessional woman, as she is described by Freud, remains the winner in that she possesses the father's worldly goods, takes care of them and cleans them thoroughly to everyone's annoyance. The advance to the oedipal level, in Dora's case, actually serves to repress that particular rivalry with the mother and is an attempt to set up a triangle with mother substitutes while leaving the anal struggle unresolved. Geahchan (1973), who is in full agreement with this description, suggests that in hysteria there is a flight from the ambivalence of the anal stage and that in its stead there is what he calls a negative identification which is still predominantly oral in nature. He points out the extent to which Dora was indeed identified with her mother and how this came out in later life. I question whether it is necessary to invent a new term for identifications which are repressed or conflicted. Deutsch's (1957) later descriptions of Dora suggest her strong identification with her mother, but one which at the time of her treatment with Freud had been repressed because of its anal content. The flight from her avoided the anal sadistic elements in such a relationship as well as in others, and Freud's symbolic interpretation of the mother's jewelry case in the dream as the female genital neglects that aspect of the container that made it a receptable for the father's wealth. Therefore, he too avoids the interpretation of the dangerous cloacal aspect of the female genital. It becomes evident from this material that Dora identified with her mother's anality but that this identification was repressed and replaced by a hostile and deprecating attitude toward her and a desperate attempt to find another object for identification, Mrs. K.

Freud's relative inattention to the role of the anal phase in Dora's difficulties was stressed convincingly by the authors of these articles. In terms of the theory of hysteria, it has led to the kind of telescoping of the oral and phallic components described by Freud and supports Green's (1973) dictum that in hysteria the breast is already a penis and the penis still a breast. Unfortunately, it seems almost as if the model of hysteria became prototypical for a certain approach to the understanding of female psychology. The dual instinct theory which was eventually translated into a separation between libido and aggression gave further reinforcement to the trend of a telescoping of the phases in such a way that phallic strivings are presumed to follow directly the oral ones and the fate of anality, if considered at all, is studied in relationship to obsessive-compulsive neurosis and problems centering on sadistic perversion exclusively, but not in relationship to the normal development of women. There, the original defense against dirt, already mentioned by Andreas-Salome seems to have remained active, and the lifting of the cover around sexuality has not extended to easing the reluctance to expand and develop further the earliest formulations regarding the anal drive components. Rather, these components tend to be studied in their sublimated forms when they have become character traits and the cornerstones of ego structures. Passive receptivity, interestingly enough, has mainly been viewed as masochism, that is, aggression directed against the self, which is a purely anal way of conceptualizing passivity and receptivity. As this view is losing in acceptability the role of the anal phase is further losing in importance, and the fact that what was being studied was a derivative of the anal drive is obscured by a new kind of terminology involving the realm of narcissism and object relations. It is to be hoped that the studies just cited demonstrate rather convincingly that it is the overcoming of the anal sadistic strivings which makes receptivity less conflicted, guilt-arousing, and narcissistically injurious.

THE SIGNIFICANCE OF THE ANAL PHASE FOR THE GIRL

From the survey of the literature, it becomes apparent that the anal phase of the girl involves a number of important developmental issues, including the separation from the mother, the mastery over her own body and to some degree her environment, ushering in the de-aggressivizing of receptivity. During this time, too, there is an important evolution in the capacity to relate to objects, leading to the turning to the father as the most important love object at the end of this phase. The drive components underlying this evolution are extremely complex in their aim, considering that they comprise both active and passive aims as well as a quality of libido in which constructive and destructive aims are so intermingled that it is difficult to separate them. As this applies specifically to the development of the girl, a further difficulty arises from the fact that the active aims of anality have been studied more extensively than the passive ones, and, therefore, the contribution of that instinctual component, which is most specifically the underpinning of later feminine sexuality, is the least well understood. Despite these difficulties, there is a certain amount of knowledge concerning the role of the anal phase in the formation of the woman's personality, and in order to appreciate it the material has been organized in such a way that the influences of each factor can be evaluated separately, even though such a separation is artificial.

THE OBJECT OF THE ANAL PHASE

According to the scheme which I would like to follow, and in keeping with some of Freud's formulations, the anal phase has its beginning before the mother has attained the status of an object. Therefore, the first object of the anal phase is a purely narcissistic one, that is, the feces. As they are expelled, they attain the intermediate status of being neither completely part of the self nor of the outside world, and subsequently, with the advent of socialization, they eventually become the vehicle for the projection of what is bad, and the love for production becomes transferred onto other objects.

The mother intervenes into this self-feces universe in an attempt to compete, in a sense, with the child over the control of the excremental product, and for her sake a pleasure is relinquished or considerably modified. This has different consequences for boys and for girls, as I discovered many years ago when I did a statistical study involving the differences men and women see between themselves and their parents, and it became apparent that there is a process taking place during the anal phase which causes this stage of development to be experienced differently by boys and by girls. The study showed that women regard themselves as less similar to their mothers than men to their fathers. This is in contradistinction to the assumption that little girls have the advantage in that their role model is present during the formative years, a view to which Stoller still adheres. The most salient of the tentative explanations is, of course, the threat to the girl were she to identify with the object, and this point of view, which stresses her phallic deficiency, while being valid, does not take into account the antecedents. As Jones and Greenacre have pointed out, whatever rivalry and deprecation of the mother there is at the oedipal level, it contains determinants stemming from the anal phase. Here we can postulate that the identification with the mother of the anal phase is often repressed because of the projected aggression which has transformed her into a feared or undesirable object. This has also been highlighted above, when Dora's inability to identify consciously with a mother seen as anally aggressive and withholding was being reexamined. The reason for this image of the mother is twofold: one residing in the girl, which we shall examine later, and the other in the necessity to assume that the mother is indeed more aggressive, controlling and possessive toward her daughter than toward her son. "I was not so much loved as manipulated," says one of my female patients. And we have reason to believe that there is a greater inhibition against manipulating a boy in the same manner, even though we also know of extreme cases in which the mother shows no inhibition. In general, however, the mother seems to be conscious that the boy, in order to become a man, must be allowed to roam and explore, and in her mind he would be a sissy, i.e., castrated, if he stayed too close to his mother.

With reference to the mother's attitude, Galenson and Roiphe say:

> . . . it is likely that the mother's activities are experienced differently by boys than by girls, not only because the genital anatomical structure of each sex provides distinctive sensations, but more particularly because the specific sex of the child provokes special and unique unconscious fantasies in the mother as she handles the infant's genitals. One has only to witness the repetitive and intense genital cleansing practiced by some mothers, in contrast to the almost

complete avoidance of the area by others, to be convinced of the impact on the infant of sexual fantasies aroused in the mother. (1977, p. 35.)

We can broaden this to include fantasies concerning the anal component, and it can be assumed that the same mother, who cleans repetitively, has different fantasies concerning male and female genitals and is more intrusive to her female child than to her male child owing to the anatomical nature of the genitals. She is also likely to be slower in converting the original identification with her baby into greater objectivation, as the child sends confirmation of its separateness.

We can see that Kesterberg's work has important implications for further illumination concerning the handling of the girl by the mother, and we can assume that some of the attitudes which she has observed in little girls are still relevant when these children become mothers themselves. Therefore, when she describes the inner genital phase and stresses the difference between boys and girls in the relationship to the doll-baby, we detect trends that agree with attitudes observed in mothers. The boy's identification seems to be in terms of the activity of the mother; he does with the doll what the mother does with him, whereas the girl tends to see herself in the doll. The doll is more subject than object, and the activity becomes secondary to something which might perhaps be called mirroring. This, it seems to me, has profound implications for the understanding of the maternal attitude of the adult woman toward her real girl baby. Folklore states that "a son is a son until he takes a wife, a daughter is a daughter for the rest of her life." The mother's feelings of possession, lack of differentiation, and identification are enhanced in the case of her daughter, and, therefore, whatever anal sadistic elements are left in the mother's character will come into play more readily with regard to female children whom she tends to equate with her own self. She may treat them with some of the tendency to dominate which she otherwise only unleashes through the superego upon her own self.

The quality of the mother, in turn, makes it more difficult for the girl to attain mastery and individuality, but logically enough, makes the need more imperative. The mother, being seen as more aggressive and intrusive, does not lend herself to being the suitable object of the girl's sadistic drive. This tends to become inhibited and turned inward. The wish to control the object is converted into self-control, a defense against the impulse and therefore impulse mastery instead of mastery of the object, and a greater need to return to introjective mechanisms in an attempt to control the object from within. These assumptions are also in keeping with observations made of girls and boys with reference to the greater speed of ego development in girls as against the accent on drive discharge behavior in boys. Girls are repeatedly described as more inhibited and showing a lowered mood. I believe that this is attributable not to their greater dependency but to the need for reassurance from the mother, whose ability to tolerate the girl's need for individuation is not experienced as reliable. On the contrary, the girl seems to attain a mastery over herself earlier than the boy, who can allow himself greater risks in drive discharge leading to greater dependence on the object's ministrations. The boy ventures more since the dependency on the mother is less destructive and can, therefore, be enjoyed longer. The girl, on the other hand, has to master in order to escape in a more radical sense. She has to master the inside of her body in order to be safe against mother's greater intrusions. Her staying closer and being "better" reassures her against the loss of the mother, which she fears because of the greater intensity of the struggle against her. The girl tends to become her own mother while the boy still tends to depend on his, but this aspect of development is often repressed, especially in those cases where the mother in reality is destructive and abnormally possessive. It can be seen, nevertheless, in the severity of the superego which bears the mark of this internalization of the mother in the anal stage, and it corresponds to the process described by Jacobson and Grunberger as the formation of the early superego.

It seems to me that these developments give an imprint to the female character, both in terms of narcissistic vulnerability and strength. The emphasis is on greater control and inwardness, possibly a greater capacity to bear pain and deprivation, and that narcissistic core which in pathology leads to an excessive need for confirmation but which in normal development contributes to a substratum of strength, stubbornness and tenacity that can be put into the service of constructive life goals. Traditionally, men have drawn upon this typically female strength.

These tendencies, of course, have different ramifications depending on the individuals involved in the process. They account for the finding that women often seem less identified with their mothers than men with their fathers, despite the persistent presence of the role model. They also contribute some support to Freud's suggestion that women tend to be more narcissistic in that they demonstrate an earlier internalization of the mothering and controlling functions of the object; therefore, identification with the mother's control seems more prevalent than with the mother's activity.

This internalization of the controlling aspects of the mother is sometimes hampered when the mother is experienced as so powerful, intrusive and unwilling to relinquish any control that escape from her domination is impossible. In that case there is a tendency to turn to the father at an earlier age for help in being freer from the mother. This introduces a triangular constellation at a time when the sadistic component is at its height and does not yet constitute a genuine oedipal triangle but rather leaves the father in the role of a pawn against the mother. The fight and rivalry revolve around who possesses the father, and it is a power struggle which does not yet concern itself with sexual gratification but with attaining strength for independence from the mother. This development is in keeping with that described by Chasseguet-Smirgel. It only needs to be added here that this process takes place earlier and with greater force (which must then be defended against, often through regression to oral incorporative aims akin to coprophagia) in those cases where no sense of mastery against the mother is seen as possible. The later the process takes place the more the libidinal, conserving and retentive tendencies dominate over the sadistic and destructive ones and the more the father can be experienced as an independent object. As a result, fewer and weaker defenses are needed against the aggression toward the father, and the idealization is not as archaic. There is, however, little reason to postulate that the process described above is ever totally benign and devoid of guilt. It is proper to normal female growth and must be integrated into the mature personality, giving it that imprint which makes it different from that of a man. There also is little support for the idea that cultural differences are apt to change this particular evolution. As background for this conviction, I have observed various modern mothers who wished to avoid the traditional role of being actively domineering or even concerned with cleanliness. The daughters still bear the imprint of a totally unresolved anal struggle, and the father's support was considered inadequate, disappointing, and eventually devalued. In particular, I would like to point to the case of mothers schooled in psychology who know how destructive harsh cleanliness training can be to a child and who, therefore, avoid the traditional and ask instead that the daughters demonstrate that they are quite uncompulsive about dirt, and want to be reassured that they are following the principles of mental health. Thus the pressure to be mentally healthy can replace cleanliness training in harshness and tyranny. It does not seem to me, therefore, that conscious changes in attitude can avoid the difficulties between mother and daughter in the anal phase.

Mahler and Gosliner say:

> We believe the stable image of a father or of another substitute of the mother, beyond the eighteen-month mark and even earlier, is beneficial and perhaps a necessary prerequisite to neutralize and to counteract the age-characteristic oversensibility of the toddler to the threat of re-engulfment by the mother. (1955, p. 209.)

But where the mother is experienced as so powerful and controlling that the child cannot free herself without help, the possession of the father in that light becomes tinged with a fecal component, since it is around the valuation of the feces as objects that the detachment from the mother takes place. When the mother seems to be the undisputed ruler, the identification with the father as a source of strength is fantasized as the possession of another internal object, whose phallic narcissistic qualities are at best doubtful, and where possession does not lead to the sense of completeness which it was supposed to produce. Clinically, this phenomenon is often seen in women who cling to a man they also devalue but from whom they cannot separate, and some of these women react to the loss of the man with eating sprees (junk food).

As to the normal introjection of the father's penis, which takes place toward the end of the anal period, as postulated by Grunberger, we must assume that it is less colored by the kind of introjection which is injurious to the object and makes it disappear, and more by the need to dominate, rule and possess, as described by Chasseguet-Smirgel. It involves the modification of the ego ideal aspects formerly belonging to the mother and, therefore, is a more phallic and less anal introjection. It is an acquisition based more on dominance than on digestion, yet, according to Grunberger, it contains sufficient aggression to lead to guilt feelings which must be resolved. When guilt is so resolved girls as well as boys are given permission to enjoy what they have, which is a narcissistic validation leading into the Oedipus complex.

Failure in this process maintains idealization which is then projected onto the father, or remains with the mother, is fused with the self, or finds an external object or ideal. Real experiences and achievements of the person often become devalued because they are compared to the pure and unadulterated ideal of the immaterial world. Objects and self are either idealized or devalued, and there is conflict when libidinal and aggressive drive components emerge toward the same object because of the inability to value appropriately the relation to the real world. Much of what we now call pathological narcissism can be seen as an attempt to escape the problems posed by the need to confront the reality of a body which is limited, mortal, and therefore, seen too much in the light of a fecal equivalent.

Paula Heimann (1962) stresses that the pleasure of the anal drive concerns the process of productivity and not its outcome, and while this is not the opinion put forth in this analysis of the anal phase, it is assumed here that it is the result of the resolution of the anal phase that productivity and control remain valued impulses and that they have been sufficiently detached from the original object so that all subsequent objects which are controlled or produced are not experienced as fecal equivalents. Or, to rephrase this in terms of Grunberger's terminology, the outcome of the anal phase should yield the ability to establish relations to objects which have an energetic quality and which lead neither to the devaluation of the object nor to fears for its safety because of this added quality.

THE ANAL DRIVE

From what has been said, there emerges an interesting paradox in the development of the girl as compared to that of the boy. In a sense she seems to surrender her anal autonomy more readily, seems to give up the pleasures of timing and control in such a way that she appears to be socialized and conformist. Mothers think in terms of girls being easier to handle at this age than boys. Yet this process of identification with the mother's requirements also leads to attempts to escape the mother's domination, as if to conform were to be free. One patient especially illustrates this kind of thinking in the following fantasy about analysis. Analysis, according to her, is like a rodeo. She is the cow and the analyst is the cowboy. If the cow is smart, she lies down quickly, lets herself get tied up, lets the cowboy have the applause, and then she is free again. It is remarkable to what degree this fantasy was ego syntonic. There was a complete absence of the desire to change and to interact in any other way than to submit passively in order to be free. In treatment she tended to experience every interpretation as a painful intrusion which threatened her sense of wholeness. Thus, the submissiveness, carried to the extreme in this case, did not involve the ability to receive from the object; it was designed to close her off from her mother. In a milder form, this is the tendency of the development of the girl's need to master and control (as compared to the boy's): The sadistic component tends to be directed toward the inside of the body or used in the form of a harsh punitive superego against the impulses (in the latter case it is already a defense). To the degree that the inside of the body becomes more important for the little girl, it paves the way for the relationship to the inner genital, feminine receptivity, and childbearing. The degree to which there is a prevalence of the anal sadistic tendencies influences the ability to enjoy body functions and leads to the problem of transferring prohibitions stemming from the anal period to all forms of sexuality and corporeality.

The inhibition against the outward direction of the need to control, to master, and to dominate, as well as the often prevalent regression to orality make it sometimes difficult to assess the role of the anal component instincts in the study of case material. Often cases are reported as if the oral and phallic conflicts are the only ones which are relevant. However, since those impulses under consideration are directed to the inside of the body, they are more difficult to detect. Nevertheless, they have a distinct character of their own. Thus the types of eating, already mentioned by Lewin, which must be considered as being coprophagic, have often been confused with purely oral derivatives. They constitute the reincorporation of an anal product rather than a feeding substitute, and we must continuously be aware of the considerable overlap between the psychosexual phases where possibly a sharp differentiation can be made only at the cost of artificiality. Thus the wish to fill the digestive tract in order to have an internal object to manipulate, to mitigate against loss, emptiness, and penetration, and to create internal pressure to calm the excitations emanating from the genitals is not primarily a wish to be nourished. It creates a feeling of fullness which negates the loss and penetrability; at worst, it gives the girl a bad inside which the mother would not want anyway and therefore gives her some sense of possession and separates her securely from the mother. Often the quality of the eating suggests its dominant aim, and patients talk about stuffing themselves with junk food and report that the enjoyment is not in the eating; as a matter of fact, they do not taste the food. Yet it cannot be accidental that food is often brown and that when the patients finally decide that they have had enough they throw the rest into the garbage. Their conscious motivation is, of course, not to be tempted by the left-overs, but this occurrence is too common not to betray the character of the fantasy as to the nature of what they were eating in the first place. The food is sometimes stolen or linked to the father, such as being the father's favorite food or meant for the father, etc. This too removes it from the center of the oral period, and the food which the mother gives lovingly. One of the patients said about the food which the mother bought specially for her father and which she was not supposed to eat since it was ''crap'' and not good for her weight: ''You have heard of penis envy, well now you are hearing of crap envy.'' Another patient was very sorry not to be able to finish a cake which a hostess served. She felt that she had eaten as much as good manners would allow and therefore stopped eating while there was still some left. She then bought herself a box of cookies which she devoured. It seemed that having to leave the cake gave her such intense feelings of loss that she had to reestablish control by buying an equivalent product, although in no way resembling the lost one, and filling herself. The fact that there was no qualitative assessment about the taste brings this into the realm of quantity and bulk rather than the need for oral gratification. Statistics gathered by the Metropolitan Life Insurance Company also support the belief that women have more difficulty controlling their eating than men. Women consistently outnumber men significantly in the category of those who are at least twenty percent above desirable weight, and Ritvo says: ''In their milder forms, disturbances of eating . . . constitute one of the most frequent complaints among women students in college health services'' (1977, p. 133). One of the main determinants of this problem in women is the reestablishment of a feeling of control directed to the inside of the body and leads to the sense of an internal object which can be manipulated and which counteracts feelings of loss, emptiness and genital excitement. The girl has a way of identifying with the active mother without becoming conscious of this, by directing the activity toward the inside of the body, which then has the status of an object.

Guilt concerning this cavity erotism of the woman, whose fixation on the anal sadistic mode has not been sufficiently overcome, leads to the tendency to reverse the relationship between container and contained. Instead of she, herself, being the menacing container, the image of the container is projected, and the outside becomes menacing in an engulfing, trapping and controlling way, while she is the threatened inside. Chasseguet-Smirgel has analyzed the impulse to jump into the void or water in terms of the reversal of the original impulse, and frequently we find the fantasy of the trap or the constriction by the rules of analysis in patients who have guilt about their wishes to dominate. In each case it involves turning upon the person the aggression which was inherent in the wish to introject the other. This sadistic fantasy must also be seen in the light of an earlier one of a libidinal nature which pertains to the oral phase, namely, the wish to be eaten or reengulfed by the mother, but it must not be confused with it since in the anal fantasy the aggression and destructiveness are evident, whereas in the engulfment fantasy the fear is that of dedifferentiation.

It is evident that the role of the contents of the body varies in meaning and that these contents, therefore, serve multiple functions starting with the link to the feeding mother, to the freeing of oneself from her, to establishing a fantasized possession of the father. But inasmuch as the anal phase confers upon them an essence which is always fecal, they risk being devalued. Trust in creativity depends to a large degree on the maturational process which detaches the impulses and the products from their derivation, which, as has been shown, is always anal in origin. Kestenberg has pointed to the fear of the little girl that her baby-doll bears the traces of the anal baby. Chasseguet-Smirgel has studied the problems relating to producing something which is experienced as a false phallus and therefore not genuine. Most clinicians have observed the tendency to devalue the concrete since it bears the traces of the manipulations originally fantasized during the anal period. These reactions are some of the most common experiences deriving from the uncertainty with regard to the product and one's ability to produce something of value. Maternal rejection is also partly predicated on the inability to give narcissistic value to the child, and it is often evident that the mother does love her child but is fearful that it does not have the objective value she attributes to it; she, therefore, manipulates and molds the child in order to make it conform to a standard which will be acceptable to others and therefore give her the right to gain the narcissistic gratification she would like from this object. In other words, she loves the child as she loved the products of the inside of her body, but she is aware that this would not be acceptable and has to be made so by various manipulations with which we are familiar. Therefore, in the case of women who have difficulty in accepting their children, it is important to assess whether or not these children are experienced as dirt and as a result have to be rejected because of the danger of being discovered loving an anal product, rather than from a profound rejection of these children. When we observe some of these "rejecting" mothers work over their children in an attempt to make them more acceptable, we can appreciate the origin of the conflict.

Similarly, even though cultural development has made women's aggression more acceptable, there seems to be a new prohibition against anality which has taken the place of the old taboo, for it is safe to say that, recently, culture has tended to devalue the feminine wish to possess and retain. With the advent of new ideas about marriage and child rearing, the emphasis has been placed on the ability of women and mothers to let their mates and children go and not to hold on to them. Such an inhibition of an impulse can lead to many manifestations of problems, for a wife or mother who would be clinging to her objects but who for reasons of a shared ego ideal does not gratify this wish, does not, therefore, mature into a woman who can modulate the wish to hold on and to let go. Instead we see her clinically as a woman who does not seem to close any muscles in around her object with the result that there is a lack of relatedness. Especially the children of these women now frequently become our patients, and they may require treatment which gives them the sense that holding on does not have to lead to the destruction which their mothers feared. The newer norms against anality in women have also prompted many so-called modern women to assume a role with regard to financial arrangements in marriage or sexual partnerships which is the reverse of the traditional one in which the woman was unconflicted about accepting money from the man in her life. The women I am describing are often relatively aggressive in the pursuit of an income of their own but excessively inhibited in exploring their wish to have some financial support from the man with whom they are sharing their lives. What seems particularly interesting in this phenomenon is that greater liberalization of the role of women has led to some gains, especially in the spheres of sexuality and professional development, but in the process other impulses have been inhibited. How much, therefore, the expression of anal cupidity toward an object has become more socially acceptable for women is a point which could be debated. It seems almost as if those women who would have formerly adopted the stance of the little woman toward a man whose masculinity they wanted to bolster are today afraid of castrating this same man anally. The endopsychic conflict against the anal drive components is almost constant, but the manifestations of that conflict are open to cultural influences.

The desire not to let anal aggression or retentiveness come into play in object relations can, of course, lead to an even better known phenomenon: female masochism. The anal component turned against the self was at one time considered so common that it seemed to many theorists to be part of normal female sexuality. In actuality, it can be seen, from everything that was said before, that it is based on a misconception which stresses excessively the anal component of female sexuality. The libidinal strivings of the normal woman are not masochistic; they do not aim toward the attainment of suffering or humiliation. Where sexuality or object relations result in this behavior pattern, strong anal fixations or regressions must be suspected. The position described as extreme submissiveness in women has been characterized by Jacobson, Reich and Fenichel as masochistic and oral. It seems to me, however, that submissiveness is the result of the defense against anal aggressiveness and stubbornness and is, therefore, more closely related to the anal phase, especially since the submission takes place to an object on whom considerable aggression has been projected and is found in women who were not necessarily weak and submissive children. In this respect too it differs from the submissiveness stemming from the passive relationship to the nurturing mother.

The confusion between masochism and female sexuality rests, of course, in a confusion between two separate stages of development which have some degree of similarity in the case of the woman. But from everything that has been said and written about the anal phase one is tempted to agree with Fenichel in his assumption that pregenital libido is suffused with aggression and that only after the pregenital stages have been overcome do libido and aggression become opposites. The passive aims of female sexuality are highly libidinized, whereas masochism contains large elements of aggression. The same kind of transition has been postulated when the change from anal incorporative aims to passive receptive femininity is considered. One is distinguished from its antecedent by the amount of aggression mixed into the libidinal aim. The attempt to separate anal erotism from sadism, on the other hand, seems futile; it appears more accurate to assume that in the course of development object relations become more highly libidinized, and, therefore, the amount of masochism present in female sexuality tells us something about the degree of anal fixation.

ANAL EXHIBITIONISM

Little has been said here or anywhere else about another component of the anal drive: anal exhibitionism. Yet it may not quite be as rare as case material would suggest, and one can observe in certain women a display of incompetence, insufficiency, or defiance that might be derived from the impulse to exhibit themselves anally. Culturally, we saw some of this with the great unwashed generation of teenagers which we have watched as a result of a certain phase of the street culture. Bergler and Eidelberg (1935) describe the cases of two women who suffered from episodes of depersonalization resulting from the defense against the impulse. Certain exhibitions of ineptitude and stupidity, which are more typically feminine than masculine, seem to tend in that direction and follow a defiant, mocking, and caricaturing pattern modeled after phallic exhibitionism but addressing itself to a display of defectiveness or dirt and other unacceptable traits. Bergler and Eidelberg make a connection between excessive self-observation and the defense against this impulse, and in this area too little work has been done, even though we have entered an era in which people continuously speculate about their motives in a kind of perversion of the analytic process. It is as if they were in analysis during most of their waking hours and give themselves tentative interpretations, which act as accusations, as to their motives. According to these authors, this kind of watching serves to inhibit the impulses of anal exhibitionism which would otherwise break through. According to them, the emergence of the wish into the preconscious is met with anxiety, followed by denial and stupidity, and eventually results in the kind of self-observation described above. In this context, it might be interesting to speculate about the effect on the little girl who complains about the lack of a penis and who is consoled by the words, "You have a vagina." If her complaint is directed at her feeling that she has nothing to show, she might eventually have the impulse to show that "nothing" in an act which incorporates a caricature of her feelings and the words of the authority. This, as well as other forms of exhibitionism, have been unduly neglected, and not much is known about them.

SUMMARY

The anal stage constitutes the phase of development during which aggressive aims dominate the libidinal drive, and the passing of this phase leads to the ascendancy of libidinal strivings toward the object and the sublimation of many of the aggressive elements into the character in terms of mastery and achievement. The wish to possess the object becomes transformed into the wish to retain and to cherish, and therefore "conquest," in the romantic sense of the word, of a love object is no longer the equivalent of its aggressive possession. With the passing of the anal phase, female sexuality and receptivity become libidinized and do not endanger the partner as they do when sadistic aims are prevalent. In terms of drive theory, the formulations of Fenichel most aptly describe the evolution which takes place. He suggests that pregenital libido is greatly suffused with aggressive aims and only gradually, during the anal phase, are the two strivings experienced as separate and at times contradictory. If at that time aggression cannot be discharged adequately, the ability to approach objective reality in a way which will make it gratifying will be greatly impaired, and there will be an excessive tendency toward idealization, spirituality, merger fantasies, and magical thinking. Grunberger's contribution to the theory of narcissism points to the necessity of the narcissistic valuation of the anal sadistic component in object relations which leads to its integration. The lack of this resolution results in devalued love relationship or an inability to find a gratifying object due to the idealization, as described by Chasseguet-Smirgel, which means that the wish aims to the attainment of the pure and the immaterial object. Since the anal impulses are turned upon the self more in the girl than in the boy, their ultimate integration into genitality is more problematic, and clinical experience yields many examples of women, even liberated ones, who are inhibited in their ability to avail themselves of a reliable and trustworthy object which they consider "theirs." In these cases the suppression of the anal component has become necessary because of its destructiveness and also because narcissism has remained at the level at which external reality is forever unsatisfying owing to its frustrating aspect. When these women exhibit a blatant orality, that level should not necessarily be considered the main fixation point but a regression caused by the defense against anality. In some cases it seems almost necessary to search for the anal components and their fate, since the clinical picture eclipses it completely.

The issue of the absorption of anal sadism into the character is the same for both sexes. This is especially true now that the realm of mastery and achievement has become more genuinely open to participation by both men and women. It is no longer incompatible for women to be aggressive in the pursuit of their own development. Almost all areas of work, creativity, and achievement have become available, and where women postulate the cultural factors which hold them back as the cause for their failure to achieve, we have, increasingly, reason to believe that the internal factors centering around the power struggle with the mother are at least as important, if not more so. It is interesting to note in this context that women patients can at times accuse a woman analyst of wanting to force them into the traditional feminine mold and thereby say in effect that the analyst does not wish them to obtain for themselves the same gratification as the analyst has from her work. The rivalry with the parent for the same right to achieve is therefore more important than the cultural factors put forth as the reason for the work inhibition.

The problem of the integration of the anal factor becomes more acute and more sex-specific in the area of libidinal object relations. It is here that passive receptive strivings are more properly feminine and must achieve the level of development in which both the receptivity and the object received are not considered dangerous either for the self or the object. As was seen earlier, the tendency of the mother toward greater intrusiveness upon a girl also leads the girl to fear intrusion and loss of body contents more than the boy. Her own sadism turned inward stresses the aggression in some of her introjective modes, which lead to fantasies in which the object is endangered during penetration. Pregnancy confronts her with the necessity of the narcissistic investment in the content of her body, and both aspects of female development—the reproductive as well as the sexual function—necessitate the relinquishment of the object and the capacity to possess and to separate, to libidinize both the filling up and the emptying out processes. Female sexuality is indeed a cavity erotism and, therefore, suffers the fate of its forerunner since both involve receptacles that can be filled and emptied and through which fullness and loss are repeatedly experienced and tolerated. In this way it resembles much more closely than male sexuality the antecedent anal phase and requires its integration as well as its surpassing.

But it is precisely this achievement of a receptive libidinal attitude that is so difficult, since the anal phase is ushered in by an active negative attitude toward the mother and her control. Passivity at this stage would mean reengulfment, whereas the active attitude leads to the desired separation from the mother. As was postulated earlier, compared to the boy there is a greater tendency on the part of the girl to internalize the mother's control and, therefore, to live out her anal sadism in terms of the control of herself and her body. Thus, in the sense that the inside of her body becomes her object, this stage is more narcissistic for her than for the boy, who tends to maintain a greater dependency on the mother's control and care. Further development, however, hinges on the possibility that the girl can find gratification and a reliable object when she attempts to direct some of the anal sadistic drive components outward. This leads to the realization that objects can be mastered and can become need-gratifying, without either oneself or the object becoming destroyed or fused in the process. It can only be restated that because of the greater identification between the mother and her daughter this is more difficult for girls, and therefore the manifestations of both the anal erotic and the anal sadistic drive components toward an external object are more threatening to the girl's need for separateness and nurturance; the need to resolve this crucial problem makes the anal phase a most fateful period of female development.

REFERENCES

Abraham, K. (1924). A short study of the development of the libido, in the light of mental disorders. In *Selected Papers of Karl Abraham*. London: Hogarth Press, 1927, pp. 418–502.

Andreas-Salome, L. (1916). Anal und sexual. *Imago* 4:249–273.

Bergler, E., and Eidelberg, L. (1935). Der Mechanismus der depersonalisation. *Internationale Zeitschrift zur Psychoanalyse* 21:258–285.

Chasseguet-Smirgel, J. (1962). L'analité et les composantes anales du vécu corporel. *Canadian Psychiatric Assn. Journal* 7:16–24.

———(1964). *Female Sexuality*. University of Michigan Press, 1970.

———(1965). Notes de lecture en marge de la révision du cas Schreber. *Revue francaise de Psychanalyse* 30:41–62.

———(1971). *Pour une psychanalyse de l'art et de la créativité*. Paris:Payot.

———(1974). Perversion, idealization and sublimation. *Int. J. Psychoanalysis* 55:349–358.

———(1975). *L'Ideal du Moi*. Paris:Tchou.

———(1976). Freud and female sexuality: the consideration of some blind spots in the exploration of the "dark continent." *Int. J. Psychoanalysis* 57:275–286.

Deutsch, F. (1957). A footnote to Freud's fragment of an analysis of a case of hysteria. *Psychoanal. Q.* 26:159–167.

Fain, M., and Marty, P. (1959). Aspects fonctionnels et role structurant de l'investissement homosexual psychanalytique d'adultes. *Revue française de Psychanalyse* 23:607–617.

Fenichel, O. (1934). Defense against anxiety, particularly by libidinization. *Collected Papers of Otto Fenichel*, First Series, 303–317. New York: W.W. Norton, 1953.

———(1939). Trophy and triumph. *Collected Papers of Otto Fenichel*, Second Series, 141–162. New York: W.W. Norton, 1954.

———(1945). *The Psychoanalytic Theory of Neurosis*. New York: W.W. Norton.

Ferenczi, S. (1923). *Thalassa: A Theory of Genitality*. New York: W.W. Norton, 1968.

Freud, S. (1897). Letter 57. *Standard Edition* 1, p. 243. London: Hogarth Press, 1966.

———(1905). Three essays on the theory of sexuality. *Standard Edition* 7:125–243. London: Hogarth Press, 1953.

———(1908). Character and anal erotism. *Standard Edition* 9:167–176. London: Hogarth Press, 1959.

———(1914). From the history of an infantile neurosis. *Standard Edition* 17:3–123. London: Hogarth Press, 1955.

———(1915). Letter to K. Abraham, May 4, 1915. In *Sigmund Freud Karl Abraham Briefe 1907–1929*. Frankfurt: S. Fischer, 1965.

———(1917). On transformation of instinct as exemplified in anal erotism. *Standard Edition* 17:125–134. London: Hogarth Press, 1955.

———(1929). Civilization and its discontents. *Standard Edition* 21:59–148. London: Hogarth Press, 1961.

———(1932). New introductory lectures on psycho-analysis. *Standard Edition* 22:3–184. London: Hogarth Press, 1964.

Galenson, E., and Roiphe, H. (1977). Some suggested revisions concerning early female development. In *Female Psychology*, ed. H.P. Blum. New York: International Universities Press, pp. 29–57.

Gargiulo, E.A. (1977). Discussion of Developmental Roots of a Special Form of Anxiety in Women by Eleanor Galenson, M.D. (Unpublished manuscript).

Geahchan, D.J. (1973). Haine et identification négative dans l'hystérie. *Revue française de Psychanalyse* 37:337–358.

Green, A. (1973). Introduction à la discussion sur les valuations actuelles de l'hystérie. Panel on Hysteria Today. *28th International Psychoanalytical Congress, Paris*. (Unpublished manuscript).

Greenacre, P. (1950). Problems of early female sexual development. *The Psychoanalytic Study of the Child* 5:122–138. New York: International Universities Press, 1950.

Grunberger, B. (1960). Study of anal object relations. *Int. Review of Psychoanal.* 3:99–110, 1976.

———(1964). Outline for a study of narcissism in female sexuality. In *Female Sexuality*, ed. J. Chasseguet-Smirgel. Ann Arbor: University of Michigan Press, 1970, pp. 68–83.

———(1971). *Le Narcissisme*. Paris: Payot.

———(1971). *Narcissism*. New York: International Universities Press, 1979.

———(1974). Gedanken zum fruhen Uber-Ich. *Psyche* 28:508–529.

Heimann, P. (1962). The anal stage. *Int. J. Psychoanalysis* 43:406–414.

Hollande, C. (1973). A propos de l'identification hystérique. *Revue française de Psychanalyse* 37:323–330.

Jacobson, E. (1937). Wege des weiblichen Uber-Ich Bildung. *Internationale Zeitschrift zur Psychoanalyse* 23:402–412.

Jones, E. (1913). Hate and anal erotism. *Papers on Psychoanalysis*. 3rd ed., pp. 553–561. New York: Wood & Co., 1915.

———(1927). Early development of female sexuality. In *Papers on Psychoanalysis*, pp. 438–451. Boston: Beacon Press, 1961.

———(1935). Early female sexuality. In *Papers on Psychoanalysis*, pp. 485–495. Boston: Beacon Press, 1961.

Kestenberg, J. (1975). *Children and Parents. Psychoanalytic Studies in Development*. New York: Jason Aronson, 1975.

Lewin, B. (1930). Smearing of feces, menstruation and female superego. In *Selected Writings of Bertram D. Lewin*, pp. 12–25. New York: The Psychoanalytic Quarterly, 1973.

Luquet-Parat, C. (1964). The change of object. In *Female Sexuality*, ed. J. Chasseguet-Smirgel. Ann Arbor: University of Michigan Press, 1970, pp. 84–93.

Mahler, M. (1963). Thoughts about development and individuation. *The Psychoanalytic Study of the Child* 18:307–324. New York: International Universities Press.

———, and Gosliner, B.J. (1955). On symbiotic child psychosis: genetic, dynamic and restitutive aspects. *The Psychoanalytic Study of the Child* 10:195–214. New York: International Universities Press.

McDougall, J. (1974a). The psyche-soma and the psycho-analytic process. *Int. Review of Psychoanalysis.*

———(1974b). The anonymous spectator. *Contemporary Psychoanalysis 10:289*–310.

Oliner, M.M. (1978). Le narcissisme: theoretical formulations of Béla Grunberger. *Psychoanalytic Review* 65:239–252.

Reich, A. (1940). A contribution to the psychoanalysis of extreme submissiveness in women. In *Annie Reich: Psychoanalytic Contributions*, pp. 85–98. New York: International Universities Press, 1973.

———(1953). Narcissistic object choice in women. In *Annie Reich: Psychoanalytic Contributions*, pp. 179–208. New York: International Universities Press, 1973.

Reich, W. (1949). *Character Analysis.* New York: Farrar Straus and Cudahy.

Ritvo, S. (1977). Adolescent to woman. In *Female Psychology*, ed. H.P. Blum. New York: International Universities Press, pp. 127–138.

Roiphe, H. (1968). On an early genital phase: with an addendum on genesis. *The Psychoanalytic Study of the Child* 23:348–368. New York: International Universities Press.

Ville, E. (1973). Analité et hystérie. *Revue française de Psychanalyse* 37:331–336.

3

Considerations About The Development of the Girl During The Separation-Individuation Process

ANNI BERGMAN

Freud repeatedly stated that he knew more about the sexuality of boys than of girls. In his paper entitled ''Female Sexuality'' he emphasized the importance and intensity of the preoedipal attachment of the little girl to her mother. He said:

> When we survey the whole range of motives for turning away from the mother which analysis brings to light — that she failed to provide the little girl with the only proper genital, that she did not feed her sufficiently, that she compelled her to share her mother's love with others, that she never fulfilled all the girl's expectations of love, and finally, that she first aroused her sexual activity and then forbade it all — those motives seem nevertheless insufficient to justify the girl's final hostility. Some of them follow inevitably from the nature of infantile sexuality; others appear like rationalizations devised later to account for the uncomprehended change in feeling. Perhaps the real fact is that the attachment to the mother is bound to perish, precisely because it was the first and was so intense. The attitude of love probably comes to grief from the disappointments that are unavoidable and from the accumulation of occasions for aggression. (1931, p. 234.)

This quotation shows that Freud had some inkling of what we now understand better by way of the study of the separation-individuation process with its regularly occurring rapprochement crisis and its necessary resolution.

I will attempt to show how issues of separation-individuation influence the development of the girl child during that period of development and beyond. A brief overview of the separation-individuation process as conceived and conceptualized by Mahler (1963, 1966, 1968) will serve as a background for the discussion of female identity formation with clinical examples of two girls and their mothers. My discussion will focus on the second year of life, in particular on the subphases of practicing and rapprochement.

The symbiotic phase is seen as the bedrock of the individual's identity which begins to be formed before separation-individuation begins. Mahler (1968) describes the mutual reflection of mother and child which, she says, reinforces the delineation of identity. Of special importance in this process is the mother's selective response to the infant's cues.

Lichtenstein, in *Identity and Sexuality* (1961), sees in the early mother-child unit, and not in its breaking up, the primary condition for identity in man. He says, "the very extremeness of the symbiotic relation of the human child to his mother—usually described as the long dependency of the human infant on the mother—becomes the very source of the emergence of *human* identity. . . . Just as an organ within an organism is both 'separate' and 'symbiotic,' the infant is one with the mother but simultaneously bears a primary relatedness of a part to a whole. . . . The organ of an organism has an identity in terms of its functions within the organism, thus the maternal umwelt (which includes the unconscious of the mother) ordains an organ-function to the child, and it is this primary function in which I see the nucleus of the emerging human identity" (p. 202). Core identity, as defined by Mahler and Lichtenstein, is most likely from the earliest time different for girls and boys.

Kleeman (1976) emphasizes the learning experience about one's gender, which he believes to be more crucial than innate differences for the formation of gender identity. From the beginning, the parents' knowledge that "my baby is a girl" organizes a whole set of cues to the infant which eventually become part of the baby girl's self experience. Stoller (1976) defines core gender identity as the sense we have of our sex. It is "the central nexus around which masculinity and femininity gradually accrete. Core gender identity has no implication of role or object relations; it is, I suppose, a part of what is loosely called 'narcissism' " (p. 61). Thus, core gender identity begins to be formed at birth; but I will attempt to show here how it develops during separation-individuation into a girl's unique sense of herself as female and how this sense of herself expresses itself by way of what may be called her identity theme.

Holland, in *Identity and Psycholinguistics* (1978), distinguishes primary identity (something actually in the individual) from the person's identity theme, which also remains constant throughout all the changes in a person's life and lifestyle but is something inferred by someone from outside. He says, "To the extent that I find it convincing to look at human lives as identity themes and variations on those themes, to that extent will I find the hypothesis of a primary identity convincing. To that extent, I can believe that the identity theme I infer from outside for someone coincides with some intrinsic unity inside the individual" (p. 177).

I intend to investigate the identity theme as it develops in interaction between mother and daughter and pertains in particular to the girl's sense of herself as female. In examples of two mothers with their girl children I will infer the girls' identity themes; thus, I will look from the outside, and I will also discuss how these identity themes seem to have been imprinted on their daughters by the mothers' perception of them as female. My clinical material is taken from Mahler's original separation-individuation study (discussed in Mahler, Pine, and Bergman, 1975). Although the separation-individuation process actually begins at the height of symbiosis and the beginning of differentiation (around four to six months of age), I will concentrate on observations of girls as they go through the practicing and rapprochement subphases which cover approximately the second year of life. I have chosen this period rather than the earliest one because, by then, presymbolic action and beginning verbal communication are more understandable to the observer; by then, through her behavior and, later, her words, a girl can give us some indications of her own dawning sense of herself as female. I will also discuss the outcome of the process during the fourth subphase "on the way to object constancy," and beyond to a time when the children were seen in a follow-up study.*

The observational study of the separation-individuation process was begun by Mahler in 1959 at The Masters Children's Center in New York, and its results have been described in numerous publications by Mahler and co-workers (1963, 1966, 1971, 1972; Mahler and La Perriere, 1965; Mahler, Pine, and Bergman, 1970) as well as in the book entitled *The Psychological Birth of the Human Infant* (Mahler, Pine, and Bergman, 1975). Mahler asked herself how normal babies attain a sense of separateness and individuality in the caretaking presence of the primary love object, the mother. She hypothesized the symbiotic origin of human existence according to which the mother and infant form a dual unity from which the infant slowly emerges in a series of steps to become a separate human being with an intrapsychic sense of constancy of the self and the object. Mahler (1971) postulated that the longing for the symbiotic mother, who was part of the self and at one time was able to provide safety and well-being, is an existential aspect of human existence and that this longing for the erstwhile all–good mother "before separation" remains with us throughout the life cycle.

Differentiation from symbiosis begins when the infant has formed a specific attachment to mother and shows a desire to explore the non-mother world. The infant does this visually and tactilely, mostly from the vantage point of mother's arms or lap. With the advent of independent locomotion at around eight to nine

*The Follow-up Study has been supported by The Masters Children's Center, New York, N.Y., and by The Rock Foundation, New York, N.Y., Margaret S. Mahler, Consultant, John B. McDevitt, Principal Investigator, Anni Bergman, Co-Principal Investigator.

months, the circles of the infant's explorations widen. As the baby ventures out further, there is more to see, more to hear, more to touch. But mother is still at the center of her world, and the baby needs to take her for granted and to return to her periodically for "emotional refueling." The elation which is characteristic of the practicing subphase (from about ten to fifteen months) derives on the one hand from the excitement of mastery and the pleasure of exploration, and on the other hand from the feeling of still being one with mother. Emotional refueling is an important phenomenon of that subphase. It describes the way in which a tired baby receives sustenance from brief physical contact with mother and has renewed energy to go forth into the world again with zest and pleasure to begin the unending explorations anew. This is a blissful time for the developing child because for a brief period of a few months the child can literally have it both ways: to venture forth into the world, to explore, to be separate, and yet at the same time to be one with mother and have the sense of safety and protection that this entails. This brings along with it a sense of invulnerability which is important to remember when we discuss the development of the little girl.

Beginning around the age of fifteen months an important change occurs when the infant, who has now become a toddler, becomes increasingly aware of her separateness. Cognitive and motor development has now advanced to a point where the illusion of unity, oneness, can no longer be maintained. The child for us in this chapter, the little girl, now often finds herself alone and painfully aware of her helplessness and vulnerability. Along with this awareness there is also a disillusionment in mother, who no longer can provide solutions as automatically as she could before. The need for emotional refueling is now replaced by a need to share with mother every new accomplishment and pleasure. But concomitantly there is also a need for autonomy and therefore a rejection of mother's help and interference. What we observe is behavior that Mahler has termed ambitendency: alternately a wish to be on one's own and to have mother present to provide solutions, only to reject them as soon as they are forthcoming. This behavior culminates in the rapprochement crisis at around eighteen months which is resolved through partial internalization and identification, as well as by turning to the father, who rescues the child from the struggles with mother. It is with the resolution of the rapprochement crisis that partial object and self constancy are attained, which make it possible for the child to feel and function more separately. One of the important shifts that happen during the rapprochement subphase is a change in mood toward a more discontented and sometimes even sad mood which has been described by Mahler (1966). Mahler hypothesized that depressive moods in women may have their origin in the coincidence of realization of sexual difference with the struggles of the rapprochement crisis, that is, with the realization of separateness and vulnerability.

In what follows I will discuss the identity formation in girls during separation-individuation from the point of view of four findings which importantly interact with each other.

1 The Discovery of Sexual Difference

It was found in the early years of the separation-individuation study that girls discover the sexual differences between themselves and boys at a much earlier age than had hitherto been thought, that is, in the early months of the second year of life; the impact of this discovery depends on many factors, some maturational, some dependent on the mother-child relationship, and some dependent on events in the outside world. Roiphe (1968) took the finding of the early discovery of sexual difference in girls further and postulated an "early genital phase" which, he believes, brings with it an important reorganization of the total personality. By way of observational research, Galenson and Roiphe (1971, 1974, 1976) have explored further the phenomenon of the early genital phase. Their findings show the impact of the early awareness of genital differences on children's subsequent development. They hypothesize a causal connection between an extreme pre-oedipal castration reaction and the later development of a basic depressive mood change in the girl. Galenson and Roiphe (1976), like ourselves, found that the discovery of genital difference takes place at an earlier age than Freud had suspected. In addition, they have described how, in girls, castration responses to the sexual difference are important organizing influences and determine not only the girl's subsequent psychosexual development but other aspects of her personality as well, and they emphasize in particular the influence of early sexual development on symbolic function.

2 Rapprochement Crisis and its Resolution in Girls

It was found in Mahler's study of separation-individuation and confirmed by Roiphe and Galenson that girls have greater difficulty in resolving the rapprochement crisis than boys; whereas boys seem to be more able to turn away from the struggle and invest the world outside with energy, girls tend to become more enmeshed in the struggle which in some cases prevents them from fully turning their energies to the outside world. For example, Donna, who was described in *The Psychological Birth of the Human Infant* (Mahler, Pine, and Bergman, 1975), as well as by McDevitt (1979), is an example of a girl who had such difficulty. Seemingly she had had an ideal early relationship with her mother, who was always available yet never seemed to be intrusive. However, during rapprochement she was unable to engage in pleasurable explorations in mother's presence because she was too anxious about mother's possible departure. She would anxiously cling to mother while she longingly watched other children play. On the other hand, when the separation was accomplished, that is, while the mother left the room for a brief period, she was then free to participate in play. It is possible to trace Donna's anxiety over separation from her mother to a series of traumatic events. Following a medical procedure during which the girl was strapped down in a helpless position, she developed a stronger-than-usual castration reaction. Donna clearly blamed her mother for what she experienced as an insult to her body. The castration conflict, combined with the ambivalence to a mother hitherto all-too-available and not encouraging of the child's separateness and individuation, seems to have contributed to a general inhibition in Donna. This was confirmed at the time of the follow-study when Donna was found lacking in assertiveness and spontaneity.

3 Identification vs. Dis-Identification

In a paper delivered at the 1979 Margaret S. Mahler Symposium in Philadelphia, Mahler (1979) drew attention to the fact that girls face the difficulty of having to identify with the same mother from whom they also have to dis-identify in order to resolve the rapprochement struggle. In all probability this is similar to what Jacobson (1964) has described. She discusses the differences between total identification based on wishes for union with the mother and ego identifications, that is, identification with selective qualities of the love object.

In order to achieve separateness, the infant, who, beginning at the height of symbiosis (around five months of age), by then differentiates mother from others, must begin to differentiate herself from mother, that is, must begin to recognize that she and mother are not one. This process which takes place within the libidinal context of the baby's relationship with both parents is only partially a perceptual-cognitive one. By the time of the rapprochement subphase, almost a year later, maturation has proceeded to such a point that realization of separateness becomes not only a cognitive-perceptual reality but has to be accepted emotionally, as well. The impact of this realization results in a rapprochement crisis characterized by the simultaneous wish for and fear of separateness and autonomy. The little boy is aided in this process of differentiation from mother by identifying with father. The little girl has a more complex task. She, too, has to emerge from symbiosis with mother and attain realization of separateness. For her, too, the father is the important "other," but she has to identify with her mother to confirm her own identity as a girl while at the same time she has to dis-identify, differentiate from her to establish herself as a separate individual. Abelin (1980) postulates three steps in the process of early triangulation — the last one different in boys and girls. He finds that at around 18 months gender identity emerges more readily in boys, generational identity in girls. Generational identity establishes the self "between two objects along one linear dimension'' and the girl's ''. . . generational self-image derives from two identifications within the mother/baby/self triangle'' (1975). In other words, the little girl sees herself as mother's baby or wishes to have a baby like mother.

4 The Mother's Attitude Toward Her Own and Her Daughter's Femininity

It is my impression that the girl's femininity and the impact on her of the sexual difference are closely connected with the mother's sense of herself as a woman and her feelings about her daughter as a girl. In subtle ways the mother communicates to her daughter what she wishes her to be, what she feels that she can be, and what she feels that she might be. The girl, on becoming an individual in her own right, has to come to terms consciously and unconsciously with her mother's conscious and unconscious expectations. Stoller (1976, p. 61), in discussing core gender identity of the girl, postulates as one of the factors of importance "the unending impingement of the parents', especially mothers', attitudes about *that* infant's sex and the infant's constructing these perceptions, via its developing capacity to fantasy, into events, i.e., meaningful, motivated experiences." Grossman and Stewart (1976) emphasize the importance of parental attitudes toward the sex of their child: ". . . to the child, the meaning of the discovery of the 'anatomical distinction' will depend on a complex variety of preparatory experiences. The timing of this discovery will be important, since the child's cognitive and libidinal levels will naturally play a part in his interpretation of this new information. Narcissistic conflicts and the child's relations to both parents will determine the final result. Parental attitudes toward the sex of the child, toward their own genitals and sexual relationships, will aid or disrupt the child's integration of the awareness of the genital differences" (pp. 206–207).

From the point of view of these four findings and considerations, we will now turn to observational data which will illustrate the complexity of female identity formation. At an early age, probably during the late practicing period, with immature cognitive capacities the girl notices the anatomical differences between the sexes at a time when the sense of separateness is not firmly established, thus at a time when mother is still expected to provide magical solutions. During early rapprochement, the renewed closeness to mother is helpful, but the rapprochement crisis demands that the girl dis-identify from mother sufficiently to become a person in her own right, and feel safe enough from fear of reengulfment to selectively identify with qualities of the mother (Jacobson, 1964). How the girl will achieve this task is importantly influenced by the mother's attitude to a girl child. This attitude of the mother is colored by her own sense of herself as a woman and by the meaning to her of a girl child. In relating to her daughter, the mother probably relives important aspects of her own separation-individuation process. The process for the girl child, which I hope to be able partly to illustrate, is unique to each mother-child pair. It will never be simple, and it will importantly shape each child's ultimate sense of herself as a woman, which will include her behavior as a mother.

The examples of two girls from an observational study illustrate the interplay between the recognition of sexual difference, the resolution of the rapprochement crisis, the vicissitudes of the mother-daughter relationship and how this is influenced by the mother's feelings about herself as a woman.

The two girls chosen for illustration of this complex interplay have in common that both of them had older brothers; thus the exposure to the anatomical difference took place naturally from the beginning within the family. Both girls grew up in families in which the father had an important role. Both mothers stayed at home and devoted themselves fulltime to their families. The manifest, openly expressed attitude toward femininity was very different in these two mothers, and it is this openly expressed attitude which is considered here as having an important impact on the children and in playing an important role in the formation of their identity themes as girls. (If we had access to the unconscious fantasies of the mothers about their own femininity during their daughters' separation-individuation process, we would add the mothers' unconscious fantasies to the complex interplay of forces we are attempting to describe.)

CLINICAL EXAMPLES

Anna and Her Mother

We first saw Anna when she was ten months old and her brother was two years old. From the beginning the mother felt ill at ease with her girl child and openly stated that she would have preferred a boy. The reason for this, she said, was that Anna's presence forced her to experience her own feelings about herself as a woman. She thought that girls and women had a hard lot in life because they always had to worry about their looks and their weight in order to please men.

Mrs. A was a very beautiful woman. Although she complained about the woman's lot in having to please men, she was on the whole more interested in, and more at ease with, male observers than female ones. She was not very sociable and did not easily talk about herself; especially, she rarely talked about her own childhood. She much preferred talking about her husband and his family.

She was in great awe of her husband's family and spent much of her time trying to improve herself in an attempt to live up to her husband's family's standards, which were highly intellectual. While Anna's mother worried a great deal about her own looks as well as her daughter's, she did little to make the child look pretty, as if there were a dawning jealousy and competitiveness with a female child. One always had the impression that mother had to work so hard at improving herself that looking after yet another female person was simply too much trouble. When Anna was thirteen months old her mother worried whether her hair would curl, and said that a boy was much easier to care for. As if in response to mother's comments, Anna began to imitate her brother and want what he had. Mother told of a poignant incident in which Anna's brother would not lend her his gun and Anna cried inconsolably. Anna's father, whom Anna loved dearly, insisted that the brother had the right to keep his gun for himself. Mother was sympathetic to Anna's plight, but, typical of her ambivalence toward females and toward herself, she could not find a solution to Anna's problem. Whereas mother said in her presence that it was better to be a boy, she on the other hand did not make any gesture to help her to assert herself vis-à-vis the boy. Thus, Anna was caught. The gun, we may assume, was already a symbol of masculinity. Although she was told it was better to be a boy, she could not get any support, from mother or father, to share in her brother's masculinity.

We have no direct evidence that Anna was aware of the sexual difference, but we would suspect that she was. This awareness may have been a particularly painful one for her because her mother expressed so many feelings about how hard the lot of a girl was. We may infer that sexual awareness may have been present from some of Anna's behaviors. For instance, she became increasingly possessive and wanted whatever her brother had. Another interesting and relevant observation made at this time was that Anna looked anxiously for her leg and seemed to think that she had lost it because she was sitting on it and could not see it.

By now Anna had already begun to show great love for her father and sometimes showed preference for him. Mother, who was always unsure of herself as a mother, immediately took this as an indication that she was not a good mother to her little girl. She could not see what was very obvious to observers, namely, that Anna was always immediately responsive to her mother's attention. Though her mood was on the whole low-key, she would immediately become active and cheerful when mother paid attention to her. Most of the time, however, Anna was quiet and subdued. In other words, Anna experienced the omnipotence and elation typical of the practicing subphase in a delayed and muted way.

When the family came back from summer vacation (Anna was about eighteen months old), mother began to toilet train her, and their relationship improved. Mother had been greatly relieved when Anna began to be more separate and autonomous because she did not feel that she was a good influence on her child. Her self-esteem as a mother was extremely low. She did not want

Anna to be part of her because she did not feel "good" as a woman. Her own negative self-image and lack of satisfaction with herself was transferred onto Anna; however, her vanity and narcissistic preoccupation with herself were not.

As Anna became more separate, an interesting phenomenon occurred within the mother-child relationship on the mother's side; that is, mother began to "hide" her own needs behind Anna's. It was striking how often Anna's mother expressed her own feelings and needs by way of talking about Anna. For example, when she was depressed, she complained that Anna never smiled; when she clearly did not feel like leaving the room for an interview, she said, "Anna will not let me go." When she herself seemed to feel tired and in need of being cared for, she told Anna to ask an observer to wipe her nose. Mrs. A's interviewer was struck by his observation that Anna's mother found it very difficult to express her own needs in a direct way. She often used words in such a way that one word undid the other. It was almost as if Anna was becoming the mother's alter-ego, a very interesting observation in view of Anna's later development. Unconsciously she was also drawing Anna closer to herself.

At the age of twenty months, Anna became toilet trained and, at the same time, according to mother, began to develop a ferocious will of her own. She became more clinging and demanding, more openly jealous of her older brother, and insisted on being right in the middle of the family. Anna referred to her brother as "the boy" rather than by his name. At the same time she began to show more active interest in being a girl. She liked to look in the mirror and paid more attention to her clothes and hair, an important identification with mother. Mother reacted immediately by expressing concern that Anna would become just like all the other little girls who were interested only in their appearance. Noticing Anna's blossoming femininity, mother again withdrew from her. She went and had her ears pierced. This could be seen as her effort to concentrate on *her* femininity rather than on Anna's. It seemed that she had experienced the spurt of her daughter's femininity as something of a threat. She dressed up for her male interviewer and seemed to compete for his attention with her daughter.

On the whole, the period of early rapprochement was a positive one for Anna, as she was able to demand more attention from her mother who responded by spending somewhat more time with her. By the age of twenty-one months, Anna was fully toilet trained, her language development was excellent, and so was her symbolic capacity as she began to express herself through fantasy play and show a lively interest in books, pictures, and stories.

At this time Mrs. A announced that she was four months pregnant. Mother's pregnancy coincided with Anna's growing separation. It came at a time when Anna was beginning to show the first signs of identifying with mother, and mother in turn seemed to be relinquishing her own needs by expressing them through Anna. We may speculate on some of the emotional significance of the mother's pregnancy at that time. Was it the creation of a new union at a time when Anna was becoming more separate? Or was it an anxious flight from an overly close relationship with her daughter which was experienced as painful, and which, from the beginning, had to be defended against?

Whatever the mother's unconscious reasons for her pregnancy might have been, Anna reacted to it by losing her pleasure in being a little girl. She began to talk about herself as either the baby or the boy. Following the birth of her baby sister, Anna went through a renewed period of rapprochement crisis. She withheld her stools, she became extremely demanding and was unhappy both in mother's presence and absence. Anna's mother became increasingly desperate, and eventually, following the birth of her third child, began to develop an obsessional fear that her hair would fall out. She was upset with herself for being so worried and described herself as extremely egotistical. She suffered on the one hand from the fear that she would lose her beauty and femininity, thus showing her wish to be feminine. But on the other hand, she blamed herself for her feminine vanity because she felt that this interest interfered with her ability to be a good mother. She constantly struggled to improve herself, and in fact it was that which interfered with attentiveness to her little girl. This seems to have been the essential dilemma for her—the burden of her femininity.

The situation of intense struggle between Anna and her mother continued throughout the third year of Anna's life. There were better times, which were often triggered when Anna was given tangible proof of love by her mother. Mother sometimes gave Anna sweets which she craved, and at times Anna showed pride in the clothes that her mother had made for her. Eventually, improvement occurred when Anna identified with her older brother and often enjoyed boy's play. She was able to take pleasure in her body. She also enjoyed all kinds of fantasy activity, and on a particularly good day she would imitate Superman. She became elated when she was able to play out her denial in fantasy. The fantasy of being Superman probably contained two wishes: one, to be a boy, the other, to be the all-powerful symbiotic mother—the mother before separation-individuation (Mahler, 1979). If this is so, it would confirm the contention of Fast (1979), who sees the formation of gender identity as a process of differentiation which requires the reunciation of the omnipotent state of being which each gender experiences in a different way.

At the end of the separation-individuation period, however, Anna continued to have a very conflicted and ambivalent relationship with her mother. She was far from comfortable with her self-image. The struggle over urine and bowel control continued, as did the struggle over her sexual identity. She alternately saw herself as Mighty Mouse and powerful, or as baby and helpless. Only on rare occasions could she pleasurably be a little girl.

It is interesting to compare impressions of Anna at the end of her separation-individuation process with those of the psychologist who tested Anna at the time of the follow-up study when Anna was eleven years old. The report states: "Anna is a pleasant, wholesome-looking, 11-year-old girl. She does not smile, she is serious, straight-laced and 'grownup.' Anna's speech pattern is clipped and precise with little voice modulation or variation. Her characteristic attitude is 'I'll do anything you ask me to do, don't worry about me, I can manage any hardship.' " When the tester asked if she minded when people smoked, she replied, "Oh, yes, but don't let that bother you. I mind naturally when my father smokes because it's not good for him, not because I mind. I really don't mind and it probably has nothing to do with my allergies. You can really smoke if you want to." Here again we find replayed the words that mother said so often to Anna when she was an infant, namely, that the lot of the girl is a hard one and that girls have to give up a lot in order to please others, especially if they want to please men. Later on in the test, when Anna was asked what kind of animal she would like to be, she said, "A bird, birds can fly, and I'd be the kind that people don't shoot. And I'd be a cardinal and make sure I'm a boy bird because he looks better."

Thus we see in Anna first a compliance with mother's wish that she not be feminine and then, at the time of the temporary resolution of rapprochement, attempts to take more pleasure in her self and concomitantly to become more feminine. Following mother's withdrawal and the birth of her baby sister, Anna showed a renewed surge of ambivalence and envy. She withheld stools, became clinging and demanding, and seemed to renounce her own separate feminine identity.

A school report about Anna described her as the kind of girl who needed a best friend with whom she could develop a twin-like relationship. Her need for a twin-like friend indicated that she probably hadn't resolved the separation-individuation process well enough to feel good about herself without the availability of another person to confirm her own separate individual identity. But the need for the twin-like friend is also reminiscent of the way in which mother had related to Anna when Anna first became more separate, namely, by hiding her own needs behind the needs of her daughter.

Mary and Her Mother

Our second case, a little girl named Mary, was chosen for the sake of comparison and contrast. Like Anna, Mary had an older brother. Like Anna, Mary had a devoted and involved father. Mary's mother, too, talked a great deal about her husband, but the relationship with her husband seemed less insecure and competitive. Mary's parents were very much a couple. Mary's mother depended on her husband for help, and he was a source of emotional support for her in the task of child rearing. She clearly expressed her pleasure in their relationship and her pleasure in being a woman. Mary's mother had had a profession before her marriage. Marriage and motherhood were clearly a choice for Mrs. M rather than a way to make up for imaginary shortcomings.

From the beginning, Mary's mother was very happy with her. She clearly stated that she was happy to have had a girl (she had had great difficulty in accepting her first baby, a boy), and she said that a girl was a gift to the mother. During the entire first year of her life, Mary was said to have been a very easy baby for her mother to take care of. An interesting change occurred around thirteen months of age, shortly after Mary began to walk. At this time the family was taking weekly trips to a nearby weekend house. On that particular weekend, Mrs. M had forgotten to bring Mary's bottle and decided that this was a good opportunity to wean her. This was the time when Mary was taking her first steps, and her older brother, who seemed to have experienced this as a threat, suddenly became quite aggressive toward her. A week later, Mary's mother reported that Mary had become aware of her brother's penis and had tried to touch it.

The taking away of the bottle, the trip to the weekend house, the beginning of walking, and the awareness of sexual difference all seemed to have coincided and brought about a pronounced change in Mary's mood. Mrs. M, in reporting on the weekend, said, "I don't know what has happened to my sweet little girl. She has always been so good and happy. This weekend she was unhappy all the time. She would lie down and cry and have temper tantrums over the slightest frustration. I took her to the doctor, but the doctor found nothing wrong with her. He thought that maybe Mary was teething." During observation time, Mary found it difficult to stay in the room. She wanted to rush out constantly, and she was very possessive about a doll carriage which she attempted to push around all morning. Here is the first indication of something that was later to take on great importance, namely, that Mary dealt with disappointment and distress by clinging to the mother-baby relationship (Abelin, 1980). This started a period of extreme jealousy on Mary's part toward her brother, Bobby. Whenever mother paid any attention to him, Mary clamored for attention and also began to imitate Bobby.

Mrs. M felt quite helpless and overwhelmed by this turn of events and found it very difficult to attend to both children equally. Mary also developed a sleep disturbance and regularly woke up in the middle of the night. Mother said that she was beginning to become aware of Mary's bowel movements, and she began to toilet train her. Mary strongly turned to her father and developed what mother called a "love affair" with him. When he came home in the evening, she would cry until he picked her up. Mrs. M was surprised by Mary's attachment to her father and said that Bobby at that age had never had a similar attachment. Mother, who considered Mary her little girl, showed signs of jealousy.

From about thirteen to fifteen months of age, Mary became more and more aggressive and possessive. She wanted not only what her brother Bobby had but transferred this aggressiveness to our Center, where she struck out at all the other children. She also became vulnerable, crying hard and lying down on the floor whenever she was hurt or frustrated. At around fourteen months, she developed a fungus infection in the urinary area. Thus, Mary seems to have been unable fully to enjoy her practicing period. This seems to have been interfered with by her awareness of the sexual difference, which coincided with beginning to walk, her brother's reaction to her at that time, and with the mother's sense of helplessness and disappointment in Mary, who was supposed to have been the "perfect little girl."

By the time the family returned to the Center after summer vacation, Mary was eighteen months old and had changed considerably. She was beginning to show a pleasurable awareness of her whole body. She seemed to have coped with the early castration reaction and penis envy by investing her whole body with pleasure. She often went to the mirror and lifted up her shirt. When mother put a new coat on her, she went to the mirror and looked at herself pleasurably. At home she liked to go around without clothes on. Some masturbation was observed when Mary attempted to press a ball between her legs briefly, apparently deriving pleasant sensations from this. Mary now turned her anger toward her mother and became less aggressive with her brother. She continued to imitate her brother and no longer wanted to wear dresses. Thus, at the height of the rapprochement crisis, Mary showed anger toward her mother and did not want to be a girl.

Sex play between the children was reported, and Mary seemed to enjoy it. Curiosity about the body and body functions was also expressed in her symbolic play (see Galenson, 1971). At the Center she teased another little boy by taking the hat off his head, crushing it, asking someone to fix it, and then putting it on her own head and laughing at the little boy. Mary became very interested in going to the bathroom. Masturbation often took the form of vigorous riding on the rocking horse. But she also frequently went to the playpen and pretended that she was a baby. When mother said that she was a big girl, Mary angrily replied that she was a baby and sat in the doll carriage. Mary's desire to be a baby at this time may have been a way to cope with her castration anxiety. She followed her brother to the bathroom, watched him while he urinated upright, and tried to do the same by squeezing herself.

By the age of twenty six months, Mary's aggressive behavior, which had begun when she had first become aware of the sexual difference, began to alternate with periods of feminine tenderness. She became quite affectionate with little boys and often kissed and hugged them.

It appears that, by the beginning of her third year, Mary had come to terms somewhat with being a little girl and had resolved her rapprochement crisis to some extent. She turned strongly to her father and began to enjoy more cooperative play with other children; however, her concern with the sexual difference remained and was shown clearly in her play and in verbal communication. She now began to be more aware of the female genital. The following play sequences illustrate this: She picked up a large ball, pointed to a dent in it, and said that it had a hole. During one play sequence at the water table, she took a pan and clutched it to her chest saying, "I have an egg beater at home but it is broken. There is another one, but it too, is broken." She put her hand into the soapsuds and said that she was making a hole in it.

During various points in the year Mary shifted back and forth between being more masculine and aggressive, and more feminine and coy. She sometimes wore dresses, and it seemed that she began to imitate mother. She was proud of a headband and didn't want to be without it. Finally, toward the very end of the year, Mary's mood seemed to shift, and she became more depressed and low-keyed. She developed a separation reaction which remained quite strong for several months, and she became more clinging and whiny and wouldn't let her mother leave.

Mary tried to woo her mother, hugging her and bringing her cookies. Once when the mother was absent from the room, Mary asked, "Where's my mommy?" When she didn't get an answer, Mary threw the mother-doll on the floor and screamed, "Mommy is thrown on the floor. I threw her on the floor."

We see in Mary, throughout the third year, a continued rapprochement struggle which centered heavily around penis envy and castration anxiety. At the end of the third year there is a suggestion that Mary gave up some of her omnipotent demands for a penis and at the same time became more subdued. It is hard to say at which point in development Mary's rapprochement struggle changed toward a more oedipal struggle with mother. But it seems quite certain that hostility toward mother increased during the third year and that the attachment to father, which had begun at around the age of twelve months, became deeper and more intense.

The follow-up study showed that Mary, at the age of eight, still struggled over the sexual difference and over accepting herself as a girl. During the tests, Mary was resentful about the demands made upon her, as though she expected to be accepted without having to give anything in return. This attitude was defensive inasmuch as Mary was actually afraid to be found lacking, and she became quite upset when she didn't know an answer to a question. She would give a spiteful, silly, or even wrong answer before she would allow herself to show that she cared enough to try to think and reflect. Mary gave no direct signs of caring what the tester thought of her. She was concerned not to reveal her defects. The tests found Mary's ego functioning to be excellent but her emotional life somewhat inhibited, with isolation and rationalization being the prominent defenses. She withdrew from situations which might evoke defeat or criticism.

At eight years of age Mary was competent and independent. Body narcissism, which had begun a little after she was one year old and peaked at twenty months of age, continued to be important. It expressed itself mainly in her interest and excellent performance in gymnastics. At the same time, she retained for herself the privileges of being the baby in the family. This was encouraged by her mother, who, in her own life, had not received enough privileges of a baby.

When her mother made demands on her, she often told her mother that she was still a baby, and her bed was filled with all her old stuffed animals.

The escape into babyhood seemed something like a shared fantasy between mother and child, a shared fantasy of symbiotic bliss when Mary was the perfect baby-gift to the mother and the mother the all-good mother ''before separation'' (Mahler, Pine, and Bergman, 1975).

She identified with the maternal aspects of mother while keeping femininity and female sexuality in abeyance. Enjoyment of her own body in sports and gymnastics could be seen as identification not only with her brother but also with her mother, who was a very active, handsome woman. The relationship between mother and daughter at the time of the follow-up study was a harmonious one.

DISCUSSION

I have elucidated some of the struggles of the little girl during the period of separation-individuation in relation to her establishment of gender identity. We assume that during the first year of the girl's life the mother has already treated the little girl in accordance with her own feelings about the child's gender. Early during her second year of life, the girl begins to recognize the anatomical difference between herself and the little boy. We believe that the recognition of the sexual difference is a developmental process. How the girl experiences and deals with what she sees depends on the state of cognitive development, on the state of self-object differentiation, and on the state of her psychosexual development — all this within the framework of her object relations to mother and father. The girl child also begins to know her own body in relation to her mother's as she begins to develop awareness of her own female identity. During the rapprochement struggle she has to assert herself vis-à-vis the mother — on the one hand to establish her separateness and begin to identify with qualities of the mother, on the other hand to establish her female identity. It is a long and complicated task, unique for each mother-daughter pair, and helped greatly by the relationship to the father, who needs to confirm the femininity of both mother and daughter.

Returning now to a comparison between two mothers and two daughters, I shall go back to the four points discussed at the beginning of this paper and compare them for the two cases presented.

1   Discovery of Sexual Difference

Anna: she first noticed and reacted to the anatomical difference between the two sexes early, probably as early as thirteen months. This discovery was colored by her mother's constant worries and complaints about being a girl and by growing up with a brother fourteen months her senior. It was not directly reported by the mother but could be inferred from Anna's behaviors.

Mary: She seems to have first discovered the sexual differences early, at thirteen months, during the height of the practicing period proper. This, combined with mother's decision to suddenly wean her from the bottle, caused temporary dampening of the elation characteristic of that subphase, as well as in increase in rivalry and aggression toward her brother.

2 Resolution of the Rapprochement Struggle

Anna: There was no real resolution of the rapprochement crisis. Following the announcement of her mother's pregnancy and the birth of her baby sister, she became enmeshed in an intense rapprochement struggle. She became severely constipated and demonstrated several of Mahler's danger signals, namely, excessive clinging and shadowing, frequent temper tantrums, and splitting of the good-bad mother image (see Mahler, 1966).

Mary: During the rapprochement crisis, aggressivity increased and was largely directed toward the mother. There was no clear resolution of the rapprochement crisis, which extended into the third year. Symbolic play revealed concern over body intactness. Mary found consolation in the relationship to her father, taking pleasure in her body, and remaining the baby in the family.

3 Identification vs. Dis-Identification

Anna: As Anna became more separate she also became more like mother, that is, more feminine. This was poorly tolerated by mother. Thus, for a while she was happiest when she dis-identified from mother and renounced her femininity to be a boy, or even better, Superman.

Mary: Mary and her mother had had a pleasurable period of symbiosis and differentiation. As Mary became more separate during practicing, she discovered her father and brother. But being not-mother in Mary's case seemed to mean being the baby.

4 Mother's Attitude

Anna: Mother communicated her conflicts over her own femininity to Anna, who then incorporated these feelings and conflicts into her self in subtle ways. Her desire to be a male cardinal whom no one would shoot is symbolic of her simultaneous wish to be beautiful, a boy, free, and unthreatened by male penetration. Furthermore, the mother showed a longing for her own mother through her tendency to use Anna as a vehicle for the expression of her own impulses and wishes. This need, in turn, was carried further by Anna who eventually showed a longing for a "bosom-friend" who it seems would help her establish an identity for herself. Although mother devalued femininity, she guarded her own femininity closely and resented competition. It seems that Anna withdrew.

Mary: Mary's mother, who professed happiness as a woman, found being a mother difficult. She had experienced her daughter as a gift to mother. But this was difficult to maintain as Mary grew up and experienced conflicts in connection with her discovery of the sexual difference. Mary seems to have internalized the mother's wish that she remain the perfect baby. At the time of the follow-up study, when Mary was eight and a typical girl with latency interests, the mother reported that Mary insisted on remaining the baby of the family. The tester reported that Mary anxiously defended against any recognition that she might not be perfect.

Both Anna and Mary, perhaps facilitated by the presence of their older brothers, showed early awareness of sexual difference. In Anna's case the awareness has been inferred. In Mary's case it was expressed directly and openly. Interestingly, Mary, whose mother was happy as a woman and happy about the birth of a girl child, struggled more actively and openly over the acceptance of the sexual difference. She found solace in remaining the family's baby and, in partial identification with her mother, in taking care of imaginary babies and her stuffed animals. She also invested her whole body with narcissistic and exhibitionistic pleasure.

Anna, whose mother experienced femininity as a task rather than as a pleasure (thus warding off underlying femininity and vanity), expressed her feelings about the awareness of sexual difference less directly and struggled less actively over its acceptance. She was happiest when she could deny her femininity altogether and pretended to be Superman. Her rapprochement crisis was more painful than Mary's. The struggle with mother was much more intense and centered around the withholding of her bowel movements and intense separation reactions. Nevertheless, she found a solution that was individual; and, eventually, she may have continued to rework separation-individuation issues by way of closeness to a girl of her own age.

Both girls experienced difficulty at the time of practicing proper and the attainment of upright locomotion. The "love affair with the world" was disturbed, was subdued—a disturbance, it seems, due to the realization of sexual difference which mother could not undo. It would seem possible that this separates the girl from the mother too rapidly and suddenly, and prevents the gradual deflation of omnipotence and illusion of oneness. If this is so, it would help to explain the prolonged rapprochement struggle of the girl. This prolonged rapprochement struggle could then be seen as the girl's wish, and often demand, that her mother remain close and available to make up for too sudden a loss during the practicing subphase. How the mother experiences the girl child and herself as a woman provides the identity theme for the girl.

In the two examples we discussed, Anna's identity theme incorporates both her mother's belief that a woman should be beautiful and that it would be better to be a man. In the case of Mary, her identity theme incorporates her mother's pleasure in herself as a woman and her mother's feeling that the perfect girl baby is the perfect gift to the mother.

Both mothers experienced difficulty with the separation of their daughters as epitomized by upright locomotion. Anna's mother expressed relief but began to hide behind her daughter; Mary's mother decided to take the bottle away, thus attempting to force her daughter to grow up faster than she was ready to. It may be that the mother experiences the daughter's growing separateness as a loss and thus reacts to it in a way that is idiosyncratic and probably connected with her own separation-individuation.

Giving birth to a girl baby may be for the mother a kind of fulfillment of the rapprochement wish for generational identity (Abelin, 1975) — which is the double wish to be a baby and have a baby, and through which the loss of the mother during separation-individuation can be temporarily undone. Her own symbiosis with mother may be reexperienced with her daughter, and thus the loss at the girl's growing separation would be a double one — the loss of the baby and the loss of the mother.

REFERENCES

Abelin, E.L. (1975). Some further observations and comments on the earliest role of the father. *Internat. J. Psycho-Anal.* 56: 293–302.

———(1980). Triangulation, the role of the father and the origins of core gender identity during the rapprochement subphase. In *Rapprochement*, eds. R. Lax, A. Burland, and S. Bach. New York: Jason Aronson.

Fast, I. (1979). Developments in gender identity: gender differentiation in girls. *Internat. J. Psycho-Anal.* 60:443–453.

Freud, S. (1931). Female sexuality. In *Standard Edition* 21:223–243, J. Strachey (tr. and ed.). London: Hogarth Press, 1961.

Galenson, E. (1971). A consideration of the nature of thought in childhood play. In *Separation-Individuation: Essays in Honor of Margaret S. Mahler*, eds. J.B. McDevitt and C.F. Settlage. New York: International Universities Press, pp. 41–59.

———, and Roiphe, H. (1971). The impact of early sexual discovery on mood defensive organization and symbolization. *The Psychoanalytic Study of the Child* 26:195–216. New York: Quadrangle Books.

———(1974). The emergence of genital awareness during the second year of life. In *Sex Differences in Behavior*, eds. R.C. Friedman, R.M. Richart, and R.J. Van de Wiele. New York: Wiley, pp. 223–231.

———(1976). Some suggested revisions concerning early female development. *J. Amer. Psychoanal. Assn.* 24:29–57.

Greenson, R.R. (1954). The struggle against identification. *J. Amer. Psychoanal. Assn.* 2:200–217.

Grossman, W.I. and Stewart, W.A. (1976). Penis envy: from childhood wish to developmental metaphor. *J. Amer. Psychoanal. Assn.* 24:193–212.

Holland, N.N. (1978). What can a concept of identity add to psycholinguistics? In *Psychoanalysis and Language,* ed. J.H. Smith. New Haven: Yale University Press, pp. 171–234.

Jacobson, E. (1964). *The Self and the Object World.* New York: International Universities Press.

Kleeman, J.A. (1976). Freud's view on early female sexuality in the light of direct child observation. *J. Amer. Psychoanal. Assn.* 24:3–27.

Lichtenstein, H. (1961). Identity and sexuality: a study of their interrelationship in man. *J. Amer. Psychoanal. Assn.* 9:179–260.

Mahler, M.S. (1963). Thoughts about development and individuation. *The Psychoanalytic Study of the Child* 18:307–324. New York: International Universities Press.

———(1966). Notes on the development of basic moods: the depressive affect. In *Psychoanalysis: A General Psychology. Essays in Honor of Heinz Hartmann,* eds. R.M. Loewenstein, et al. New York: International Universities Press, pp. 152–168.

———(1968). *On Human Symbiosis and the Vicissitudes of Individuation,* Vol. I, *Infantile Psychosis.* New York: International Universities Press.

———(1971). A study of the separation-individuation process and its possible application to borderline phenomena in the psychoanalytic situation. *The Psychoanalytic Study of the Child* 26:403–424. New York: International Universities Press.

———(1972). Rapprochement subphase of the separation-individuation process. *Psychoanalytic Q.* 41:487–506.

———, and La Perriere, K. (1965). Mother-child interaction during separation-individuation. *Psychoanalytic Q.* 34:483–498.

———Pine, F., and Bergman, A. (1970). The mother's reaction to her toddler's drive for individuation. In *Parenthood: Its Psychology and Psychopathology,* eds. E.J. Anthony and T. Benedek. Boston: Little, Brown, pp. 257–274.

———(1975). *The Psychological Birth of the Human Infant.* New York: Basic Books.

McDevitt, J.B. (1979). The role of the internalization process in the development of object relations during the separation-individuation phase. *J. Amer. Psychoanal. Assn.* 27:327–43.

Parens, H., et al. (1976). On the girl's entry into the oedipus complex. *J. Amer. Psychoanal. Assn.* 24:5:79.

Roiphe, H. (1968). On an early genital phase; with an addendum on genesis. *The Psychoanalytic Study of the Child* 23:348–365. New York: International Universities Press.

Stoller, R.J. (1976). Primary femininity. *J. Amer. Psychoanal. Assn.* 24:59–78.

4

The Inner-Genital Phase — Prephallic and Preoedipal

JUDITH S. KESTENBERG

Though woman's role in the social and economic world has changed over time, her basic internal organization as a real or potential mother, provider and lover or wife has undergone only superficial alterations. From time to time there occurs a shift in emphasis from one or another of these three womanly tasks and they take on different forms as the standards for motherhood, woman's work and her role in relation to man change. Under the average expectable conditions of our present culture the adult woman is capable of integrating various aspects of femininity, seeking fulfillment for some, fully or partially sublimating others or dividing her life span into successive stages of feminine productivity and interest.

In seeking to trace the developmental lines of femininity, we need to revise the traditional developmental hierarchy of libidinal phases which does not give justice to feminine phases in either sex and does not distinguish between man's and woman's phallic modalities. To revise the sequence of developmental phases, we must keep in mind that the outlines and shadings, if not the substrate, of a given phase may be obscured by an overlapping of phases or by constitutional and/or environmental influences upon phase progression. Moreover, precursors of certain traits can be seen before they become dominant in a given phase, and isolated advances of certain ideas and functions can feign the advent of a phase before there is a confluence of functions to support a specific developmental task.

Feminine modalities such as receptivity, taking in and nurturing are less conspicuous than masculine intrusivity. Perhaps this factor has played a role in the view that woman's development evolves in the shadow of masculinity. Freud's idea, that maternality is derived from phallic wishes and active modalities, helped to preserve the anonymity of the inner genital in children of both sexes and the neglect of the unseen genitals as zones for drives and originators of modalities.

My first description of an early maternal phase that follows the pregenital and precedes the phallic phases (1956a, 1956b) brought into focus the externalization of vaginal impulses onto maternal play with dolls. I have since renamed the maternal phase ''inner-genital'' because of further data indicating that inner genital tensions contributing to the development of maternality are dominant at that time in both sexes (1967b, 1968, 1971, 1974, 1975, 1976). More recently (1976b, 1979b) I have reexamined the phases that follow the inner-genital — the phallic-negative, and the phallic-positive oedipal phases — which highlight two other feminine attitudes, those of a worker-provider and a sexual partner of man, respectively. This chapter recapitulates my revision of the hierarchy of developmental phases and traces the three basic aspects of femininity, their biological core and their developmental lines. To do so, I shall briefly discuss the influence of inner-genital and outer-genital (phallic) modalities in pregenital phases. This will serve as a framework for the clinical description of the prephallic, proeodipal inner-genital phase in the girl. I will introduce the topic with a brief account of my clinical sources and methodology, as well as of my classification of phases.

COLLECTION OF DATA, METHODOLOGY AND CLASSIFICATION OF PHASES

I have based my view on development upon clinical data derived from the following sources: cross-sectional and longitudinal observation of infants, children and adolescents, as well as adults when they become parents; memories and reconstructions from the analyses of adults, adolescents and latency children; and the analyses of preschool children from the ages of under three to five or six (Kestenberg, 1975).

Since 1953 I have been engaged in a longitudinal study of three children from birth on, one of whom has since become a mother herself (1965–1967; with Sossin, 1979). This study served as a pilot for the development of a system of movement notation from which a Movement Profile (MP) was constructed (Kestenberg, 1975). The MP was designed in correlation with Anna Freud's (1965) developmental assessment.[1] It was given to infants, toddlers and preschool children as well as to some children in latency and adolescence on five Israeli Kubbutzim (1969–1970). This work helped me to establish an MP developmental sequence and test the validity of my phase classification.

[1]The Movement Profile (MP) consists of nine diagrams representing the ratio of movement patterns covering the expressions of drives, affects, self-feelings, responses to stimuli, styles of relating, defenses against drives and against objects, modes of adaptation to reality and modes of relating to constant objects. The first profiles of three girls, then three years old, were constructed in the Hampstead Clinic and subsequently three more profiles of girls of this age were made in the Child Development Center in New York (Courtesy of Dr. Peter Neubauer).

In my work at the Center for Parents and Children, sponsored by Child Development Research (1972–present), I have had occasion to observe children of both sexes throughout their entire early development, through the inner-genital phase and into the phallic, and many more as they made the transition out of pregenital phases into and through the inner-genital phase (twenty-two girls altogether). Movement profiles of most of these children and their mothers were constructed from movement patterns, and some were constructed several times at different ages.[2]

In order to see development in as many of its aspects as possible I have paid special attention to data concerning growth of organs and changes in hormones in childhood and adolescence (1961, 1967b, 1975, 1979).

From all of these sources —from analyses, psychoanalytic observations, developmental assessments, clinical findings, movement profiles and hormonal changes — I have come to view the sequence of developmental phases differently than many other psychoanalysts.[3] An outline of my classification of phases follows:

Childhood

1. The *Neonatal* period can be considered the first *inner-genital* phase. It is initiated by a "genital crisis" of the newborn (Pratt, 1954) which is caused by an overflow of maternal hormones into the neonate's system. As with all other

[2]Ages of the subjects varied. Since this paper deals only with girls I am listing only the following: two girls were seen from eighteen months to two years, nine months; six girls were seen from two to three years; four between two-and-a-half to three years; one from eighteen months to three-and-a-half years; one from birth to three years and three months; two from approximately seven months to three years; three from three to four years and one from two months to four years. I have follow-up data on about half of them. Some of the girls were only children, others had older siblings, and others were followed while their younger siblings were growing up.

[3]I can cite several factors which may account for different perspectives on developmental phases.

What I have seen and described as a phase has often been sub-subsumed under the existing division of Freud's libidinal phases, oral, anal and phallic. Because of the fact that each phase contains elements of the other phases and that phases overlap, some psychoanalysts (e.g. Greenacre, 1954; Benedek, 1974) look at phases in very broad outlines and do not delineate them in accordance with very specific developmental tasks as I do.

Research findings on the development of female organs and hormones (Kestenberg, 1961, 1967b, 1968, 1975, 1979), though not yet conclusive, have added to my conviction about the existence of childhood phases in which the inner genitalia play a decisive role. This may not be convincing to those who would rather keep analysis entirely distinct from anatomy and physiology.

The notation and scoring of movement patterns plays an important role in my assessments of a phase. Becoming aware of the ratio of different movement patterns helps to see the overlapping of phases or transitions between them. One sees the contributions of both inner-genital and phallic components to pregenital phases, as well as the influence of pregenital modalities on a predominantly inner-genital or phallic organization. The predominance of inner-genital rhythms and of

inner-genital phases that will follow (resolving similar problems on a higher order), this phase begins with a disequilibrium that is resolved via the integration of internal and external stimuli. Under the guidance of the nurturing mother, the genital modalities recede, making way for the oral dominance of the next phase.

2.   *Pregenital phases* are characterized by the dominance of oral, anal and urethral component drives and their derivatives. During these phases inner-genital and phallic modes contribute their share to the formation of gender characteristics while at the same time dominant pregenital trends leave their imprint on the antecedents of genital sexuality.

3.   The *inner-genital phase* (prephallic and preoedipal) begins with a *disequilibrium* in which pregenital and early genital drives and derivative ego functions vie with one another. The ensuing *integration* of pregenital and phallic drives and allied ego functions under the aegis of inner genitality is aided by the child's identification with the mother, who acts as an external organizer, reinforcing and guiding inner genitality, the internal organizer of that time. Externalization of inner genital impulses is the mechanism which underlies their sublimation into maternal behavior and the wish to be a mother. The former dyadic relationship is now replaced by a triangular "girl-baby-mother" relationship.

4.   The *phallic-oedipal* phase can be divided into two sub-phases:

a).   The *negative-oedipal*, in which outer genitality flourishes at the expense of the acknowledgement of inner genitals, whose existence is now denied. The wish to please the mother by giving her a child combines with competition with the father as provider and love object of the mother. The identification with the father succeeds that with the mother to provide a new external organization. Pregenital forms of penis envy are now subsumed under a phallic-intrusive penis envy, with fantasies of an external penis growing out of the clitoris. Inner genital tendencies become subordinated to phallic ones in such a way that the wish for a baby becomes subordinated to the wish for a baby-bearing penis.

---

feminine movement patterns in the three-year-old adds considerable credence to the delineation of an inner-genital phase at that time. A predominance of phallic rhythms and masculine movement patterns are seen in the early phallic phase.

A combination of phallic and inner-genital type rhythms and their derivatives constitutes the early core of heterosexuality. Correlated with the prevalence of these combinations is the fantasy of an inner penis in the positive-oedipal phase. The resulting representation of the shape of the inside is a phallus-like structure. Her endowing the uterus-vagina with phallic features had led me to look upon the girl's positive-oedipal phase as phallicized rather than phallic. Thus I can agree with Blum (1976 and personal communication) that the positive-oedipal phase is a cradle of one important aspect of femininity, and with Gray (1976) who looks upon the vagina as the erogenous zone of this phase. However, I have to add that the feminine sensuality that develops at this time is typical of normal female bisexuality (Kestenberg and Marcus, 1979).

b). The *positive-oedipal, phallicized* phase, in which sensuality threatens to break through the barrier of denial of the introitus as entry to the vagina. A fantasy of having an inner, hidden penis co-exists with a desire for penetration and being filled by the father's penis. The child-wish of that phase emerges from the internal phallus fantasy. Inner genital modalities are phallicized and the representation of the shape of the inner genital shifts from that of a female to a male baby. A new form of identification with the mother ushers in the feminine superego.

5. *Latency* is a phase in which repression of incestuous wishes for penetration and impregnation is reinforced by a complex of defenses. All three feminine attitudes of maternality, competitiveness and sensuality become consolidated in the ego and in the superego.

6. *Adolescence* can be divided into prepuberty, a phase of growth, and a phase of differentiation that ends with a preadult phase of consolidation (Kestenberg, 1967b, 1968, 1975). Adolescent genitality is ushered in with a *new inner-genital phase in prepuberty*. A reintegration of pregenital and genital modalities is based on the acceptance of inner genitals which becomes the basis for resolution of penis envy and oedipal strivings in *mid– and late adolescence*. Throughout adolescence there is a progressive trend to restructure and coordinate the three basic feminine attitudes which play an important role in the emergence of feminine identity and the feminine ego ideal. A new edition of the superego ushers in the stage of adult developmental phases.

7. *Adulthood* (Erikson, 1950; Benedek, 1959; Furman, 1969; Kestenberg, 1975, 1976) highlights efficiency, achievement in work and sensuality in the establishment of adult love relationships while maternal wishes are postponed and sublimated. Pregnancy is an *adult inner-genital* phase which brings to fruition the childhood wishes for a baby from all preceeding phases (1976). In successive *developmental phases of parenthood* the sublimation of inner genital impulses takes on new forms as requirements for the baby's bodily care change. Body contact becomes less important with time and maternality eventually manifests itself in functioning removed from bodily intimacy. *Menopause and Senescence* brings on a final renunciation of the desire to procreate. Productivity and competition may bloom again and sensuality need not be lost. The wish for a baby arises on a new level and culminates in the satisfaction of grandmotherhood.

PHYSIOLOGICAL CORE AND ENVIRONMENTAL INFLUENCES

The three aspects of femininity are backed by three hormones in the female body: (1) Sensuousness complementary to man's, triggered by estrogens; (2) The capacity to carry a fetus, sustained by progesterone; and (3) The energy and strength to pursue sex and work, enhanced by androgens produced by the ovary and the adrenal gland. The thalamus acts as an overseer and regulator of their interaction with end organs and with the rhythmic centers which mediate between soma and psyche. Roughly speaking, there are three organs which respond selectively to these hormones. Estrogen is the principal agent responsible for vaginal lubrication; the uterus only responds to progesterone when primed by estrogen while the clitoris enlarges and becomes more active under the influence of androgens (of which testosterone is one) (Kestenberg, 1975, 1979).

In childhood, small quantities of estrogen and androgen are secreted, the former reaching somewhat higher levels in girls. A great many follicles develop from time to time up to a certain point and become atretic before puberty. This presupposes a periodic increase in estrogens, a prelude to later periodicity. There is some evidence that, by the age of two-and-a-half or three, there are changes in the ovaries and in hormones which may be correlated with an upswing of inner-genital activity (Kestenberg, 1967b, 1968). In four-year-old girls androgens are said to increase more rapidly than in boys (Dorfman, 1948; Kestenberg, 1975) while estrogen secretion rises much more slowly (Nathanson, 1941). Not only are there centrally controlled differences of hormone constellations in girls and boys, but their influence differs depending on the nature of the end organs on which they act. The clitoris, though phallic, erectile and accessible to palpation, can never become a phallus. All parts of the female genitals except the external labia are technically internal, because they are covered by mucous membranes.

Procreation can only become a reality when adolescent fertility is ushered in by the cyclic secretion of different quantities of estrogen and progesterone to insure ovulatory menstrual cycles. The secretion of sex hormones in childhood may be an important aspect of the feminine core in the very young. It may well serve as a primer of the immature organs, readying them for their mature functioning long before it materializes.

In successive developmental phases the bisexual components of womanhood begin to take shape. Inner-genital tensions in the prephallic phase serve as a primer for internal sexuality that eventually leads to procreation. Psychological priming for motherhood is accomplished through the externalization and desexualization of inner-genital impulses, which alongside with the girl's identification with her mother form the core of maternal sublimation. The degenitalization (in pregenital phases) and the desexualization (in the prephallic, inner-genital phase) of inner-genital impulses may well be necessary safeguards against premature flooding with genital sexuality. They stand the child in good stead when, in the phallic phase, fulminant phallic impulses threaten to overflow into inner organs. In the negative, phallic-oedipal phase, clitoric impulses along with the child's identification with the father support the wish for a male child and prompt the girl to be competitive. The foreboding of mature feminine sexuality in the phallicized, positive-oedipal phase represents a blending of feminine bisexual components which will become an important ingredient of woman's adult heterosexuality.

The difference between boys and girls is expressed in the boy's greater muscular mass, his greater vital capacity and his more rapid motor development (all contingent upon higher androgen levels). The girl may be less aggressive than the boy, but she is frequently more outgoing and more responsive to kinesthetic and auditory stimuli. The latter characteristic may have a relation to the girl's higher estrogen levels.

Parents treat girls differently than boys, not only because of their individual predilections and adherence to proscribed role models, but also because they respond differentially to their gender differences. For example, the boy is more prone to turn his aggression outward (Kestenberg and Marcus, 1979) while the girl is more apt to inflict pain upon herself (Freud, 1924; Chasseguet-Schmiregel, 1976); at the same time, she is more capable of seeking narcissistic supplies than the boy, and she tends to increase her well-being (and later her self-esteem) by attunement with another person (by adopting the ideal qualities of her love object). These are some of the reasons that make a parent more likely to be rough with the boy and protective of the girl.

The preponderance of inner genital discharge in mother and child creates a kinship between them. This kinship promotes a primary feminine identification which may well be one of the sources of "primary femininity" described by Stoller (1976). Individual and cultural differences in parents support the development of one or another of the core aspects of femininity. Responses to biological characteristics can reinforce or inhibit them, but they cannot alter them completely.

THE ROLE OF INNER-GENITAL AND PHALLIC MODALITIES IN PREGENITAL PHASES

Just as all organs are present from the start, so are all functional core modalities[4] which differentiate along with id and ego differentiation. Oral, anal, urethral, inner-genital and phallic modalities are coordinated with tensions and sensations emanating from internal and external organs, their mucous membranes and related skin and muscle groups. Inner-genital and phallic modes are reinforced or inhibited by hormonal changes and by external stimulation or lack of it. Inner genital influences tend to initiate pregenital phases. Their gradual forms of

---

[4]We use the term "*modalities*" in the same sense as Erikson (1950, 1959). However, because of our experience with the observation and notation of movement patterns (Kestenberg, et al., 1971, Kestenberg and Sossin, 1979) we are also guided by such drive-modalities as rhythms and attributes of tension-flow, both initiators of later maturing patterns which serve defenses and adaptation. In

excitation have a mitigating effect on pregenital sadism, which increases with frustration and tends to combine with abruptly rising phallic-sadistic components.

It is likely that vulvo-vaginal engorgements and vaginal lubrication (according to Masters and Johnson (1966), a homologue of male erection) accompany *neonatal* suckling at the breast and recur periodically in female infantile states which correspond to those in which newborn boys have periodic erections (Wolff, 1966). Both inner genital and phallic discharge forms are present during the neonatal period but the former predominate and both soon become subordinated to oral drives which become progressively more differentiated and dominant. A moratorium on genital gratification (albeit incomplete) is in the offing. Out of the ashes of the inner-genital symbiosis of pregnancy there arises the external dual symbiosis of the nursling and her mother (Mahler et al., 1974).

---

addition we are guided by modalities of relatedness as observed in changes of body-shape, the cradle of later maturing patterns, serving the expression of constant relationships. For the benefit of readers interested in the differences between inner-genital and outer-genital patterns, their derivations and the affine patterns of relating we list the following definitions:

Inner-genital rhythms are characterized by gradually rising tension which changes from low to high intensity when aggression becomes a feature of this discharge form, as for instance in uterine contractions. Low intensity of tension is correlated with a lengthening in the body-shape, and correlated with gradual tension-increase in bulging. High intensity goes together with shortening which helps to expel body contents.

The inner-genital core-modalities (graduality and low intensity) influence the choice of passive forms of adaptation (indirect, light and decelerating efforts, such as can be seen in floating). Correlated with them are open forms of shaping which promote exposure to people and things (spreading, ascending and advancing). When high intensity prevails, lightness is substituted by strength (as in wringing) and ascending by descending.

Outer-genital (phallic) rhythms are characterized by abruptly rising tension, reaching high intensity, but also observable in low intensity (a sign of lessened aggressivity). Correlated with them are shape-changes serving output and ejection of body contents through hollowing and shortening. (Note here that bulging and lengthening are conducive to intake, e.g. taking in into the body). Libidinal phallic discharges in low intensity are correlated with lengthening. The aggressive phallic core-modalities (abruptness and high intensity) influence the choice of active forms of adaptation (direct, strong and accelerated pattern, as can be seen in punching). Correlated with these are closed forms of shaping of the space around us which serves protection from people and objects (enclosing, descending and retreating). When a more indulging form of adaptation prevails, lightness is substituted for strength (as in patting or dabbing) and ascending is more likely to occur than descending.

The development of femininity and masculinity implies bisexuality which is composed of a mixture of inner- and outer-genital modalities and their derivatives. For a treatment of this subject see Kestenberg and Marcus, 1979.

The Oral Phase

As orality becomes dominant, it borrows some of its sensuality and receptivity from the inner genitals; at the same time, its rhythm of introjection and projection becomes a model for similar processes in other parts of the body, for receptivity and release, for the capacity to retain and expel, to yield, to be filled to capacity and to let go. Later fantasies of oral intercourse and the equation of food = baby are based on these primarily oral and inner-genital influences. At a time when the baby girl is still using her mouth as organ of exploration, she alternates between licking and mouthing a doll and tasting it. As an act of early love she may mouth a younger baby.

With the heightening of aggression in the oral-sadistic phase, there is also an increase in phallic activity. Ejection becomes more abrupt, serving as a model for the head shake of negation and for instant projection. Looks become sharp and penetrating, reaching and kicking become more direct, banging a favored past time, and motor activity leads the child into the practicing phase (Mahler et al., 1975). On seeing the genitals of a male, the girl wants to grab them and eat them as if they were food, a breast or a bottle. This forms the substrate of oral penis envy.

The Anal Phase

Towards the end of the oral–sadistic and into the beginning of the anal phase there is an increase of behavior characteristic of later feminine attitudes. The shy baby girl, seeing a stranger, hides her face and peers at him in a charming, girlishly seductive way. This is a time when she may discover the vulva (Kleeman, 1976), but at this point she is not yet able to distinguish between adjoining organs and openings and her vulvo-vaginal and anal sensations have a tendency to fuse. It is difficult to say which of the cavities, the vaginal or the anal, has rented out space to the other (Andreas–Salome, 1916). Once more there is a participation of inner genitality in the formation of a new libidinal zone. When the anal sphincter contracts volitionally, the urethral sphincter and the laminal muscles of the vagina follow suit. The levator ani, the perineal and gluteal muscles begin to act in consort with the sphincters as the baby girl pulls up her rear end, rubbing it when she sits on the floor or slides, and wiggling it when she crawls. The pulling up also includes the vaginal orifice, and the short periods of holding and releasing include also the tightening and relaxing of the end portion of the vagina.

When the toddler girl begins to tighten the anal sphincter rather than play with contraction and release, when she begins to maintain the contraction of the levator ani and the perineal muscles, she develops a sense of something solid inside. Within this solid cluster lies also the tightened vagina acting as an auxiliary to the ano-rectal region. In coordination with the tightened inside, the whole body can pull up and stiffen in an erect stance.

The more extensive the participation of large muscles in learning to remain erect and to hold, and the more intensity needed, the more aggression is used in the prevailing discharge forms. The anal-sadistic rhythm, "accumulating, holding and pressing out," draws from oral, urethral and vaginal modes of pulling in, retaining and releasing. At the same time it leaves a permanent mark of its own on the functions and representations of the mouth, the urethra and the vagina. Food is now held much longer for chewing and churning; urine is retained along with feces and the vagina held in and squeezed by thigh pressure. In addition, the pressure of the fecal column in the rectum has an effect on the state of excitation in the vagina.

Becoming cognizant of feelings and pleasant fullness, the child pulls up her shirt, pats her belly and sometimes says there is a baby inside. She does not yet distinguish clearly between total body sensations, excitement, organs and body products: Feeling full becomes associated with losing her behind (which encompasses also her genital, often included in the global term "tushy"); the loss of sensation, the loss of feces, begins to symbolize the loss of a baby (Klein, 1932); and losing balance and falling signify the loss of all products as well as the collapse of the emerging "total self." Each release from holding may feel like a loss of the middle of the body which no longer feels full and heavy. Each fall signifies a loss in stability, which is identified with being full and therefore erect.

The conflict between the wish to hold and the wish to release generates more aggression. An influx of phallic drives at this time favors rapid release: Not wanting to part with is now counterbalanced by wanting to get rid of. This type of anal-phallic discharge increases peristalsis abruptly and may cause diarrhea and tummy aches. The disgust with loose bowels merges with an anal-sadistic form of penis envy. When the little girl sees a boy's penis now, she readily equates it with a fecal column. Having begun to differentiate between up and down, she does not yet distinguish properly between front and back. Having feces and having a penis is associated with possession and control. Loss of feces and being dirty and smeared is associated with the vagueness of fading inner-genital tensions. A resentful awareness of a disadvantage of being small and unformed rather than big and shapely, marks this pregenital precursor of penis envy (Galenson, 1971; Galenson and Roiphe, 1974). The oral envy of food represented by breasts merges with the predominant anal envy of fullness and volume and with the unclear inner-genital sensation of swelling and the phallic sensation of erectility. However, a precursor of a positive (rather than a negative penisless) gender identity is based now on the concrete association of a big, full belly with the big bellies of pregnant women.

The anal-sadistic phase comes to a peak in the anal-sadistic struggles of the "terrible twos" (Gesell, 1949). In her throwing of objects, her temper tantrums and her incessant getting into things, the little girl releases also a good deal of phallic-clitoric discharge along with the anal-sadistic. But her angry behavior may reveal precursors of aggressive feminine qualities. She whines, argues and uses words, rather than limbs, as weapons. She becomes cruel to dolls and babies. In her anal-sadistic conflict with her mother she also struggles with the baby she has equated with feces.

The Urethral Phase

With the beginning of the urethral phase, which is sometimes quite short in girls, there is a general mellowing of the girl's disposition. Inner-genital drive components now outweigh the transitory phallic onrushes and fuse with increased urethral strivings.[5] The proximity of the urethral to the vaginal opening makes for an easy overflow of excitations from one to the other; every wiping and cleansing encompasses both. The external sphincter of the short female urethra is not effective in holding urine back. Once it enters the urethra urine begins to drip out. Tightening thigh muscles and wiggling as a form of closure lead to a urethra-vaginal masturbation. Urethral forms of fluid holding and release are influenced by, and in turn influence, vaginal modes of retaining and letting go of lubricating fluids. By the time the little girl becomes concerned with training for urine control, she may become aware of a vaginal serous or mucous discharge (frequent during and after colds and infections), which she does not distinguish from urine.

The urethral and inner-genital modes of retention share the quality of gradual changes in tension which promote a distension of elastic, hollow organs. A little girl can distend her bladder for a long time without feeling pressure. This constitutes passive rather than active retention. When she lets go, urine comes out gradually either dribbling or flowing, wetting the external genital or the thighs (depending on the child's position). Passive distension and letting go evoke fears of drowning in one's own fluids in the toilet, or losing all body fluids by leaking.

The idea of losing something else as the urine flows out and is flushed down the toilet is sometimes associated with a fear of losing a very tiny baby. Experimentation with bathing dolls, which is at its peak at this time, constitutes both an outlet for urethral pleasures mingled with inner-genital and phallic components, and a sublimation of these tendencies to become a part of maternal preoccupation with washing and wiping of the baby.

Envious of the boy's capacity to "shoot," aim and stop the flow of urine as he stands facing the toilet, the girl tries to stand up and bends down to see what

[5]The female urethra has the same cell composition as the vagina, and both are subject to the influence of estrogen.

she is doing when she urinates. This increases her aggression and her competitiveness with boys and brings on an influx of phallic modalities. A fear of being abruptly filled with water or urine—to the point of bursting—is a precursor of later fears of penetration. The girl's ability to contain fluids and close off access to her inside counterbalances the discontent of the urethral precursor of penis envy. When she develops pride in lieu of shame, her self-esteem rises. Learning to discriminate between the two organs of excretion and becoming aware of what is front and what is back, she accepts herself as someone who sits for defecation and urination and this helps her to differentiate her own gender identity from that of boys (Fast, 1979). At the end of this relatively short phase the little girl is less aggressive than the boy and her urethral-sadistic shooting fantasies are more easily counterbalanced by the inward-directed wishes of the inner-genital phase that follows.

THE ROAD FROM THE DYADIC RELATIONSHIP IN PREGENITAL PHASES TO A TRIANGULAR-MATERNAL ATTITUDE IN THE INNER-GENITAL PHASE

As long as pregenital channels are available for genital discharge, and the genital tensions are not too intense, the infant or toddler girl is able to rid herself of them without direct genital satisfaction. When aggressive pregenital and phallic discharge forms increase at the end of each pregenital phase, termination of old and anticipation of new pleasures are experienced with a sense of urgency. Acting as bearers of continuity, long-lasting, inner-genital discharge forms facilitate the smooth transition into the next pregenital phase by neutralizing the sharpness of pregenital and phallic discharge forms. In this process, libido is shifted from the genitals and the inner-genital tensions become degenitalized, paving the way for the undisturbed differentiation of phase specific ego functions.

Throughout development, discharge modalities, adaptations and defense mechanisms evolve within the framework of human contact. Each discharge form or mode of adaptation calls for a corresponding mode of relating. The admixture of inner-genital drives with pregenital ones promotes receptivity, curiosity about people and reaction formations, all in tune with empathy and the desire to please. The admixture of phallic drives with pregenital ones promotes intrusiveness, curiosity directed to the external world and identification with the aggressor, all serving individuation and independence.

During pregenital phases, the predominant dyadic attachment to and identification with the mother is intertwined with spurts and threads of attraction for and identification with the father (Abelin, 1971; Burlingham, 1973; Kestenberg, 1974; Ross, 1975). Whenever aggressive outlets are sought, the father (or men in general) becomes an interesting companion or play-mate. Both precursors of negative and positive oedipal leanings are also in evidence, especially when older babies and toddlers turn to one parent when they feel rejected by the other.

Alongside the development of relationships to primary objects there develops a sense of self and a feeling for people and things. Towards the end of the oral phase the child begins to see herself as a baby and her mother as a baby-feeding mother. Food comes from the mother and makes the inside of the baby feel good. It is a prototype for a third object, interposed between mother and child. In the anal phase feces gain prominence as a link to the mother, and in the urethral phase urine becomes the intermediate 'third' object (Kestenberg, 1971). All three — food, feces and urine — have shapes, consistencies and colors which can be used to represent what is inside the body, what fills it, moves in it, bulges out, retracts, presses and pushes or squirts out. By so doing each of these "objects" seems to have an independent existence; separation from them underscores the idea of another being that can be taken away. While separation-individuation proceeds, the infant and the young toddler girl successively learns to feed herself, to hold in her food, feces and urine and to control their intake and output. These objects which link her to her mother feel as if they were a joint product. Only gradually are they substituted for by play objects which — at first — are not far removed from their originals.

In the oral phase, the little girl mouthes her doll; in the anal phase she smears and throws it and in the urethral phase she floods it. The image of the baby, created by the girl, is built on self-perception as well as on the perception of the products that come in and out of her body. Externalization from inside out is modelled after the experiences of spitting, defecating and urinating. Because inner-genital sensations yield no product, there is a greater need for them to be externalized and to be made into a living link between the inside and the mother: *a baby* (Kestenberg, 1971). The external genital can be touched and might not be externalized, if not for the fact that the clitoris is elusive and one can think of it as a tiny baby that hides.

In transition to the inner-genital phase, an irregular overflow of inner-genital waves can regenitalize the (previously degenitalized) pregenital drives and unbalance the neutralization of the phallic drive. The effect is a regression to earlier drive positions with external genital (phallic) components vying with pregenital and inner-genital ones. This multi-drive onslaught creates a drive diffusion, similar to that seen in the transition from latency to adolescence (Kestenberg, 1967a). The resulting overflow of excitations from one organ to another, with a concomitant shifting of discharge modes has a direct influence on the child's image of herself and her relationships to others which also keep shifting and blurring.

Even with successful separation-individuation (Mahler et al., 1975) constituting a firm basis for the development of a multi-dimensional self- and object–constancy, the little girl is at a crossroads. All previous flaws in the development of individuation become aggrandized now. The little girl is no longer a baby, but she is not yet a big girl who can bring order into the chaos of old and new stimuli, and into the onrush of thoughts and words which defy her understanding. In the process of giving up her babyhood, she is trying to recreate what she once had in a baby of her own, but pregenital representations of the baby vie now with phallic and inner-genital ones. She feels something inside,[6] live, warm and exciting like a real baby and like her mother. She externalizes it, shifts it upward and confuses it with rectal and urethral sensations. Unaccountably she loses her excitement and unaccountably it comes back again, making her feel full rather than empty. She may become envious of the boy who has something live, warm and baby-like that he can keep on the outside all the time. This inner-genital "penis envy" does not concern the phallus alone but rather the configuration of penis and testicles in which the image of a baby is perceived (with the penis as the nose and testicles as eyes or cheeks). The girl's quest for an inside baby alternates and fuses with the wish to have one outside and with wanting to be a baby herself and become her own mother. To grow into a mother and to shrink adults (especially the mother) into a baby are dyadic solutions which intermingle with the newly created triangle, "me-baby-

---

[6]The controversy regarding the existence of sexual feelings in the little girl's vagina (Freud, 1931, Horney, 1926) is still alive. Kleeman (1971) described how early the little girl discovers her vulva and there is no doubt that the clitoris is handled in early childhood. Masters and Johnson (1966) have demonstrated that external sexual excitation cannot proceed without the physiological participation of the vagina. However, that does not mean that the adult woman, masturbating on the clitoris, must be aware of the engorgement in her vagina. There is no doubt that in some cases vaginal sensations reach the level of perception in childhood (Fraiberg, 1972), but there is no evidence that the little girl can, without help, localize the excitement emanating from her vagina in the same way that she perceives and localizes clitoral feelings. Barglow and Schaefer (1976) rightly object to the equation of excitations, tension, biological urges and vaginal desires. Inner-genital tension—in my usage of the term—refers to changes in the elastic tissue of the vagina and uterus; they can be experienced as pressures or waves of tension-changes radiating through the body. Excitations refer to the building up of intensity of feelings, perhaps based on engorgement. None of these are experienced by the little girl as "vaginal desires". On the contrary, in the inner-genital phase the vagina achieves representation as an organ primarily through the externalization of tensions, excitations, urges and impulses on objects of the external world, such as the baby doll or a shoe. The representations of the creative inner-genital are constructed from colors, shapes and designs which correspond to poorly localized stirrings, but derive their structure from experimentation in action and thought. The representations of the inner-genital in the phallic phase derive their shape from the penis or a phallic baby. Perhaps the wish to be penetrated in the positive oedipal phase comes closest to what in the adult woman we call a "vaginal urge".

mother.'' Father, siblings, friends and relatives come into the orbit of this triangle in various ways. The child may play that she is daddy in anticipation of the negative-oedipal triangle, or that she is mommy to a baby she shares with daddy as a foreboding of the positive-oedipal phase, but the central issue in her relationships is shifting from the dyadic ''mother-me'' (or father-me, sister-me, friend-me, blanket-me) to a triangular ''mother-baby-me'' constellation.

THE PREPHALLIC, PREOEDIPAL INNER-GENITAL PHASE

This phase can be divided into a long period or several bouts of *disequilibrium* caused by regressive and progressive forces vying with one another and into long or several shorter periods of reintregration which steady the child before phallic concerns begin to overwhelm her in the next phase.

Pregenital drives do not all participate equally in the regression; previous failures in taming some drives and/or the breakdown of precarious defenses against them bring one or another pregenital drive expression into the foreground. In addition, phallic components are not equally represented in the drive-disequilibrium that ushers in the inner-genital phase.

All psychic functions, whether concerned with the organization of drives, the formation of the body image, the representation of multifaceted relations and gender identity or with defensive and coping actions and thoughts, are now in a state of disequilibrium. This gives the child and her mother a second chance to resolve unsolved infantile problems, and this task may become the central issue in the ensuing id and ego reorganization. Regressive behavior evokes regressive defenses, such as introjection, projection, negativism and massive denial. Externalization, the passing on of excitement, argumentativeness and nagging, the foremost defenses of the inner-genital phase (Kestenberg, 1975), merge with short-lived repressions and other defenses that come and go.

Externalization is favored because new, more advanced perceptual experiences (visual, auditory and tactile) foster the transition to an external focus. This is balanced by the increasing capacity to internalize in the form of representations and memory. However, the internalization of the two- to four-year-old girl in the pre-conceptual stage (Piaget, 1951) is still dependent on external referents. She cannot immediately understand new experiences and she assimilates them in fantasy in accordance with memories of the past which she cannot always distinguish from present day reality. She accommodates her internal representations and her actions to external models by imitation, drawing and impersonation. Before she can organize objects in a new multi-dimensional way, a great many things she has learned before impinge upon her for which she has no spatial distribution to give them perspective. She is beginning to ask how, where and when but she is not always ready to absorb answers. Moreover, she still employs action-thinking and asks questions more through movement language than through words. It is up to the mother with whom the child identifies, to organize her maternal functions in such a way that she can help the girl to make order out of her internal chaos.

The developmental task of the child in the inner-genital phase is to overcome the disequilibrium that initiates this phase, to integrate the inside with the outside, the old with the new and to create bridges between the past, the present and the future. In this task she is aided by the integrative influence of inner-genital drives and of maturing cognitive ego functions (acting as internal organizers) as well as by the integrative influence of her mother (acting as external organizer).

The Disequilibrium

The more traumatized the girl had been as an infant (through illness, seduction, permissiveness or undue restrictions), the more likely she is to suffer from an intense and prolonged disequilibrium which initiates the inner-genital phase. The more capable the mother is in guiding the girl towards leaving babyhood behind and the less new stress there is currently, the smoother the transition into the inner-genital phase. A family which fosters dependence or selectively encourages lack of control over oral, anal, urethral or phallic drives can camouflage the inner-genital phase to such an extent that inner-genital influences cannot be easily discovered outside of analysis. However, confusion between present and past, and between early and present needs, will be seen at this time regardless of the nature of the clinical picture. The independent little girl clings and screams for her mother, her sleep becomes disorganized and she may create scenes about food or use retention of feces or urine as masturbatory procedures. She nags her mother, provokes her by asking questions impossible to answer and caricatures her mother's actions in exaggerated identification with her. In the following vignettes I shall highlight a few of the many forms in which the disequilibrium manifests itself, and I will try to demonstrate the role of the mother and father in the maintenance or resolution of the disequilibrium.

The following is an example of disequilibrium in a child with an oral-sadistic fixation, whose parents currently encouraged urethral-phallic interest.

At the age of two years and four months, M was weaned and trained and quite advanced in her speech and her sociability. In contrast with her intellectual advancement, she had a low frustration tolerance. She grabbed things from other children and dropped them just as quickly. When thwarted she bit and hit them. The administration of a movement profile revealed a developmental fixation at the end of the oral phase. Strong oral-sadistic needs, coupled with the grandiose conviction that everything she wanted was automatically hers, vied with urethral-sadistic components. Flitting to and fro, stopping to grab and running away, M wanted to be contained but literally bit the hand that held her. At the age of two-and-a-half, she alternated in an erratic, unpredictable way between running like a two-year old who loses control over direction and dancing in rhythm to music in a gradual, flexible feminine manner. She also began to retain urine by gradually distending her bladder, using it as a masturbatory equivalent. A maternal interest in babies was evident only during the few moments she stopped flitting. At home, she became preoccupied with the question, "Do you have a penis?", which she repeatedly asked anyone who came her way. In recounting this, her mother smiled in an embarrassed way. Both parents seemed to interpret this interest as flattering to the father, who habitually invited M to see him shave and urinate. M rewarded him by telling visitors how big his penis was. At that point most of the children in the center became very interested in babies and where they grew before they came out. M began to put sharp objects inside her genital and watched her mother's excited concern. M's mother was encouraged to disapprove by saying that M should not hurt herself. Soon after, M surprised her mother by asking whether she, the mother, had a baby in her mouth. M was beginning to mellow, but the inner-genital modes which were expressed in dancing and becoming interested in and gentle with babies were still vying with oral-sadistic and urethral components. Her disequilibrium was subsiding in a special way characteristic for M. She had "good" weeks or days when she wanted to be good and share the interests of the other children instead of being a biting and flitting toddler who antagonized children and adults. These advances were interrupted by "bad" days of renewed regression which could be traced to recent frustrations or more frequently to seductiveness on the part of adults with which M could not cope.

The transition from the urethral to the inner-genital phase can come in spurts or gradually; it can be accelerated or decelerated depending on constitutional differences, previous experiences and parental attitudes. When a mother is pregnant at the time that the little girl is entering the inner-genital phase, she herself is in that phase (Kestenberg, 1976) and her own integrative efforts have a special effect on her first child. As she is trying to resolve conflicting feelings revived from her own childhood, the mother consciously or unconsciously directs her daughter's concerns about babies and big girls. The resulting precocious development may encompass the disequilibrium and short-circuit or reduce it to periodic spurts of confusion. Through identification with her mother, the young child can become a relentless organizer and clarifier.

C's mother had been prematurely cast in the role of the older sister when her own mother had delivered a baby before C's mother was two years old.

Repeating her own mother's experience she became pregnant again when C was eleven months old and had just been weaned.

At fifteen months, C, under the unspoken guidance of her mother, pointed to her own belly when we talked about the baby inside mother (Kestenberg and Buelte, 1976). She became maternal and gentle with children, some older than herself. At seventeen months she was seen hiding a doll under her polo shirt. C's mother was anxious about her toilet training as she did not want to have two diaper-babies to care for. As C was anxious to please her they both had worried looks on their faces. C talked to herself at night repeating three words: C, baby, mommy.'' Her mother feelingly said that an undue burden had been placed on one so young. When the baby arrived, C, then nineteen months old, ignored mother and baby and busied herself training a doll (named C) on the pottie. She was taking over the concern of her own mother in relation to herself and was leaving the new baby to her mother.

Sharing the concerns of her pregnant mother and destined to relive her mother's early childhood, C developed great strength and not only trained herself, but entered the inner-genital phase before the age of two. Her capacity to assimilate and integrate new experiences grew by leaps and bounds, and she met each sign of disequilibrium with a relentless pursuit of re-equilibration. In identification with her father she entered the negative-phallic-oedipal phase at the age of three and a half. Her closeness to him after the baby was born facilitated this progress.

Trying to safeguard the young girl's babyhood, a mother, feeling guilty about the new pregnancy, may delay the progression from the pregenital to the inner-genital phase. The problems she and her husband try to resolve anew during the second pregnancy may become the source of a shared confusion. Regressive defenses may be called upon as a response to shared anxiety and as a method to circumvent a disequilibrium.

L's mother became pregnant when her daughter was two years and five months old. She had been the youngest sibling in her own family and had no experience coping with a baby other than L herself. She seemed to identify L with her older sister. She felt guilty because she was "cutting short her little girl's babyhood," and could not get herself to train her.

In identification with her sensitive, childless aunt, L was easily offended. She clung to her mother like a child in the rapprochement phase (Mahler et al., 1975), but did not protest when she was left in the playroom without her. However, she would resist approaches of other children and adults and would play with her legs spread widely and toys placed between them, muttering to herself. She sucked her finger as if she were in a daze. Moody and unpredictable at home, L refused to give up her diapers although she had demonstrated her ability to toilet herself on a few occasions. With the firmness of a mother or an older sister speaking to a child, she informed her mother that she would use the toilet on her third birthday, and not before.

During the reading of a book about a new baby, L pretended not to hear, especially when we read about a grandmother who came to stay with the older child. She ignored our question: "Who will take care of you when Daddy takes Mommy to the hospital?" Mother then revealed her uncertainty about the plans for her absence. Both parents vacillated between wanting to ask the grandmother to come and stay with L and leaving the child with the mother of L's friend J (a little boy). L sensed her parents' conflicting feelings about entrusting L to family or friends. She shared their fears and interpreted them in her own way. She was afraid that her mother would no longer be hers when the baby came. Instead she would have to accept J's mother as her mother. Both J's mother and her own

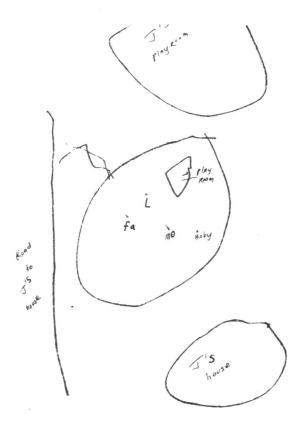

Figure 1. L draws the two separate houses, J's and hers, but J's playroom is much bigger and located outside the house.

mother reassured L in this respect. The parents realized that they would have to pursue one plan for which L would be prepared.

When the parents decided to bring L over to J's mother's house before going to the hospital, I drew two houses (L's and J's) and connected them with a line. This line indicated the road on which they would drive. Another line led from J's house to the hospital. Inside each house I placed the respective occupants, indicating that first L, and then the baby, would return to their house. (Grandmother was to arrive the day after the delivery). L had me repeat the drawings many times. At home she began to draw imitations and elaborations of my drawing (Figure 1) and continued to do so several times a day until her baby sister arrived from the hospital.

It should be noted that L rounded out the houses into circles and ovals. In Figure 1 she made a separate "play room" for J, while her own "play room" was inside her house. This shape seems identical to the one L drew six weeks later (see bottom of Figure 7a) when she was struggling with representations of containing and protruding organs.

Gradually L began to think of herself as a big girl, but she still tested her parents' attitude about it. On her third birthday (two months before the baby was born) she tried to renege on her promise and demanded to keep her diapers. We helped L's mother to be firm in her demand that promises be kept. Almost overnight L's disequilibrium seemed to disappear. Her previous interest in dancing, which had alternated with her saying she was a boy, returned and her interest in dolls increased. With the newly gained freedom from worry about separating from the mother, L embarked on the task of integrating the past, the present and the future.

Integration as Means of Resolving Disequilibrium

In the analyses of three year-old girls one sees a regression to all previous developmental phases. While this produces a disequilibrium, it also serves in recalling events from babyhood and toddlerhood which need to be clarified and reinterpreted in light of later experiences. Only then can they become integrated into the prevailing inner-genital maternal organization. Two processes evolve which enable the girl to accomplish the integration: (1) Kinesthetic and visual memories are externalized in actions for which meaning is sought; and (2) Sensations and feelings are reproduced and played in a new key through the externalization of inner-genital strivings. In undisturbed development, doll play is the principal outlet for the externalization of memories and feelings, derived partly from pregenital and phallic drives, but primarily from inner-genital drives. The little girl is able to seek the right shapes, designs and colors to represent feelings inside the body and link them up with things of the past and present well before she can ask questions and think of alternative answers. Regressive behavior alongside with nagging comes into the foreground in situations where problems of the past cannot be resolved. It is then that the professional adult co-integrator, with the aid of the parents, helps to reinstate the processes necessary for the integration of the past with the present.

At the age of three, D was nagging and clinging like a baby. This so infuriated her mother that she was unable to help D out of her disequilibrium. At this point, D entered analysis. Shortly after she began, D started to show signs of drive regression which intermingled with sporadic genital advances to her father, who took the place of her mother in providing bodily care (Kestenberg, 1969, 1971). In the midst of a regressive bout D wet herself and refused to have a b.m. Putting a doll on the toilet instead, she wet herself again and announced that she wanted to be a baby. Added to her confusing and unpredictable behavior were incidents in which she behaved as if objects and people from important past events were to be found in the present. D complained that she could not find the dress her mother had worn more than a year earlier when she went to the hospital to deliver a baby. She asked about the nurse who had taken care of her baby sibling. The reconstruction of events surrounding the birth of the baby took some time, leading us through a detour into even earlier events of D's babyhood.

She seemed to count all her losses: her weaning, her mother's absences, the furniture she had before the family moved and the renewed loss of the mother to the baby. At the same time as she traced (through its shape and color) a chair in which she had been held for bottle-feeding, she looked for shapes and colors with which to conceptualize and build her own body image.[7] She searched for a shape for a long time until she saw tulips in my garden. She remembered flowers and animals around a house not her own in which she slept at the foot of the bed and saw something on her father which looked like a flower. To identify the place in time she told me that there was no place for the baby there. Her father could now recollect a resort they visited when D was twenty months old. D wanted me to draw, identify and name the father's organ she had seen: the "tushy-flower" she recognized when she turned my drawing of a tulip upside down. No doubt, her careful observations of scrotal contractions — which use the gradual changes of the inner-genital rhythms (Kestenberg, 1965–67, 1975) — aided her in the choice of this organ as a model for the externalization of her own inner-genital rhythm.[7] Yet, anal components of penis envy played a role in this choice as well.[8]

[7] Proof of the meaning of the shapes she drew or asked me to draw came later when she produced organized images of her inside (see illustrations). She selected colors painstakingly and was not satisfied until she found the right shape and color. At this time she would acknowledge that her genital had color and feelings but was intent on finding external objects, especially those she could no longer see, to represent visually what she had inside.

[8] Much later, when D had begun to deny her inner and concentrate on the outer genital, she equated her vulva with a daisy and her external labia with an inverted tulip (her father's scrotum).

Once D, with the help of her father, could reconstruct what had happened when her mother was pregnant, gave birth to the baby and came home (Kestenberg, 1969), she was able to work on the integration between the internal and external parts of her body image. Central to this was her creation of a baby out of her own inside. The unseen, unknown inside was like her past. She felt it, could visualize it as a baby in colors and designs, but she needed external aid to give it shape. Touching a doll lightly, with inner-genital stroking rhythms, she was not satisfied with its rigid boundaries as a representation of her inside. Yet the ebb and flow of the waves of inner-genital excitement she felt gave her no sense of a contained, solid organ. In addition, pregenital oral, anal and urethral representations in colors and shapes (white milk in a bottle, brown feces, yellow urine) all interfered by merging with inner-genital images. To help her differentiate between anal, urethral and inner-genital structures, I offered a term "baby-house," an image acceptable to her. She utilized it to bring into focus the genital as the main container of the baby and the mother (Figure 3), and integrated it with spatial representations of the rectum and the clitoris. The outline of the "house" was patterned after that of the outer labia, but it also had depth, drawn from the feelings of something inside.

When in transition from the inner-genital to the negative-phallic phase D had completed the major work of integrating her pregenital, inner-genital and phallic component drives; her drawings became more complex and in them she was able to demonstrate the differences between her inside and outside. This came about in the following way: D was jumping on the office couch in two distinct ways: she jumped up and down, changing tension abruptly, or she jumped and fell on a pillow, gradually settling there before the next jump. One

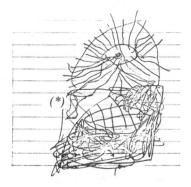

Figure 2. D jumps, draws a design, but refuses to explain what it is. It may be a house. ("What is it?") "Nothing." ("Is it a baby?") "No." ("Is it a house?") Perfunctory agreement. (*) See figure 3.

day she explained to me that the first type of jumping was ''button'' jumping (pointing to a button on the couch), but she had no words to explain the second. In response to my request to draw what she meant D produced a composite picture (Figure 2) of what turned out to be a schema of her inside, but in keeping with her incipient denial of her inner-genital, she said it was ''nothing.''

After further analysis of her old wish to create a baby out of feces and of her need to mix up the anal opening and the introitus, D drew two separate pictures, one to represent the ''pillow'' jumping (Figure 3) and the other ''button'' jumping (Figure 4). One can easily see that the composite picture (Figure 2) has been divided into two, with the button (sun) on top placed within a bounded frame and encircled by designs almost all of which are phallic in appearance, with only some oral, urethral and inner-genital components added (Kestenberg,

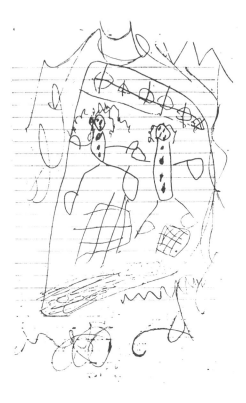

Figure 3. Two weeks after drawing in Figure 2, D explains to me the difference in feeling between two types of jumping. This design illustrates how she feels inside when she falls on a pillow. The forms represent a baby and a mother in a baby house.

1965–67). Crossing radials represented the radiation of her excitement outward (Figure 4). The bottom of the composite picture was enlarged in Figure 3. The dark (anal) area on the bottom was considerably reduced and separated from the criss-crossed shapes above. Instead of one pear-like shape, there were now two criss-crossed squares. The frame, bounded by designs, was identical with that seen in the lower part of the composite picture. In approximately the same location as the small figure in Figure 2(*), D began the drawing of the baby in Figure 3. By depicting the mother separately from the baby, D expressed her new fantasy that she was holding hands with the mother inside her genital, in her "baby-house." To combine the inner genital with the now more prominent clitoric representation, she put buttons on baby and mother, with mother having one more than the baby. In addition, the baby's hair had a predominantly phallic design. The scribble surrounding the now almost completely isolated inner genital kept changing in character, with small phallic configurations on the bottom, inner-genital waves on the sides and combinations of both on the top.

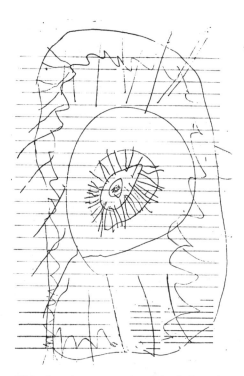

Figure 4. This drawing represents D's feeling from outside, from the "button" (clitoris) which she experienced when she jumped up and down without falling. To my question whether it is the sun, she agreed without conviction.

The small shaded area at the bottom of the house is no doubt anal; the top section of several half-circles and triangles with a line in the middle probably represents a multiplication of a crossed out orifice. There is evidence that the criss-crossed squares above the darker base represent shapes suggested from deep feelings inside the vagina. When asked about deep feeling directly, D drew a boundary line with two ovular and one pyramidal multi-dimensional figures, criss-crossed like the squares (Figure 5).

With my help, D had built up an integrated image of her inside and her outside. With the developmental task of the inner-genital phase completed, she began to woo her mother like a suitor. She invited her to see the leaping into space which she practiced in my office and she was eager to finish her treatment to please her mother.

Central to the girl's integrative effort is her concentration on the baby and the baby doll she animates in fantasy. When she ceases to feel warm and alive inside, she becomes disinterested in her doll. When her inner-genital tensions mount, she gets angry at her inside and attacks the doll. All these feelings are interrelated with the girl's relationship to her mother and her identification with her. When she feels rejected or abandoned by her mother, she likens it to a loss of the illusory baby inside of her. Closeness to the mother, feeling alive inside and having a baby to share with the mother are all signs of life. Being left, losing feelings inside and childlessness signifies the death of the mother, of herself and of the baby.

At the end of this phase there is always a disillusionment and a feeling of loss. The depression about the loss of the illusory baby (Kestenberg, 1956a,b, 1968) may occur earlier when it is reinforced by the daily observation of the live baby-sibling who belongs to the mother. The girl may feel that she has an empty

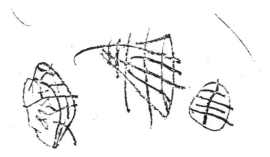

Figure 5. Asked what she feels way inside, D drew three "multi-dimensional" shapes, but the boundary for their contours became hazy on top, petered out on one side and abruptly stopped on the other.

container, useless and in danger of being thrown out. Fortunately there are various ways open to her to cope with her fears and her losses through an upsurge of creativity.

Preoccupied with her fear that she would lose her mother to the new baby, L neither wanted to leave her own babyhood nor did she want to acknowledge her own wish for a baby. She was the only girl we have seen in the Center who did not point to her belly to show that she is pregnant like her mother. However, her repetitious drawing of separate houses proved to be over-determined, not only separating her from J's family but also representing her mother's and her own pregnant body. Her interest in dolls seemed to wane, but she expressed the hope for a baby sister, a duplication of herself, typical for girls in the inner-genital phase. However, once more L's wish for her own baby suffered a setback when her parents convinced her that she should instead hope for a baby boy.

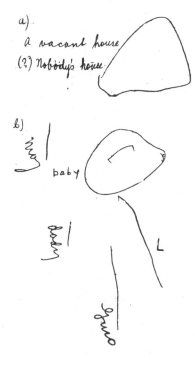

Figure 6.   A few days after the baby came home from the hospital, L made these drawings to indicate that the baby was not inside any longer, and that she, L was closest to the baby and the most important. Note also that the baby, though born, is still in an enclosure(b). Note also the relative lengths of the lines representing people close to the baby.

L was happy when her mother came home with a sister, Lottie, and named her new doll Lottie. She was nice to the new baby, but mistreated her doll and attacked older babies in the Center. When I visited L shortly after the birth of the baby she took me aside and drew an empty enclosure, commenting soberly: "It is a vacant house" (Figure 6a). I asked her what that meant and she explained: "Nobody's house." She then drew all the family members, with the baby still housed in a container and herself represented by a long line adjoining the baby, while mother and father were removed and shorter than L (Figure 6b). She revealed her understanding of a container for babies inside the body. Yet, at the same time the newborn baby seemed to her to be still inside a container that came out as well and left mother's body "vacant." She seemed confused and sad, yet knowledgeable.

In the next few weeks L drew almost incessantly (see a sample of her drawings in Figure 7). In many of these drawings one could recognize attempts to deal with the outside and the inside. Her scribbles, used alone or as boundaries for rounded container-shapes, betrayed her preoccupation with the varieties of excitement she felt. Phallic forms intertwined or alternated with inner-genital waves, but hollow containers still predominated as central themes. Six weeks

Figure 7.   Six weeks after the birth of the baby, L drew shapes, bounded by designs in which phallic protrusions alternated with or combined with inner-genital waves. On picture(c) phallic leaps were crossed by a horizontal wave, and underneath a shape, typical for a younger child, repeated containment in several layers. The latter predominates over other shapes.

after the birth of her sister, L dedicated a drawing to me (Figure 8). She explained that it was something to hold heavy things so they wouldn't fall. She had added the dimension of weight to her image of a baby-container. Her new experience of holding a baby "too heavy" for a little girl might have brought it into focus. She may have also learned about holding things up and down from watching her friend J's "ballies."

For some time the children in the Center had been preoccupied with death. They played out an incident in which a dead bird was buried by getting buried in leaves and coming alive again. L was afraid to be buried. At home she composed sad stories about a little girl left all alone by her parents. At last, she was able to formulate a question that had been on her mind for a long time. She wanted to know where her deceased paternal grandmother was. Told that she was very old and very sick and died, she revealed in a drawing that she had connected death to the absence of a baby inside, causing the container to be old and used up. She drew an old, worn *"carrot-shoe,"* empty and withered. Her sadness about losing her mother the way her father had lost his, and about losing the baby inside the carrot-shoe (a symbol for the vagina) would shift into anxiety. In response to a fairy story she heard she began to write about a witch who caged her parents. For a few weeks she rejected her mother and asked her father to sleep with her. This brief inroad into a phallic, positive-oedipal attitude was followed by an equally short negative-oedipal stance. L became maternal to her baby sister and, in identification with her mother, reported the baby's progress with great pride. By the time she was three-and-a-half she played with many dolls and told her mother

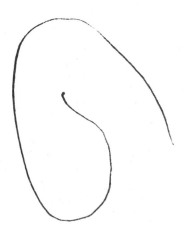

Figure 8.   L's drawing six weeks after the birth of her sister. She said it was something to hold heavy things so that they would not fall down.

that they were not real babies, but around this time she inadvertently revealed her fantasy that she was pregnant and had to consult her mother's obstetrician.

Fear of abandonment and the knowledge that her parents wanted a boy had interfered with L's creation of a baby, but in her play, her drawings and stories she was able to express her creativity. She kept her illusory pregnancy secret. Unlike many other children who connect empty insides with the death of the illusory baby, she discovered the existence of a feminine container whose uselessness she connected with death.

As the inner-genital phase progresses, inner-genital drives increase, but thoughts become more organized and the child becomes less dependent on ready-made objects for externalization of impulses through action. On the one hand, the girl nags more and more in response to inner-genital tensions with which she cannot cope; on the other hand, she becomes intensely involved in the process of creation of designs expressive of her feelings and of shapes to give them structure. Dissatisfied and whining at one moment, she may, in the next, become highly creative and reproduce the result of a long process of integration in stories and pictures. Her creativity is concerned with making a baby and letting it grow into a big girl. Thoughts about the baby's (her own) origin in the past and its transformations within a spatial context evolve from kinesthetic and visual sensations and perceptions, and the new concepts become even more complex when they include data regarding space, weight, volume and time. It is not unusual for short-lived positive or negative oedipal fantasies to invade the predominant preoedipal relationship with the mother, especially in girls whose triangular "girl-baby-mother" relationship has been invaded by conflict.

When A was three-and-a-half years old, she played with dolls a great deal, but she never admitted that she wanted a baby of her own like her eight month old sister. Her movement patterns and demeanor indicated that inner-genital and phallic tendencies vied with one another, but the former predominated. At periodic intervals, A would become very excited; she would nag her mother, scream and shake. At other times she would jump and leap, getting excited without becoming frustrated. She would periodically complain about "tummy aches," especially during meals.

A clung to her mother, but she was also greatly attached to her father and, at the age of three years, seven months told me confidentially that she will marry him when she grows up. At this point she denied wanting a baby of her own, but six weeks later she tested mother by demanding a baby and screaming. When told that to get a baby she first needed a husband to marry, she screamed louder, insisting that mother must not marry daddy but leave him free to marry A when she grew up so that she can have babies. It became evident that A did not allow herself to wish for a baby in the present and that she camouflaged her urgent baby-wishes by relegating them into the future. Marrying the father, at this point, was the only means of getting a baby. It did not occur to her that anyone else could be a husband. Yet, the matter was on her mind and one day she did fourteen consecutive drawings concerned with the inside and the outside, and with big and heavy, small and light attributes of animals and people.

In explaining what she drew, A had trouble formulating her thoughts and was rather defensive about revealing them. The first picture (Figure 9, 1) "a bleed under the skin," was also "a kind of turtle inside." In the second picture A had made thick scribbles in the midline; she called it "a line inside a line" which reminded me of a patient who thought of her uterus as a line and of the children who drew people as lines (see Figure 6) (Kestenberg, 1956b). In the third picture there was a protrusion out of the circle and there seemed to be a division between body and head. A proclaimed quickly that it was "inside of a tiger" and that she liked the stripes outside better than the "skin-bleed" inside. The fourth picture seemed to have a head, extremities and perhaps a tail and it was dubbed "inside a hippopotamous". A had to think a long time before she named the fifth picture. She repeated the previous title, but she was not satisfied. At last, in the sixth picture, a baby seemed to emerge—a baby partially enclosed by a protruding belly. A said quickly: "People inside people" and looking up she added by way of an explanation: "Mommy had me inside."

Having revealed her thoughts about her mommy's inside, she stopped talking about it and called the remaining pictures "lion" (7), "a man. . . an Indian" (8), "a light" (9). She clearly was veering away from women, but her urge to create a baby interfered. She was reluctant to explain picture 10, most probably a representation of pregnancy, and said that it was a pencil. To

Figure 9.   At the age of three years and seven months A drew this series of pictures. When she finished, she told me that she had been inside of her mommy for twelve years. She became perturbed wondering where she had been before. She reassured herself by the thought that she had always been in her mommy.

1.   A bleed under the skin. A kind of a turtle inside.

2. *Line inside of a line.*

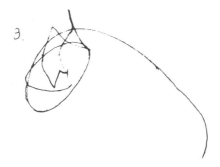

3. *Inside of a tiger. Bleed skin inside. Stripes outside.*

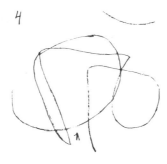

4. *Inside of a hippopotamus. I like outside better.*

5.   *This is the inside of a hippopotamus.*

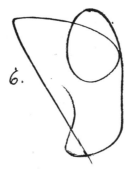

6.   *A people inside of people. A bleed. Mommy had me inside.*

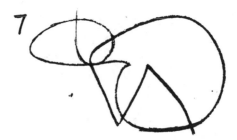

7.   *A lion. RRR.*

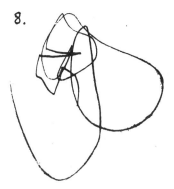

8. *Indian. A man. Indian.*

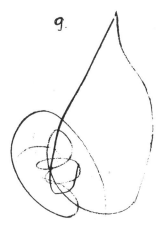

9. *A light.*

substantiate this claim she drew a very small, hardly visible line at the bottom of the page. Picture 11 was "a queen," 12 "a hippopotamous" again and 13 "a giraffe with a long neck." Just then a mother of a toddler passed by and I asked A to make a picture of her, but at the end it turned out to be a likeness of a little girl, A herself.

I have included this series of pictures to illustrate the thought processes of a girl in an advanced stage of the inner-genital phase. Successive attempts to represent the inside and to fathom out the evolution of a baby were counterbalanced by

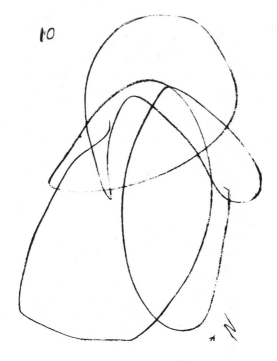

10.   *This is a pencil. Draws a pencil on the bottom.*

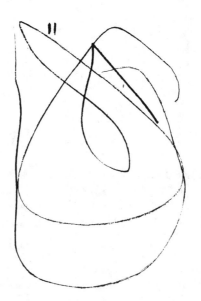

11.   *A queen.*

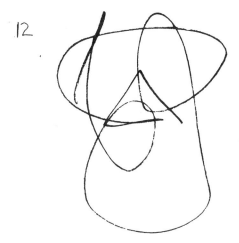

12

12.   A hippopotamus again.

a tendency to conceal this interest and to substitute for it thoughts about men and phallic symbols. How a child's conceptualization of making a baby is connected with fears of death can be illustrated by A's further thoughts. A had retraced her own origin from the ''bleed inside'' to her present status of a girl with long hair. Immediately after, she told me that she wanted to be twelve-years-old and that she had been in her mother's inside for twelve years. On thinking where she might have been before, she became anxious and wanted me to tell her that she had always been inside her mother. She had connected not being anywhere with death and worried that either she or her mother would die. A few weeks elapsed before A began to show an interest in nurturing the baby. She wanted to know what would become of mother's breasts if they were no longer needed for the baby. Would they go away?, she asked. She began to quiz her grandmother about her mother's early childhood. The persistent need to establish the continuity of her roots extended to her own perpetuation in children. She said that she would have many children when she grew up. A was not eating too well and asked her mother whether (the mother) had used the food she ate to feed the baby when it grew inside of her. When her mother drew the uterus as separate from the intestines, A understood the drawing but needed more time to absorb it. At no point did she ask how babies got inside, a question usually asked in the positive-oedipal phase when wishes for and fears of penetration gain in importance. It was noteworthy that only a few weeks after she completed the drawings A behaved as if she did not recognize them. She seemed embarassed and proclaimed that they were scribbles drawn by another girl. Only the ''lamp'' was her own drawing. The denial of the inside had begun and the shining, conic light, a phallic symbol, was here to stay. When L drew the ''carrot-shoe'', A

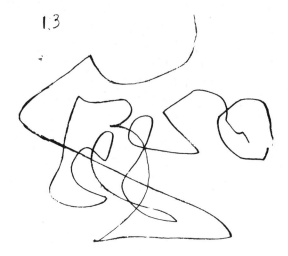

13.   *A giraffe.*

14.   *That's nothing. A little girl (?) Me.*

drew one too, but hers was almost entirely shaded in, leaving only a very small empty space. By closing off her inside and becoming interested in the outside, A warded off her fear of death. In a self-portrait at the age of three years and ten months (Figure 10) she illustrated her entry into the phallic phase, during which she stopped worrying about her own and her mother's death.

Having progressed in her ability to verbalize and integrate thought and action, the little girl who nears the age of four is capable of constructing an integrated image of her reproductive inside and her outside genital. This forms the base for what is becoming a core of her self-representation in the context of a continued existence, encompassing the past and the future. However, when regression persists due to a need to repeat traumatic events from the girl's toddlerhood, the inner-genital creation of the baby, the central issue in her gender identity, becomes arrested in pregenital ideation.

Figure 10.   A's self-portrait at the age of three years and ten months, attesting her entry into the phallic, negative oedipal phase.

G,[9] three years and four-months at the start of her analysis, and the youngest in her family, had no model for thoughts about pregnancy and they never became as clearly demonstrable as they were in D's, L's or A's cases. G's babies were literally "bathed in fluids." She was making babies out of paper which she pasted into small squares and brought to her mother. She made baby shapes out of clay as well. All these activities would combine with tea parties, with cooking and washing and they would invariably end up in floods. She bathed clay in water, making circles in gooey material. Paper got wet and tea was spilled. A pool of liquid seemed to envelop G and things around her, including the analyst. She refused to be weaned and trained, filling herself up with milk from the bottle and flooding her bed with urine.

When the analyst pointed out that she did not like to be wet and the mother began to wean and train her, G began to be interested in growing up. The indiscriminate flooding ceased and it became possible to trace its origin from an operation performed on G when she was twenty months old. At that time, her mother had to apply compresses while giving her the bottle and G had diarrhea while being fed. Working through the trauma of the operation, G tried to connect it with present day events. She would act out the role of the mother while the analyst became the child. She played at scolding her bad unruly child, repeating a recent scolding by her mother, but she tinted it (so to speak) with urethral features. She used dolls to represent the primal scenes she had experienced recently, but her creation of the baby was linked with her operation. In the process of integration of the past with the present, she recreated herself as the baby who was bathed in fluids from outside and inside. Once she could divorce babyhood from operations and flooding, she progressed rapidly into the phallic phase. In identification with her father she intruded upon the analyst, trying to "bop" her. At the same time she changed from a whining, irritating child to a charming girl who wooed her mother.

THE END OF THE INNER-GENITAL PHASE

Toward the end of this phase it becomes apparent in what manner pregenital forms of relatedness had become incorporated into the inner-genital relationship. The oral anaclitic bond to the mother remains in the girl's feeling that she needs her mother when she is sick or frustrated. Anal-sadistic ambivalence plays a role in the girl's argumentativeness and verbal barrages. The urethral sequence of hate followed by love is incorporated into the girl's progression from resenting her mother (for neither letting her have a real baby nor be a baby any longer) to lovingly forgiving her. The greater the intensity of sensations of hunger, colic,

[9]I am grateful to Dr. Ildeco Mohaczy for allowing me to use this material.

abdominal and pelvic pressure, pain upon defecation, anal itching and burning upon urination in infancy, the more ready the girl is to experience intense genital tensions as threatening and the more hateful she becomes. Conversely, the more pleasurable her memory of satisfaction at the breast, of relief from anal or urethral pressures, and the more sensuous her oral, anal and urethral experiences in the past, the more ready she is to enjoy waves of inner-genital fullness (radiating from inside) and the more loving she becomes.

The externalization of inner-genital impulses mollifies the little girl's yearnings for her lost babyhood and for the ideal mother of her infancy. The interpolation of the baby (in lieu of the genital) between mother and child creates a triangular relationship which dilutes anxiety and hostile feelings, deflects them and promotes identification with the mother. However, when inner-genital tensions increase and urgently call for relief, "tummy-aches" increase, externalizations cease and sublimations falter. The girl nags her mother, whines, screams, argues and passes on her excitement on to her, taxing her patience and tolerance. The provoked mother becomes angry and thus justifies the girl's hatred of her. At the same time, the little girl mistreats her doll over and above her need to repeat the unpleasant experiences of the past and the present. Unable to externalize, she can no longer endow the doll with the live qualities of a baby. Angry at her own nagging inside (experienced by A as "skin-bleed" or "a slow moving turtle"), she is also angry at her mother whose insides are hers ("because she had been there"). Wanting desperately to get rid of intense tensions that cannot be localized, she also wants to get rid of the baby associated with them. Death wishes toward her own live excitement (Fraiberg, 1972), and toward the mother and the baby who personifies it, become prominent at this time. They merge with bad wishes toward younger siblings. In some instances, the transformation — in fantasy — of the animated doll into a dead baby becomes a symbol for feelings of deadness (loss of sensation) in the genitals (Kestenberg, 1956, 1975). At other times there is a feeling — akin to mourning — because the container for the baby is empty and worn, ready to be thrown out. These feelings and fantasies are preludes to an escape from the genital dissatisfaction which generates denigration of the baby-bearing inside and self-hatred. In the process of self-exploration the little girl discovers her introitus at a time when her anger at babies merges with the fear of her inside. Frequently the discovery of the hole becomes a landmark separating the inner-genital phase from the phallic-oedipal. The ensuing denial of the introitus is reinforced by an isolation of the vagina from the external genital and by a creation of an illusory penis which seals the opening.

The availability of the external genital, especially the clitoris, acts as a lightening-rod that frees the girl from the need to hold on to excitement for a long time. However, because the clitoris cannot enlarge like a penis, intrude or penetrate and because it disappears at the height of excitement (Masters and

Johnson, 1966), it does not serve as a true phallic organ. The disappointed girl may revert to indirect masturbation through thigh pressure or through holding back of urine, a latent activity which permits her to maintain the fantasy of an illusory penis.

The calmer the inner-genital phase, the greater chance the girl has to develop a good image of her creative inside. This process of the formation of the self can be quite silent, with the child using play, stories and drawings to connect externalized feelings with shapes, colors, and objects which become the bridges between her outside and her inside. Yet, despite her efforts to represent her productive inside, she does not achieve a sense of organ-belonging as the boy does. In a way, her image of herself remains an open system subject to shifts and changes in keeping with the requirements of future changes in cycles and states, such as pregnancy, post-partum- and lactation-periods. Whereas in the prephallic-inner-genital phase the father is primarily an aide and an adjunct to the preoedipal mother, in the phallic-negative oedipal phase he becomes an organizing object in his own right. The girl admires him, identifies with him, hates him and competes with him, trying to outdo him in his ability to provide. Whereas in the inner-genital phase the child's concept of the father's genitals encompasses the testicles and the phallus, in the phallic phase the erect, large phallus becomes an object of true penis-envy. As successor to the baby that filled the inside, the girl's illusory penis — fashioned after the father's penis — closes off access to the inside. At this time, the triangle "girl-baby-mother," shifts to an oedipal triangle, "girl-father-mother," with the mother as the love-object and the father as a rival. With the realization that the clitoris will not grow into a penis or baby, the girl's illusory penis is shifted in fantasy into the place in her inside where the baby was. The open system of the internal genital phase is re-evoked and balanced by an admixture of phallic attributes. When in the phallicized, positive-oedipal phase the little girl turns to her father for love, she once more dreams of pregnancy, but at this time the sensuality of impregnation is a more crucial issue than being pregnant or having a baby. At this time, the primary triangle becomes girl-mother-father with the father as the love-object and the mother as the rival.

SUMMARY AND CONCLUSION

I have attempted to demonstrate the role of the inner-genital phase in the development of the girl's maternal image of herself. More extensive treatment of this topic has appeared elsewhere (1956a,b, 1962, 1967b, 1968, 1969, 1971, 1975, 1977, 1978b). Here I described the emergence of this phase within the developmental line of maternality and brought it into perspective with two other feminine developmental lines, the first culminating in the negative and the second in the positive-oedipal phase.

From these three lines stem the three basic feminine attitudes, the tender-maternal, the efficient-competitive and the enticing-sensuous. These attitudes alternate, differentiate, combine and become integrated within the total personality of the adult woman. On a higher level, they are repeated in adolescence and incorporated in adulthood into: (1) woman's fulfillment in motherhood or equivalent creativity; (2) her competence to provide and cope with the world in or outside of her immediate home environment; and (3) her fulfillment in a constant heterosexual relationship.

In a brief outline I tried to show the mutual influences of pregenital, inner-genital and phallic drives in pregenital phases and to trace the antecedents of the inner-genital phase and the phallic phase that follows.

All drive modalities are present in infancy. By combining with pregenital tendencies and becoming subordinate to them, inner-genital and phallic-clitoric drives become degenitalized. In each pregenital phase, an influx of phallic impulses fosters active aggression, differentiation and separation. A wave of inner-genital impulses seems to mellow the aggression and to usher in new libidinal phases by enhancing a reintegration of old and new dominances. Phallic-aggressive drives, combining with pregenital drives, are at the core of the pregenital precursors of penis-envy. Inner-genital drives contribute their share to pregenital representations and wishes for a baby. Phallic modes foster identification with the father and inner-genital modes foster identification with the mother. In infancy and toddlerhood, one can see how combinations of inner-genital and phallic drives underlie the early sensuousness that presages its adult form.

The wish for a child comes to a peak in the inner-genital phase. At this time, the preoedipal relationship changes from a predominantly dyadic to a triangular grouping of the ''girl-baby-mother'' trio. Via the externalization of inner-genital tensions and impulses, the girl can sublimate her drives, converting them into the drive-derivative function of maternality. Out of the disequilibrium that initiates this phase, there arises a reintegration of pregenital and inner-genital drives and a new organization through which the past is understood in the light of the present and the future. By assuming the role of a mother to a baby, the little girl recreates not only her own babyhood, but also the mother of her infancy. In this process, she builds an image of her procreative inside, modeled after the shape of a baby. It is difficult for her to understand that she has a container without a content. When she finally grasps the fact that she has no baby inside, the empty container becomes worthless and she feels dead inside.

When the girl's capacity to sublimate fails, she nags her mother, arguing with her and trying to pass her excitement on to her. At the end of this phase, she blames her for the loss of the illusory baby and temporarily turns away from her. Giving up her "live" baby she simultaneously denies the existence of her introitus, opening up the way for repression of the vagina as an organ. When phallic-clitoric tendencies increase, she enters the phallic-negative oedipal phase. With phallic penis-envy reinforcing the denial of the introitus, she leaves the preoedipal relationship behind and becomes the father's rival for the mother. Her fantasy of growing a penis (in lieu of the baby) is supported by masturbatory pulling on the clitoris and the labia. Adorned with an illusory penis she can now forgive her mother and she can generously offer to give her more babies than the father had given her. The newly developing triangular relationship centers on the oedipal triangle "girl-father-mother" and the baby, now phallic in nature, becomes an adjunct of this relationship. What was once a narcissistic union of "mother-baby-girl" transforms into a more object-directed love affair, first with the mother and then with the father. Precursors of this type of love, seen in pregenital and inner-genital phases, seem pale in comparison with the passion of the oedipal girl which so often withstands all efforts at sublimation.

Phallic tendencies in the girl are at the core of her bisexuality, but they are not masculine in nature. For instance, they can never be as outward-oriented as they are in the boy and the identification with the father is less deep-seated than that with the mother. The turn to the positive-oedipal phase may occur very quickly. In the renewal of her identification with the mother, she treats her as a rival, vying with her to be more alluring to the father. The external illusory penis transforms into an internal phallus which fills the vagina and gives it phallic qualities. The container becomes re-sexualized and the wish to be penetrated exists side by side with the fantasy that a penis is already inside. The image of the inner-genital becomes phallicized. The combination of inner-genital and outer-genital drives serves as a core for the immature heterosexual sensuality of the girl in the phallicized, positive-oedipal phase.

With the repression of incestuous wishes there occurs also a repression of the image of the inner genital and of the wish to be penetrated. In a drive-derivative form, the latency girl consolidates her femininity, drawing from pregenital as well as from the three early genital phases.

The inner-genital phase serves as a transition between babyhood and girlhood. It introduces the capacity to sublimate inner-genital tensions without subordinating them to pregenital impulses. Armed with a reservoir of sublimations, the phallic-oedipal girl is safeguarded against genital-sexual acting out. Sublimations, deepened, diversified and consolidated, serve the latency girl well when she begins to feel the impact of anatomic and hormonal change before the advent of adolescence. Among typically feminine sublimations, interest in nurturing stands out as a fountain from which various derivations of maternality spring. In the inner-genital phase in prepuberty, a reorganization of drives, with the inner-genital leading, brings on new forms of sublimation—the baby once more playing a central role in the process. In later phases of adolescence the already available sublimation of the desire for a baby becomes a mainstay in the reformation of psychic structures. In adulthood the fulfillment of the wish for a baby has an already solid underpinning of sublimations which safeguards the real child against premature sexualization by the nurturing mother.

ACKNOWLEDGMENT

To my granddaughter Afruz Amighi who helped me with this paper.

REFERENCES

Abelind, E.L. (1971). The role of the father in the separation-individuation process. In *Separation-Individuation*, ed. J.S. McDevitt and C.F. Settlage, New York: International Universities Press, pp. 229–252.

———(1977). The role of the father in personality development. In *Panel Discussion Tape of the San Francisco Institute Extension Division*. New York: Aronson, Psychotherapy Tape Library.

Andreas-Salome, L. (1916). "Anal" and "sexual." *Imago IV.*, pp. 249–273.

Barglow, P., and Schaefer, M. (1976). A new female psychology. In *J. Amer. Psycho-Anal. Assn. Supplement-Female Psychology*. 24:305–350.

Beard, R.M. (1969). *An Outline of Piaget's Developmental Psychology for Students and Teachers*. New York: Basic Books.

Benedek, T. (1974). Discussion of presentation at panel: *Parenthood as a Developmental Phase*. I.M. Marcus, chairman, Meetings of the American Psychoanalytic Association, Denver.

Blum, H. (1976). Masochism, the ego-ideal and the psychology of women. In *J. Amer. Psycho-Anal. Assn. Supplement-Female Psychology*. 24:157–191.

Burlingham, D. (1973). The preoedipal infant-father relationship. *The Psychoanalytic Study of the Child*. 28:23–47. New York: International Universities Press.

Dorfman, R.I. (1948). Biochemistry of androgens. In *The Hormones*. eds. Pincus, G. and Thieman, K.V. New York: Academic Press.

Erikson, E. (1950). *Childhood and Society*. New York: Norton.

———(1959). *Identity and the Life Cycle*. New York: International Universities Press.

Fast, I. (1979). Developments in gender identity: gender differentiation in girls. Int. Journal of Psychoanalysis. Vol. 60/41, pp. 443–495, 1979.

Fraiberg, S. (1972). Some characteristics of genital arousal and discharge in latency girls. *Psychoanalytic Study of the Child*, 27:439–475. New York: Quadrangle Books.

Freud, A. (1965). *Normality and Pathology in Childhood: Assessment of Development*. New York: International Universities Press.

Freud, S. (1924). The economic problem of masochism. *Standard Edition* 19:157–70. London: Hogarth Press, 1961.

———(1931). Female sexuality. *Standard Edition* 29:225–43. London: Hogarth Press, 1961.

Furman, E. (1969). In *The Therapeutic Nursery School.*, ed. A. Katan, and R.H. Furman. New York: International Universities Press.

Galenson, E. (1971). A consideration of the nature of thought in childhood play. In *Separation-Individuation: Essays in Honor of Margaret S. Mahler.*, eds. J.B. McDevitt, and C.F. Settlage. New York: International Universities Press., pp. 41–49.

————, and Roiphe, H. (1974). The emergence of genital awareness in the second year of life. In *Sex Differences in Behavior*, eds. R.C. Friedman, R.M. Richart, and R.M. Van der Wiele. New York: Wiley, pp. 223–231.

Gesell, A. (1940). *The First Five Years of Life*. New York: Harper.

Gray, S.H. (1976). The resolution of the oedipus complex in women. *J. Phila. Assoc. Psycho-Anal.* 3:103–111.

Greenacre, P. (1954). Problems of infantile neurosis. *Psychoanal. Study of the Child*. 9:18–24. New York: International Universities Press.

Halverson, H.M. (1940). Genital and sphincter behavior of the male infant. *J. Genet. Psychol.* 56:95–136.

Hartmann, H. (1939). *Ego Psychology and the Problems of Adaptation*. New York: International Universities Press, 1958.

Heiman, M. (1976). Sleep orgasm in women. In *J. Amer. Psycho-Anal. Assoc. Supplement-Female Psychology* 24:285–304.

Horney, K. (1926). The flight from womanhood. *Int. J. Psycho-Anal.* 7:324–339.

Katan, A. (1961). Some thoughts about the role of verbalization in early childhood. *Psycho-Anal. Study of the Child*. 16:184–88. New York: International Universities Press.

Kestenberg, J.S. (1956a). Vicissitudes of female sexuality. *J. Amer. Psycho-Anal. Assoc.* 4:453–476.

————(1956b). On the development of maternal feelings in early childhood. *Psycho-Anal. Study of the Child*. 11:275–291, New York: International Universities Press.

————(1961). *Menarche*. In *Adolescents*, eds. S. Lorand, and H. Schneer. New York: Hoeber Press, pp. 19–50.

————(1962). Panel on theoretical and clinical aspects of overt female homosexuality. Reported by C.W. Socarides. *J. Amer. Psycho-Anal. Assoc.* 10:579–592.

————(1965–67). Movement patterns in development I, II, III. *Psycho-Anal. Quarterly*. 34:1–36, 34:517–563, 36:356–409. Reprinted by Dance Notation Bureau, New York: 1976.

————(1967b). Phases of adolescence with suggestions for a correlation of psychic and hormonal organizations, Part 1. *J. Amer. Academy Child Psychiatry* 6:426–463.

————(1968). Outside, inside, male, female. *J. Amer. Psycho-Anal. Assoc.* 16:457–520.

————(1969). Problems of technique in child analysis in relation to various developmental stages: prelatency. *The Psycho-Anal. Study of the Child* 24:358–383. New York: International Universities Press.

————(1971). From organ-object imagery to self- and object-representation. In *Separation-Individuation: Papers in Honor of Margaret Mahler*, eds. J.B. McDevitt, and C.F. Settlage. New York: International Universities Press, pp. 75–79. Reprinted and revised in *Children and Parents* (see below).

————(1974). Notes on parenthood as a developmental phase. In *Clinical Psychoanalysis, Downstate Anniversary Series*, vol. I, eds. S. Orgel and B. Fine. New York: Jason Aronson Publishers, 1979.

————(1975). *Children and Parents: Psychoanalytic Studies in Development*. New York: Jason Aronson Publishers.

————(1976). Regression and reintegration in pregnancy. *J. Amer. Psycho-Anal. Assoc. Supplement—Female Psychology*. 24:213–250.

————(1976b). *Phases of Feminine Sexuality*. Psychotherapy Tape Library.

————(1979). Eleven, twelve, thirteen. In *Contributions of Psychoanalysis to Human Development*, eds. S.I. Greenspan and C.H. Pollock, National Institute of Mental Health (In press).

————(1979a). The three faces of femininity. *Psychoanal. Review* Vol. VI/3, pp. 313–335.

————et al. (1971). Development of the young child as expressed through bodily movement, I. *J. Amer. Psychoanalytic Assoc.* 10:746–763.

————, and Buelte, A. (1977). Prevention, infant therapy and the treatment of adults. *International J. Psychoanal. Psychotherapy.* I. Towards understanding mutuality. VI:367–396. II. Mutual holding and holding oneself up. VI:367–396.

————, and Marcus, H. (1979). Hypothetical monosex and bisexuality. A psychoanalytic interpretation of sex differences as seen in movement patterns of men and women. Vol. II. Self-in-Process Series, eds. Nelson, M. and   enberry, J. New York: Human Sciences Press.

————, and Sossin, M. (1979). Movement Patterns in Development II. *Epilog and Glossary.* New New York: Dance Notation Bureau.

Kleeman, J.A. (1976). Freud's views on early female sexuality in the light of direct child-observation. *J. Amer. Psychoanal. Assoc. Supplement —Female Psychology* 24:3–27.

————(1975). Genital self-stimulation in infant and toddler girls. In *Masturbation from Infancy to Senescence*, eds. I. Marcus, and J. Francis, New York: International Universities Press, pp. 103–106.

Klein, M. (1932). *The Psychoanalysis of Children.*. London: Hogarth Press.

Mack Brunswick, R. (1940). The preoedipal phase of libido development. *Psychoanalytic Q.* 9:293–319.

Mahler, M., Pines, F., and Bergman, A. (1975). *The Psychological Birth of the Human Infant: Symbiosis and Individuation.* New York: Basic Books.

Masters, W.H., and Johnson, V.E. (1966). *Human Sexual Response.* Boston: Little, Brown.

Nathanson, I.T., et al. (1941). Normal excretion of sex hormones in childhood. *Endocrinology* 28:851–865.

Piaget, J. (1951). *Play, Dreams and Imitation in Childhood.* New York: Norton.

Ross, J.M. (1977). Towards fatherhood: the epigenesis of paternal identity during a boy's first decade. *Int. Review of Psychoanalysis.* 4:327–348.

Stoller, R.J. (1976). Primary femininity. *Amer. J. Psychoanal. Supplement —Female Psychology* 24:59–78.

Wolff, P.H. (1966). The causes, controls and organization of behavior in the neonate. *Psychological Issues V,* no. 17., New York: International Universities Press.

5

A Suggested Developmental Sequence for a Preoedipal Genital Phase

LAURICE GLOVER AND DALE MENDELL

Contemporary psychoanalytic theorists have significantly altered formerly accepted hypotheses regarding female psychosexual development. They emphasize the very early roots of femininity, with the girl viewed as entering a phase of genital development out of a matrix of pre-existing sources and awarenesses of her femininity. When discussing early origins of female development, contemporary investigators stress multiple determinants such as cognitive, psycho-physiological and identificatory processes. Thus, Stoller (1976) concludes that sex assignment at birth initiates a process of core gender identification which is probably irreversible by the age of eighteen months and Kleeman (1976) emphasizes the primary, organizing effect of the child's early linguistic ability to label herself a girl. Both theorists, plus other observers (Blum, 1976; Kestenberg, 1975; Parens et al., 1976), also consider that parental attitudes, bodily sensations and identifications with the child-bearing mother contribute to a very early feminine self-representation.

These conclusions regarding the nature of female sexual development raise serious questions with respect to the traditional Freudian formulation (1925, 1931, 1933) that femininity is primarily an outcome of the discovery of the penis during the phallic phase and of the consequent castration shock. According to contemporary theory, the girl has evolved a feminine core gender identity by this time; in fact there has been some question about the use of the term "phallic phase" to describe the period of the girl's advance into genital sexuality.

Writing on the "phallic phase," Edgcumbe and Burgner (1975) refer to the girl's focused awareness of her genital apparatus and its functioning, and to the potentialities and effects that this new genitality has on herself and others. Frankel and Sherick (1979) find three and four year old girls distinctly different, in both fantasy and activity, from their male peers. Parens et al. (1976) believe that the little girl's "visible sensual activity . . . is an expression of her *primary constitutional feminine disposition* . . . Speaking only of her phallic preoccupations . . . does not take into account what we have found to be the *dominant* factor of the girl's awakening genital sensuality . . . Direct observation leads us to question the view that the feminine activity . . . is defensive or reactive'' (p. 83). They add that there is a weakness in Freud's view that the boy's heterosexuality is activated by a psychobiological force, whereas the girl's is activated by a narcissistic injury. Therefore, Parens et al. renamed this period the ''protogenital phase,'' which they observe emerging from the third year of life.

Similar concerns[1] about the nature of the girl's developing psychosexuality, ego apparatus and object relations led us to review material gathered from our adult analytic patients. We did an indepth study of a few individuals, primarily of unconscious derivatives stemming from dream material. Our findings suggest that there is a discreet phase in female psychosexual development, occurring between the anal and oedipal periods, in which the dominant zone is the genital and the dominant task that of defining oneself as female. When describing this phase we have decided to substitute the term ''preoedipal genital'' for the less appropriate term ''phallic.''

In the next section of this chapter we will review selected literature. Then we will discuss the methodology of our study. The body of the paper will consist of a presentation of the preoedipal genital phase as it appears to have occurred in our subjects. We will conclude with a discussion of a few prominent issues in the field. In presenting our data, we hope to make a contribution to the further understanding of a major stage in the development of female sexuality.

REVIEW OF LITERATURE

Freud's later papers (1925, 1931, 1933) introduce the concept of a phallic phase succeeding the oral and anal stages. The phase is named phallic as it is hypothesized that only one genital organ, the penis, is recognized by children of

---

[1]Our major divergence from Parens et al. (1976) is in regard to the timing (a) of this developmental phase and (b) of entry into the oedipus complex. Akin to Frankel and Sherick (1979), who observed ''protogenital phase'' behavior in nursery school girls occurring 6 months to a year later than did Parens et al, we hypothesize that children as young as those observed by Parens et al. (and by Galenson and Roiphe) are still primarily involved in anal phase development and we would speculate that Parens et al. may have been observing precursors of preoedipal genital behavior. In addition, we believe that oedipal phase development does not occur until after the major task of the preoedipal genital phase—consolidating a sexual identity—has been resolved, and would interpret much of what Parens et al. speak of as oedipal phase behavior as preoedipal attention to one *or* the other parent. We emphasize these points because we do not think that children as young as two and a half years old have the ego or object relational capacities to engage in oedipal phase relationships. In this last matter we have been influenced by Edgcumbe and Burgner (1975), whose investigation of preoedipal development grew out of their studies of object constancy; their views are summarized in this chapter's Review of Literature.

both sexes; the vagina is unknown until puberty. According to Freud, both boy and girl reach the phallic phase with identical libidinal stands: with the surge of libido to the genitals the original passive desire for the mother changes into an active, thrusting urge towards her, accompanied by penile or clitoral masturbation. A new interest and curiosity in regard to genitalia lead children to compare their respective organs and to discover that the girl does not have a penis. "[She] knows that she is without it and wants to have it" (1925, p. 252). Upon the girl's recognition of the inferiority of the clitoris as a source of gratification she develops the castration complex; she stops masturbation and develops an envy of the penis; her original love of the mother turns to hatred for having been made without a penis, and the girl turns to her father in hopes of receiving a penis and a penis-baby from him, thus initiating the Oedipus complex. The three tasks of female development involve changing from activity to passivity, from mother to father as love object, and from clitoris to vagina as erogenous zone.

Deutsch (1925, 1930) and Bonaparte (1951), elaborating on Freud's concepts, perceive the necessity of changing activity to passivity and clitoral to vaginal cathexis in order to achieve femininity as frequently insurmountable obstacles in female development. If, as they reason, the clitoris is simply a rudimentary male organ, then clinging to "clitoral sexuality" would prevent a girl from moving beyond the phallic stage, with continuing active attachment to the mother and "masculine protest." Deutsch (1944-45) believes that the girl, having no adequate genital organ with which to express phallic urges, turns her phallic strivings inward, becoming passive and masochistic.

Brunswick (1940), with Freud as collaborator, adds that phallic masturbation is repressed not only because of the girl's castration complex but also because the true object of clitoral activity is the mother, who has denied the girl a penis and forbidden masturbation. Brunswick also points out that the wish for a baby, based on the primitive identification of the child with the active mother, much precedes the discovery of the anatomical differences and the wish for a penis; rather, the girl wants both baby and penis and, "in the course of normal development the impossible is given up and the possible retained" (p. 245). She also acknowledges the possibility of early vaginal sensitivity "of anal origin," but believes that its role is very minor in comparison to that of the clitoris until puberty. Although Freud did note the girl's pre-phallic attachment to and identification with her mother, he neglected its importance in establishing a "developmental continuity" (Schaefer 1974, p. 474) out of which further feminine growth evolves.

Unlike Freud, Horney (1933) and Jones (1932, 1935) see the little girl as female from the start, having knowledge of her vagina, with the clitoris as an integral part of the female genital apparatus. They do not consider the phallic phase to be a normal developmental step, but instead view it as a secondary neurotic structure which the girl creates out of her oedipal fears, e.g., the fear of the father's large penis destroying her small genital; in this case the girl represses vaginal awareness and transfers it to her clitoris, the external sex organ, in order to protect her fragile inner genital. (More extensive reviews of Freudian theory and of dissenters from that theory can be found in Chasseguet-Smirgel, 1970; Kleeman, 1976; Moore, 1976; M. Bergmann, this volume; and many others.)

Contemporary thinking diverges considerably from Freudian theory on a number of issues. The persistence and urgency of the little girl's wish for a baby is no longer thought of as stemming from her disappointment in the lack of a phallus. Rather, the girl's wish for a baby is currently seen as deriving both from central phase-specific female concerns (Kestenberg, 1975; Parens et al., 1976; Benedek, 1970) and from identification with the powerful, beloved mother. According to Blum (1976) "Motherhood is . . . a core feminine wish and not secondary or compensatory" (p. 176).

Observations of masturbation in little girls (Kleeman, 1975) demonstrate that it is not confined to the clitoris; all portions of the genitalia appear to be explored, including clitoris, labia, vulva and the opening of the vagina. Both Greenacre (1950) and Kestenberg (1975) hypothesize early inner-genital sensations in girls, initiated by a mouth-genital innervation in the suckling infant and continuing with vaginal sensations primed by sensations in the adjacent bowel and anus. Kestenberg (1975; this volume) posits an inner-gential phase following the anal and urethral phases in which the girl is intensely, though globally, aware of her "creative inside." Nevertheless, the question of whether the young child forms a mental representation of her vagina is still unresolved. Clower (1975) suggests that the vagina is not cathected until puberty; on the other hand, Horney (1933) claims that "the undiscovered vagina is a vagina denied." Whatever future findings indicate, it is no longer feasible to assume that infantile sexuality is solely clitoral.

Contemporary thinking is also moving away from the idea that the clitoris is a masculine organ; it is now considered an integral part of the female genitalia, appearing to act as a conductor of sensuality to all portions of the genital apparatus (Masters and Johnson, 1966). Gillespie (1969) suggests that clitoral excitement may accompany a wish to be penetrated, rather than a wish to penetrate. Although, during the course of development, the clitoris may be focused on defensively, to suppress internal genital sensations (Horney, 1933), the defensive use of an organ does not define its original function.

To quote Moore:

> . . . Freud's (1933) statement that both sexes seem to pass through the early phases of libidinal development in the same manner (pp. 117, 118) is not supported by these observations. In particular his pronouncement that the sexuality of the little girl is of a wholly masculine character (Freud, 1905,

pp. 219) and that her masculine clitoral sensitivity must be given up for the vagina in order to achieve femininity at puberty, are untenable.

. . . The beginnings of gender identity (occur) before the phallic phase and before castration anxiety, penis envy and the Oedipus complex exert their greatest influence. (1976, pp. 289–290).

According to Freudian theory, the turning point of the phallic phase was the discovery of the anatomic difference; the resulting penis envy marked the beginning of feminine development, with the girl turning from her mother to her father to seek the desired penis. However, many current writers have challenged the concept of penis envy as the major determinant of feminine development (see Chasseguet-Smirgel, 1970; Panel, 1976; Blum, 1976; Barglow and Schaefer, 1976; Grossman and Stewart, 1976; Lachmann, this volume; and many more). To illustrate briefly: Kleeman (1976) and Stoller (1976) do not consider penis envy to be "the initiator of feminine gender identity"; Blum (1976, p. 186) states that it can not be regarded as "the major organizer of femininity"; Spielman (Panel, 1976, p. 641) believes that "there has . . . been a mistaken emphasis on penis envy as a primary organizing force in both female ego development and object relations" and that this has led to the unfortunate result of regarding women's intellectual or physical achievements as displacements from genital concerns.

Frankel and Sherick (1979) observed that three and four year old girls were absorbed in play activities and fantasies different from those of their male peers; they do not find that "female development involves an essentially masculine, phallic phase" (p. 306). Edgcumbe and Burgner (1975) believe that the phallic phase, characterized by a shift into genital sexuality, is primarily concerned with the shaping of a sexual identity. Penis envy, by sharpening the perception of differences, aids girls in accomplishing this task; girls are impelled to renounce the role of the opposite sex as they engage in the comparison with others so characteristic of the phallic phase. Regarding penis envy and the phallic phase, Edgcumbe et al. (1976) state: "rather than postulating that recognition of her lack of a penis forces the girl to abandon a masculine position for a feminine one, we suggest the less biased view that awareness of the significance of physical sexual differences between children and adults aids both boys and girls in consolidating their sexual identity" (p. 59).

The "phallic" phase is often referred to in the literature as the "phallic-oedipal" phase, as it is usually assumed that the child who has entered a phallic phase drive position, with a surge of libido to the genitals, has therefore also entered the triangular oedipal relationship and is rivalrous towards one parent while simultaneously desiring the other. Summarizing the Freudian position, LaPlanche and Pontellis state, "The phallic stage corresponds to the culmination and dissolution of the Oedipus complex" (p. 309). (The issue is not as clear cut in girls as it is in boys; it will be discussed more fully later in this section.) However, in 1975 Edgcumbe and Burgner proposed separating the preoedipal portion of the phallic phase from the later oedipal portion. Calling the preoedipal portion the phallic-narcissistic phase, as suggested by Anna Freud, they reserved it for that part of development when the genitals have become the dominant erotogenic zone, but when the most pronounced drive components are those of exhibitionism and scoptophilia, when the dominant mode of relating is still dyadic and when the issue of shaping one's own sexual identity is prominent. They see the ''phallic-narcissistic'' child as using the genital organs primarily for exhibitionistic, narcissistic and comparative purposes, to gain the admiration of the object and to consolidate sexual identity by increased identification with the parent of the same sex.

> It is characteristic of the child's relationships in the phallic-narcissistic phase that sexual wishes and fantasies toward an object are expressed within what is still essentially a one-to-one relationship. The third person may be seen as an unwelcome intruder in this exclusive relationship, as in earlier prephallic phases of the mother-child relationship, but this intruder has not yet been awarded by the child the full status of the oedipal rival. (1975, p. 167).

Not until the tasks of the phallic-narcissistic phase have been fulfilled can the child move easily into the oedipal stage and establish a truly triangular relationship with the parents, which presupposes a relatively mature level of relationship to self and object, of drive activity and of acceptance of the irreversibility of the fact of being female and having a female body.

Closely related to the question of whether there is a preoedipal phallic phase, and to questions concerning the nature of that phase, is the issue of the negative oedipal phase. Traditional theorists agreed that the girl enters the negative oedipal phase concurrently with the beginning of phallic drive development, i.e., that the girl assumes an active phallic stance with her mother as love object and her father as rival; the girl has no impetus to change love objects until she discovers her lack of a penis and, disappointed and hostile, turns to her father in hopes of gaining a penis and/or a baby as a substitute for the missing phallus. However, while Lampl-de Groot (1927) considered the girl's negative oedipal phase to be part of the Oedipus complex, similar in all respects to the boy's positive oedipal phase, Freud (1931, 1933) and Brunswick (1940) place the girl's negative Oedipus complex in the preoedipal phase.

The entire concept of a negative oedipal phase preceding the positive oedipal complex has been questioned by theorists such as Edgcumbe and her colleagues:

The question of timing of entry into the oedipal phase seems to rest largely on whether entry into the positive oedipus complex is taken as the beginning of true oedipal development, or whether the negative phase in girls . . . is also included as oedipal rather than preoedipal. In either view there is an implicit assumption that entry into the phallic-drive phase is accompanied by some form of move to triangular oedipal relationships. This assumption . . . may be one of the factors which biases our observations and obscures our understanding of behavior early in the phallic phase, since it makes us look for sexual attraction to one parent and rivalry with and hostility to the other . . . : we may confuse preoedipal with oedipal rivalries . . . .(1976, pp. 39–40.)

Edgcumbe et al. studied girls in treatment at the Hampstead Clinic and found that, while the Oedipus complex proper appears to contain both positive and negative aspects, they could not find a specific negative oedipal phase preceding the positive oedipal complex. They conclude that it would be more appropriate to describe the early portion of the phallic phase as narcissistic rather than as negative oedipal.

We suspect that, in addition to the conceptual difficulty of equating a change in drive development (shift into genital sexuality) with a change in object relations and identifications (triangular oedipal relationship), the confusion around the concept of a negative oedipal phase stems from Freud's hypothesis that the girl is pushed into the oedipal phase due to narcissistic disappointment and rage with her mother, and that she would otherwise have no reason to change her love object from mother to father. A corollary assumption is that, until the oedipal stage, she has accorded no more importance to her father than to any other-than-mother acquaintance (Lampl-de Groot, 1928). However, contemporary studies indicate that children's attachment to the father is early and specific, and that they turn from mother to father repeatedly during the preoedipal period, both in order to obtain an ally in separating from the mother and in order to find excitements and satisfactions not obtained from the mother (Abelin, 1971; Panel, 1976).

In Edgcumbe et al.'s data, most subjects moved into the positive oedipal phase with minimal difficulty, save for those girls who had an absent or unresponsive father, or whose mothers did not provide them with a suitable model for feminine identification. Rather than viewing the phallic phase girl as turning to her father out of humiliation and rage towards her mother, we find it more feasible to think that her growing awareness of her genital sexuality leads her to define herself in two major ways: by comparison and identification with her mother and by contrast with the complementary object, her father. Once she has defined and delimited her own sexual identity, her entry into the oedipal stage is immeasurably facilitated.

THE STUDY

Method

In seeking additional information and clarification about the period of the girl's advance into genital sexuality, we reviewed our records of the dreams of six adult patients with neurotic character structures. Of the six, four had completed their psychoanalyses before this study was conceived. All dreams reported by these six analysands during their regressive repetition of the developmental period between the anal and oedipal phases were examined for this study.

In utilizing data culled from the psychoanalyses of adult patients in order to further understand the psychic reality of a childhood developmental phase, it is not expected that adult patients literally replicate their original childhood experience. Rather, it is assumed that they repeat that experience with individual disguises and revisions (Blum, 1980). It is to be hoped that penetrating these disguises and revisions and complementing them with data from the literature on the psychoanalytic observation of children will aid in gaining a fuller understanding of a "preoedipal genital" phase.

The decision to use dream derivatives in this study was based upon the immediacy and intensity with which dreams reflect the regressive activation of conflicts during the psychoanalytic process (Garma, 1978). Our patients' dreams were studied for their yield of unconscious derivatives of drive, ego and object relational elements as they appeared to emerge during the developmental period between the anal and oedipal phases. (The senior author has worked extensively at elucidating the meaning of dream derivatives in clinical settings. Elaboration of the theoretical bases underlying such work can be found in Glover, *Listening: Unconscious Derivatives as they relate to Session Themes*, in press.) Validation of these findings relied upon the internal consistency of the data rather than upon corroboration with the analysand's free associations and memory traces, as it does in reconstructive work. (See Appendix A for an illustrative sample of the analysis of dream derivatives.) As an added check on our observations, we examined ongoing reconstructive work with patients not included in the sample and found similar developmental themes.

We would like to stress the exploratory nature of this study. At the time we began to review the records of our patients' dreams, we had formulated few hypotheses regarding the nature of female preoedipal genitality; in addition, four of our six patients had already completed their analyses. Therefore, we were surprised to discover a sequence of four specific themes emerging from our analysis of derivatives, a sequence which was observed in all of our patients.[2]

[2]With the exception of (1) a portion of the sequence dealing with the genital mother (the initial portion of subphase three, as defined at the end of this section) and (2) instances where the patient had been sexually traumatized as a child. In the latter instance, the usual sequence of events did not appear in the derivatives until the area of trauma (including the associated after effects) had been worked through.

While the unanimity of themes among our patients point to the possibility of a valid developmental sequence, we realize that our findings are based on a small sample and on the observations of only two clinicians; in addition, despite our lack of explicit hypotheses, we are aware that unconscious bias on the part of the analyst can influence the content and timing of analytic material. Nevertheless, we decided that our material warranted presentation at this point due to its potential for contributing to the understanding of a complex and important period of development. Further clinical and observational investigation is needed to ascertain the validity of the themes we have noted and of the discreet phenomena within them.

Our thematic material suggests that, prior to the oedipal phase, there is a developmental period where the genitals are the dominant erotogenic zone and where there is a dominance of concern (a) with the female sexual apparatus and its functioning, (b) with the establishment of a differentiated female sexual identity, and (c) with female modes of relating to others. We believe that the emergence of such a constellation is psychobiologically predetermined and is based upon internal maturational factors as well as upon external stimuli and would therefore be considered an epigenetic developmental phase.

As indicated earlier, we consider the term "phallic" to be inappropriate for a developmental phase which, in females, is concerned with female anatomical structures and with establishing a female indentity, and which contains specifically female fantasies. We therefore substituted the term "preoedipal genital" as being far more accurate a description of this phase. As it emerged in our data, the proposed preoedipal genital phase follows the anal phase and is succeeded by the Oedipus complex. Our proposed schema has both similarities and dissimilarities to those reported in the literature; it encompasses both the periods of Kestenberg's inner-genital phase and Edgcumbe and Burgner's phallic-narcissistic (or preoedipal phallic) phase; thus, we assume, it should describe the child of approximately 2½ to 4½ years of age. Throughout the body of the paper we will note certain agreements and disagreements between our observations and those of other contemporary investigators.

Our material indicates that the suggested preoedipal genital phase consists of four sequential developmental subphases, as follows:

First, a focus on inner bodily sensations and a beginning awareness of the female sexual apparatus.

Second, a focus on the father in specifically gender terms, with an awareness of femaleness in relation to his maleness.

Third, a focus on and identification with the mother's genitality, within the context of sexual differentiation from her.

Fourth, a focus on the total genital self; comparisons with others in order to obtain narcissistic gratification and evaluation; organization of component instincts into an increasingly mature genital drive; formation of a consolidated sexual identity.

Each of the four subphases of the proposed preoedipal genital phase will be presented with an introduction and a summary. Quotation marks indicate illustrative use of our raw data, the dream material.

First Subphase

During the first subphase the girl begins to focus on her own body's specific genital organs and capacities. There is a heightened awareness of each of the female genitalia, a sorting out of the differences between the anal orifices and products and the genital, and a concern as to whether or not "everything is present and not damaged." The girl's perception is primarily focused inward and used in the service of assessing her own body components and eventual sexual capacities. Libido is directed towards the inner self, as if the girl has withdrawn libidinal cathexis from the object representations of mother and father. There is a vague awareness of her mother as a strong, protective figure and occasional glimpses of her father waiting for the moment when her sexual maturation will begin to unfold and she can begin to be *"his* little girl." This inward focus, with a concentration on the fantasized baby inside, has been noted by Kestenberg (1975) in her discussion of the inner-genital phase, and is perhaps behaviorally evidenced by Frankel and Sherick's (1979, pp. 299–300) three-year-old girls when they quietly draw and paint, or play at examining and treating those who are hurt.

The girl's inner-genital subphase opens with the beginning awareness of parts of her body that are sexual or somehow related to "having babies like Mommie does." She explores the inside and the outside of her genital body, discovering through touch or through muscular tension the vagina, clitoris, and labia. She is also somehow aware that there is "a place inside myself" that is hollow—"a dome—like a honey comb"—that can carry something—"like a suitcase." Whether by inference or by identification with her mother she associates this inner place with fecundity: "A big hand bag with a baby in it," "a marsupial pouch," "a tiny bassinet in orange and brown velvet." Either by putting her finger inside herself, or by playing with siblings and friends, she discovers the receptive vaginal passageway: "a corridor," "a drive way," "an entrance and exit." She finds the labia and thinks of them as protective curtains: "I fixed the blinds so you couldn't see into the room outside." She delights in the pleasure of beginning sexual arousal when she strokes her clitoris. It not only is a way of initiating inner genital sensations - "a bunsen burner in front of the door"—but it helps her to consolidate her own physical and emotional sense of self—"a button which helps me to find my way home." It is also good for helping to reestablish a sense of body-self in the presence of anxiety: "a pacifier."

Along with these awarenesses the girl realizes that the clitoris is different from the phallus of her boy-acquaintances. She knows that it is much smaller— "a small part in a play," but the primary differentiation is functional. The phallus is seen as something which penetrates, whereas the clitoris is seen as something which arouses both clitoral and inner-genital excitement— "a cherry in whipped cream instead of a screw driver with a cherry." These findings are consonant with Clower's statement: "The fact that anatomically [the clitoris] is a true homologue of the penis and that it has been traditionally considered the 'female phallus' has obscured understanding of its function, which is totally limited to initiating or elevating levels of sexual tension. The clitoris serves *only* as an erotic focus for sexual stimulation. This capacity is biologically determined, (and) manifest in the preoedipal girl" (1976, p. 112).

The beginning stirrings of genital sensation mobilize a counter-wish to withdraw or to retreat to earlier emotional levels. Thus, the girl speaks of "things which can't be named" which are "powerful and elusive" within herself, and then of the anti-instinctual impulse "everything is locked up" and "I'm in a mental state of not wanting to let anything in nor let anything out." She tries to halt the developmental surge by imagining herself as "the sleeping beauty" or "in a coma." But the genital impulse continues to emerge: "I wanted to break the glass to get out."

She is anxious about the beginning experience of exhibitionistic impulses, "of being found out, revealed, exposed." But she delights in them as well, taking joy in "parades, parades." In addition, she is frightened of being overwhelmed by sexual response which is too strong for her still-developing ego structure. "I was drawing back from the man in fear—not of him, but of the airplane, the horse." Similarly, she is anxious about "falling" or "hanging off a cliff and hanging on." A number of writers (Fraiberg, 1972; Kramer, 1954; Barnett, 1966) have described girls who turn away from genital stimulation at approximately this time due to anxiety over intense excitation resembling, but not the same as, that of an adult; a transient loss of ego boundaries appears to have threatened the girls and provoked repression of genital stimulation.

There is a narcissistic quality in this subphase as the genital libido is focused on the self; the feeling is of "being in touch with myself," and of "shelter." (Themes of inwardness develop later in the protogenital phase and are extended to the arenas of religious interest and creative activity. There are beginning echoes of these themes in references to "my soul" and "deeply felt" experiences.)

There is very little reference to the mother or father during this subphase. The girl's feeling is "like 'leave me alone!' " When she is aware of the mother, she usually sees her as "protecting me with her strength"; occasionally she experiences her mother as joining her in a regression to the symbiosis of the oral phase: "going back to the woman." The girl views her father as supporting the development of her genital sexuality; he may be a benign figure: "the priests opened up caves of magnificent paintings" or a frightening one: "it was the man who kept a knife in a wound to keep it open."

As the girl continues to explore the genital parts of her body, she begins to contrast that which is genital with that which is anal. The fact that both areas encompass orifices is confusing; there ensues a sorting out of the specific body contents, qualities, and activities connected with the genitalia, and those connected with the anus.

The girl notes that "there is one hole in front and another hole in back." She is aware that the front hole has to do with urine or vaginal discharge, the back one with feces: "the water was all dried up and we came to the mud." She uses defecation as an analogue for vaginal receptivity: "I was skiing up hill while the others struggled down the hill," and uses images of reversal of direction to indicate something coming into the body rather than going out of it: "the ducks were swimming downstream; they turned around and swam the other way." She sometimes refers to the vaginal orifice as bigger, older, and more dangerous than the anus: "The apartment was bigger but old; it had holes that were dangerous, and you could fall down."

The girl playfully combines genital and anal products: "*statues* of Beauty and the Beast"; genital and anal sensations: "kids were *banging* on things"; and genital and anal activities: "she was *cleaning* with water," but then feels anxious that anality may contaminate genital development. "The toilet overflowed with shit all over my feet" refers to interference with phallic activity; "roaches were coming out of holes in the plaster" refers to interference with inner-genital activity. Greenacre (1948) notes that inappropriate defecation is condemned more sternly than eneresis, and that such condemnation can aid in repressing genitality. Kestenberg (1968) adds that the inner genital is not easy to localize. "The inner-genital girl fuses anal, perianal and introital sensations and repudiates the inner genital as she repudiates anality and the anal baby; she fears all of her inside will fall out during defecation (delivery)" (p. 508).

On the other hand, the girl fears that the growing awareness of genital sexual impulses may interfere with her newly acquired capacity for independent functioning, the ego's legacy from the anal phase. "A sports car wheel caught one of my shoes" reflects this fear, as does "I had to jump over a hole to get to the path."

The closing portion of the inner genital phase is a time of inventory. The girl determines what sexual equipment is and is not present, assessing whether there has occurred in some vague, undefined way damage to the capacity to function genitally. She is involved with questions of damage to vagina, uterus and the fantasized fetus. "A big part of my jaw fell out, full of teeth and blood" reflects concern about the intactness of the vagina. "Something was wrong with the pipes in my kitchen—I was looking at the walls and they were blistering" refers to questions about the uterus. The damage to the potential fetus may either be due to natural defects—"It was a retarded baby with a big head"—or to the destructiveness of others—"They took cuttings of the plants in the courtyard." The girl may also evidence concern about the fate of the baby she will ultimately birth: "the female lambs were led to slaughter."

The girl assumes that she is supposed to have male, as well as female, genitalia. "I felt castrated: something had been sticking out of my body, something visible and tangible—aggressive, almost like a weapon—pleasurable to use. I had the feeling everyone had conspired to take it away." Perhaps she has a penis hidden inside of her body? "There were hidden pennies under the sixes." The aggressive and penetrating qualities of the penis are especially emphasized, and in that regard the inadequacy of the clitoris by comparison. "I had small knives; the man had a kitchen knife and he stabbed me." Not only the penis but the testicles are found absent: "I was in a tennis competition. I kept missing the balls."

While references to male genitalia are far less frequent than are references to female genitalia, at this point in development the little girl seems to feel that the human being was meant to be hermaphroditic. In terms of Fast's "gender differentiation perspective" (1979), the girl is initially in an undifferentiated period with respect to sexual characteristics and only gradually learns to recognize and accept her sexual limits. "The loss of maleness seems to represent to the girl . . . the loss of unlimited potential. To have maleness (or male genitalia) would make her complete. Her wish is not to be male instead of female, but to be unlimited instead of female" (p. 448).

The girl also questions her own capacity for sexual responsiveness. Will she be capable ultimately of such response, or will she be too frightened of emotional and physical genital contact? "The house was empty. There were alcoves in my room, but the woman was frozen and in pain on the fire escape." Will genital experiences be pleasurable or sad? "The cover was white painted flowers: underneath was the face of a clown." Is it safe to be sexual? "I was driving up a steep hill with snow. The car was skidding until it came to a resting place." What will her mother's response be to her developing sexuality? "Mother didn't want any bums sleeping on her doorstep." And her father's? "A girl and her mother were going somewhere and they needed passports."

With these questions, the girl leaves the initial subphase of inward concern and focus, having explored the qualities of her inner physical and emotional world. With her inventory of her inner-genital world as a basis for a beginning sexual identity she is ready to turn her attention to her father as a genital, sexual being. The inwardness she has just experienced will not return until the final moment of the preoedipal genital phase, when she begins to confront the questions of fecundity and birthing.

Second Subphase

During the second subphase the girl turns her attention to her father as a sexual being, including his genital sexual interest in her and hers in him. In the literature this theme is often referred to as oedipal in nature. However, we do not consider it oedipal as the emotional task of the subphase is not to win the father from the mother, but rather to become familiar with the complementary male figure and to develop a female sexual identity vis-à-vis his maleness. There is not yet any hint of competition with the mother, who is used (in a silent, inconspicuous way) as a supportive figure throughout the subphase. Our data are consistent with Fast's (1979) "differentiation framework" which "suggests that as the girl recategorizes her experiences in gender terms changes occur in her relations to each parent . . . she must learn to relate to the father now as specifically male in relation to her own self as female . . . The relation to the mother is an independent source of support for her femininity as she develops her cross-sex relation to her father as masculine" (pp. 451–452).

During the initial part of this subphase, there is a heightened awareness of the father's body, especially of his penis. There is a generalized fear of being damaged and also the suggestion of a frozen immobility, an emotional and physical paralysis. The middle part of the subphase is one in which the girl delineates her own (and, by inference, her mother's) psychological and physical defenses against the overpowering male. She then is prepared to deal with more specific anxieties: penetration anxiety as a response to the sexually phallic male and the fear of being mutilated by the angry phallic male. These are followed by a brief identification with the aggressor male and then by the realization that the father needs her as a female counterpart to his maleness, that he is "there for her"[3] as a female and will take care not to hurt her.

The final part of the subphase encompasses the shift of libidinal instincts and ego processes from passive to active. The girl develops the capacity to act as well as to be acted upon in her sexual interests: The inner genital focus shifts to the outer body, and the phallic identification from the genitalia to the entire body. She demands support from her father in these efforts and claims his protection against any dangers from the outer world she may encounter in her newly developed active mode. The subphase closes with a joyful awareness of her own beginning genitality and with an appreciation of her father's phallic qualities as both attracting and supporting her developing sexuality.

---

[3]Max Geller (1969). Personal Communication.

The initial feeling state of this subphase might best be described by the words "penis awe." The father, the prototype male, is seen as huge in size, primitive and invincible. The large size may refer to the father's body—"the man was oversized, super human, bigger than life"—or to his penis—"the abominable snowman emerged from the woods; he was called Big Foot." The primitive qualities of the father come to life with the image, "he was a man with two heads, two faces, the evil gorilla and the vampire with awful eyes, glowing and magnetic." He is also magically invincible: "a male monster, seven feet tall; a man stabbed him, but that didn't mean he was dead."

Greenacre (1953) discusses the phenomenon of penis awe as a mix of "intense admiration, a feeling of strangeness, with little sense of the possibility of possession, sometimes an element of fear . . . aggressive feelings . . . are suspended and diffuse, and may be converted into worshipful submission . . . or into states of considerable excitement" (p. 176). She suggests that penis awe is the result of viewing the adult penis, particularly erect or erecting, an awareness sharpened up to age four or five with the increase of genital feelings. Greenacre believes that the timing of viewing is crucial; if a contemporary is viewed first, envy is most likely, if an adult male, awe is the usual result. Our findings suggest that penis awe may be a normal developmental phenomenon rather than an accidental occurrence, as it was present both in girls with opportunities to observe young brothers and in those not exposed to contemporaries.

The awe of the phallic father is accompanied by a state of intense terror, suggestive of emotional and physical paralysis. The differentness (foreignness) of the male combined with his superior strength and his capacity to stimulate sexual responsiveness in the girl all call forth images of being damaged or even killed.[4]

While the girl's fears of genital damage are similar to those she experienced in the last part of the inner genital subphase, she now attributes the damage to the powerful phallic father or to her own awakening sexual response. However, there remains a vagueness as to the exact manner in which the damage is brought about. That theme develops later in the sub-phase.

There are references again to possession of both male and female genitalia. The father may be held responsible for castrating the girl, because of his sexual need for her: "The man wanted to talk with me; he had eaten one of my arms." Or he may injure her vagina: "The woman's mouth was pale and scarred" or her clitoris: "her ear was a little red and raw stump." The strength of the father's phallic sexuality may stimulate an uncomfortably intense awareness in the girl of her own sexual impulses: "the driver of the boat shook the boat so suddenly I fell off"—or—"the man got into the car and it started careening up and down the

---

[4]It is similar to the feeling response reported by women unexpectedly exposed to a male exhibitionist. There is a sense of complete powerlessness, immobility, and the need to stare at his penis as if physically forced to do so.

street." He might even damage her capacity for fecundity: "The man was a foreigner and a killer of children."

Accompanying the beginning vivid awareness of the father's masculinity are the first thoughts of weddings and of becoming a bride. There is a curious sense of helplessness, passivity, and childishness, which still does not reflect oedipal derivatives. The father's adult state is contrasted with the girl's tender years and there is as yet no mention of competition for the father: "I was trying out for a play—my part was as the bride—I just stood there"; "I was getting married in a child-like outfit."

As she becomes aware of the possibly damaging aspects of the awesome phallic father, the girl begins to delineate the various psychological and physical weapons she can use to defend herself against physical or emotional injury. Former terrors are mastered by turning a passive response into an active one, in part by identification with the mother's intra-psychic and interpersonal defenses, in part by using methods of coping and self-defense learned in earlier psychosexual phases.

The girl's favorite weapons are words and attitudes designed to challenge the father's sense of self as a genital male, or to manipulate his phallic sexuality and aggressivity. Emotional castration or ridicule of the father is illustrated by such statements as "the mother had a male attendant who was very weak." In addition, the girl may withhold phallic narcissistic gratifications: "I refused to sing the Star Spangled Banner" or attack his self-image: "The man was fat and bald." When threatened by the father's phallic aggressivity, she may try to stimulate his phallic sexuality; thus there is the statement, "a group of men were playing cards [release of phallic aggression]; I took off my clothes and excited them [being enchantingly seductive in part as a defense]."

The theme of the closure of the vagina appears for the first time, either as a defense against the physical approach of the male or as a defense against the girl's own overpowering sexual response. The former is seen in the statement "This guy wanted to be with me; I closed the door," the latter in "There was a stampede of wild horses; I had to get away to a small cottage; I closed the door and kept the horses out." Horney (1933) and Jones (1932) speak of the girl's repression of vaginal impulses due to narcissistic anxieties in regard to attacks on the inside of her body.

The girl also identifies with her mother's role as nurturer in order to explore its possibilities as a weapon against the powerful male. "We were feeding the guard whipped cream to get him sick. He was lying on the boat bunk bed exhaling little puffs of whipped cream." She begins to see herself as one who can feed or withhold food: "The leaves and seeds from trees on the ground are a source of energy to him." Through identification with her mother as well as her own projections, she becomes aware of her father's vulnerability to separation anxiety and realizes that she can use it as a weapon: "The woman died; my father was crushed by her death and couldn't function for a while." "Leaving a man is the best way to hurt him."

There are probably many other self-protective devices available to the girl in her attempt to assuage her terror about the genital aspects of her father.[5] Their relative absence from the literature may reflect a misinterpretation of these phenomena as defenses against penis envy, i.e., envy of the penis defended against by belittling and attacking activity. However, penis envy does not seem to be present at this point in our material. The girl's feelings towards the penis are still those of fear and awe in the context of complementary, rather than comparative, object relationships towards her father.

With the confidence developed both from an awareness of her capacities to defend herself if necessary and from a somewhat more differentiated object representation of the father, the girl begins to deal with more specific anxieties. Where she had previously responded to the phallic father with an essentially global terror, she now feels safe enough to identify specific "threats." These are four-fold: anxiety about penetration, anxiety about castration (displaced to body limbs), anxiety about being intruded upon sexually, and anxiety about seduction with an over-exposure to her own sexual response. Only after these anxieties have been clarified and dealt with is the little girl able to view her father as a positive genital figure.

Penetration anxiety is the specific female genital anxiety, the one most frequently experienced and expressed by the girl. This is the fear that the entry of the thrusting, powerful penis into her vulnerable vaginal cavity will injure the vaginal wall and tear her apart. Horney (1933) speaks of the size of the father's penis in contrast to the smallness of the girl's body, with the resultant possibility of pain and hemorrhaging. Greenacre (1953) describes "an active terror of the organ on account of its size and the fear that to be penetrated by such an organ would be to be split or torn apart by it" (p. 179). Barnett (1966) adds that, due to the little girl's awareness that the vaginal cavity lacks the protection of voluntary muscular control, "penetration via that organ remains a constant threat" (p. 131).

Examples of this phenomenon from our sample include "the elevator kept going through a solid wall" and "the door had been hacked open with a heavy screwdriver"; also "The bears were on their hind legs with their paws up. I was frightened. Whoever was in charge didn't have good enough control of them;

---

[5]She may also attempt to cause her father to turn his aggression against himself, by playing on his oral and genital narcissistic needs. "The man was on top (phallic) of a big Christmas tree (oral) on top of the steeple chase at Coney Island (phallic); I was worried he was going to impale (castrate) himself." There is the beginning reference to her own identification with the (aggressor) male. "It was supposed to be a picture of Blue Boy but it was of me."

they looked like powerful men.'' These fears have the quality of helplessness, but not of the paralysis experienced earlier in the subphase.

In our sample, castration anxiety is usually connected with the girl's withholding a sexual or nurturing response sought by her father; i.e., ''castration'' is seen as an angry retaliatory response to her unavailability. The castration fantasy may include displacement to the limbs of the body: ''The man in the truck came. I said I didn't want to stay there because somebody might come while I was asleep and chop me up with an ax—dismember me.'' (Here the girl is unavailable because she is asleep). Or the castration may be symbolic in nature: ''My mother was playing her organ; the town bully made cutting remarks.'' (Here the mother is unavailable because she is masturbating.)

The anxiety of being intruded upon sexually is connected with the feeling of being helpless and used, or of being taken from. Most of the themes are connected with the anxiety of being robbed: ''a guy got my wallet and took everything out of it,'' ''my purse was stolen,'' or ''the boy wanted the keys to my apartment.''

The fourth anxiety is that of being overwhelmed by her own sexual response to genital stimulation. ''There was a fire—I could see a woman and hear her screaming.'' The specific fear is the fear of the loss of ego boundaries such as is experienced in orgasmic states. ''I was going to wash the floor, but the water had overflowed and caused the floor to collapse.'' The father is often seen as dangerously seductive. ''I walked on my hands over a stream. On the other side of the archways were rapids. My father said to go on. It was very dangerous; I was going to drown.''[6]

As a result of these anxiety responses to her own excitement, the girl may draw back from vaginal to clitoral sensations. ''I decided to go into the snack bar instead of the restaurant.'' The clitoral excitement is seen as easier to control than is the vaginal excitement. ''I had an image of dipping my toes into the water as a prelude to going in. The water was like the water at Bali, but it was calm.'' Barnett (1966) suggests that a return to clitoral masturbation helps to achieve and maintain repression of conscious vaginal sensations.[7]

As she is dealing with the specific anxieties related to penetration, castration, intrusion, and seduction, the girl may attempt, for a short time, to

---

[6]Water is a frequent symbol for female genital sexuality. Another example of the dangers of seduction is ''I was near the water. There were a lot of very high waves. It was frightening. My mother and sister were telling me to run away.''

[7]In instances where the girl has been traumatized earlier by genital interaction with the father or a fathering figure, there now occurs a recapitulation of anxiety themes from earlier points in the developmental sequence. In the instance, for example, where the girl had been masturbated by the father's finger, the penetration anxiety was prematurely experienced by a yet too immature ego structure. Until some of the penetration anxiety was worked through at this moment of the developmental sequence the earlier anxieties about physical damage to the genitalia, the anal-genital confusion, and the passivity of the helpless bride could not be brought under the sway of the ego.

identify with the (aggressor) phallic father: "I was going to try out for the lead in a play. I would be Jonathan Adler." This identification is in the service of self protection. "A girl gave me an umbrella to defend myself with." But the father encourages her to identify with his projected, idealized, female imago rather than with his phallic aspects. "My father was driving the car. I was afraid he would hit some cats walking down the street. Then *I* was driving. I almost hit a kitten. My father said, 'No, no, you must care for her and feed her.'"

The girl becomes increasingly aware of the phallic father as pleasantly exciting, giving, protective, and supportive. She experiences him as more able to understand her than her mother can. "The [male] teacher perceived me as I really was." He is seen as protective of her female genital interests: "The man was masquerading as a blind man to protect the bank." And, even more frequently, as actively encouraging her developing femaleness through his giving gifts of adornment to her as a male to a female: "The man had gone to another land to get treasure, gold rings, for me." There is a beginning sense of delighted receptivity towards her father as a genital being.

In the final part of the subphase, the girl moves beyond a passive sexual position to an active, aggressive receptivity and begins to demand a degree of phallic protectiveness, sexual response, and active support for her femaleness from her father. The inner-genital world is moved outward onto her body as a whole and into interpersonal situations. The identification with the phallus is displaced to the entire body as it moves through space.

The shift from passive to active in libidinal aim is seen most clearly in the beginning interest in voyeurism. "I would like to photograph men; I would be more in control." There is an accent on seducing rather than being seduced: "The man was interested in another woman, but *I* seduced *him*." This sounds like an oedipal statement, but the motif is one of having the power to seduce him who seduces. These phenomena may be combined: "I was making a movie. The images were surreal and abstract, as if energy was pulling things in while other things were moving past."

Rather than fearing her father's phallic aggressivity, the girl begins to welcome it: "There was a giant man seven feet tall. I liked him a lot and didn't feel threatened." She takes in his strength and makes it her own: "He came over with a syringe and filled me full of heroine." (Heroine is a double entendre.) Or she experiences his phallic qualities as there *for* her: "My father puts his arms around me. The feeling was, I could lean against him."

Welcoming her father's strength, the girl demands his protection against danger: "My father's flashlight protected us like firelight protects against animals." She uses him as she begins to separate sexually from her mother: "I was next to the water; a crab (my mother) got hold of my foot. I couldn't get it off, but my father helped me." She is angry if he is not actively supportive of her other developmental steps. "I never got support from my father when I was interested in a boy.'' If he is passive, she is upset that he is rendered impotent via-à-vis her needs: ''The man had a scar on his face; he was passive like my father.''

Now, instead of being frightened by her own sexuality, the girl begins to stimulate it. She engages in masturbatory experiences alone or with a boy. ''An insect with the head of a cockateel (penis) and the body of a fish (vagina) was polluting the grounds: I put it in the pool.'' She may use her father to reassure her or to acknowledge the acceptability of her sexual interest. ''The boy masturbated me in the hallway to the restaurant. I ran home without my pants to show my father.''

At this point the girl is able to transfer her inner-genital world with its qualities of inwardness and concentration on selfhood into the outer world. Perhaps the best description is found in the dream image, ''There was a lady who dominated the whole subway car with her presence.'' The focus shifts from inwardness to outwardness: ''I couldn't pee and couldn't shit because people kept calling me or knocking on the door.'' She feels an ineffable power which is sensed by others: ''She was a Medea-like character, having to do with religion, ethics, and philosophy.'' Often it is associated with the possession of religious powers: ''I was held captive by a group of men. I have a can of bug spray and anoint them with it in the sign of a cross.''

In traditional theory these feelings of power and presence are understood as a defensive substitution of the body for the missing penis. Our material suggests that it may be, rather, a transfer to the outer world of inner-genital feelings. Indeed, it need not come as a surprise that the girl who is accepting of and pleased with her inner-genital physiology and activity will feel similarly towards her body as a whole.

However, there is a type of phallic displacement which is evident in this part of the sub-phase, the displacement of the identification with the phallus-moving-through-space to that of the body-moving-through-space. One purpose of the displacement may be to maintain emotional proximity with the father. ''A girl was tied to a boy with rope on her wrists; she jumped from the ground to an upper window. A woman with several men around her jumped onto the roof.'' This particular aspect of identification with the phallic father is seen frequently in the later developmental sequence of the preoedipal genital phase.

A common theme linking all of these drive and ego elements is that of the girl's shift from a passive to an active mode, with a sense of excitement at her capacity to master her own and others' genital sexual strivings. Interestingly, a theme which runs clearly throughout all of our material is that as the decisive psychosexual events of the preoedipal genital phase are experienced, the subjective representational world becomes more clearly articulated and structuralized (Stolorow, 1979); this increase and consolidation in the stability of self and object representations bolsters the child's sense of self esteem and of active mastery of herself and of the objects in her environment.

To summarize the second subphase, the girl passes through several libidinal, aggressive, ego, and object relational shifts. Initially she is aware of the father as able to hurt her or to forcefully awaken her own sexuality with his frightening phallic strength. In order to protect herself, she delineates her own repertoire of defenses against the too-powerful male. She then becomes aware of and deals with more specific anxieties, e.g., penetration anxiety as a response to the sexually phallic father and castration anxiety as a response to the aggressively retaliating father. The father is occasionally seen as seductive; sometimes the girl draws back from vaginal to clitoral sensation, to avoid overstimulation. There is a moment of identification with the aggressor phallic father, followed by a realization that the father wants her to be a female, not to identify with him.

At the end of this subphase the girl's genital instinctual impulses shift from passive receptivity to a demandingly active receptivity. Instead of being frightened by her father's sexuality, she seeks to entice him and to use his phallic strength for her own needs. She enjoys masturbation, with deliberate stimulation of her own sexual responses. She shifts her focus from the inner-genital world to becoming the central figure in the outer world of herself and others. She displaces the identification with the phallus-moving-through-space to the body-moving-through-space. She ends the subphase in a state of joy in her own sexuality, a fairly comfortable acceptance of her father's sexual responses to her, and a beginning refinement of her feminine identity vis-à-vis the male.

Third Subphase

The third subphase is characterized by the girl's awareness of and interaction with her mother as a genital sexual being. Until this moment in her development, the girl has been only peripherally aware of her mother's genital sexuality. Now she brings into focus the mother's feelings about her own sexuality and femininity. She is also interested in her mother's sexual responses to men and compares her mother's functioning with her own experiences. In focusing on her mother's genital sexuality, the girl becomes particularly aware of the mother's anxieties, defects and developmental lacks. She compares her mother both with other adult females and with her father's image of the ideal female. The initial portion of the subphase thus takes on a highly individualized sequence of emotional events, depending on the particular negative aspects of the "genital mother" which must be worked through by the girl in order to proceed to the next developmental step. (The positive aspects of the "genital mother," e.g., rhythmicity, are kept as unchanged elements of an identificatory process which started at a much earlier age.)

In the middle part of the subphase the girl deals with the mother's destructive impulses towards the daughter's genital sexual interests. The mother attempts to maintain the pregenital emotional closeness that will be lost once the daughter has advanced to a mature sexual position in which she prefers contact with a male to that of her mother. Both overt aggressive threats against the girl or the male she prefers, and covert homosexual seductions are used by the mother in her attempts to subvert the daughter's maturing sexuality. The girl's own anxiety about the approaching psychological separation from the mother adds to her expectation of destruction; themes of dying and death become prominent.

The subphase closes with the process of sexual separation from the mother, with a consequent experience of individuality and of sexual identification as a female being with a female body. There is the sense of "owning one's own body"[8] and of that body possessing distinctly female genitalia. The father is seen as a background, supportive figure throughout this process, encouraging the girl's sexual separation from the mother. Phallic identification, with themes of movement through space away from the mother, is used in the service of separation.

Our material is congruent with Fast's (1979) "differentiation framework." To quote: "She learns to relate to her mother as a same-sex person, to identify with her without losing self-other differentiation, to maintain an object relationship without the intrusion of notions of narcissistic unity . . . her relation to the father provides a needed separateness from the mother as she elaborates her identifications with and same-sex relationship to her" (pp. 451–452).

With the security provided by a beginning comfort in her own sexuality and the feeling that her father is "there for her" as a female, the girl turns her attention towards her mother's particular intrapsychic and interpersonal style of expressing genital sexuality. Previously, through early identification, she had made use of her mother's knowledge and coping mechanisms in her exploration of her father's phallic sexuality. Now, in order to facilitate her own sexual growth both by selectively identifying with those aspects of the mother which contribute to further feminine development and by attempting new resolutions of problems the mother has not solved, the girl focuses on her mother's limitations, anxieties and developmental lacks. She observes her mother's feelings about her father as a mate and as a male figure, and her mother's responses to the daughter's developing genital interests.

Since the girl needs to discard and modify negative aspects of the internalized "genital mother" in order to attain a separate sexual identity, she must deal with the specific, unique model of sexuality which her particular mother provides. Therefore this is the one place in our study where the universality of discreet developmental tasks breaks down. Interestingly, although there are also many models of male genital sexuality, the impact of the father's particular sexual style seems less specific to his daughter's developmental

[8]Frank M. Lachmann (1970). Personal Communication.

schema. The characteristic form the father's sexual impulses assume is not in and of itself as important to the girl's maturational progress as is her perception of whether or not her father is responsive and supportive of her developing femininity.

Within this small study, four strikingly different feminine styles were expressed by the mothers of our six subjects. One mother was seen as castrating of men due to penetration anxiety, and another as passively dependent with her mate. A third mother was experienced as rejecting and withdrawn in relation to the father, while the fourth was seen as "a strong woman" married to "a weak man". These differences in their mothers affected both the daughters' perceptions and reactions to men and the emotional processes necessary to the resolutions of these reactions.

In the first instance, the maturational problem was that of shifting from the attitude of penetration anxiety, with resultant wish to castrate the male to that of a more trusting receptivity. In order to accomplish this, the daughter used her own perceptions of her father's capacity for tender warmth to counteract her mother's perception of the father as dangerous (a distorted perception based on the mother's experience with her own father). The daughter's perception received validation from other family members, enabling the girl to reject the negative aspects of the "genital mother."

In the second instance, it was necessary for the girl to find a way of handling dependent and narcissistic needs differently from her mother's style of passive dependency vis-à-vis her husband. The solution was found by shifting to the genital arena for satisfaction of narcissistic needs, as well as by substituting genital for oral receptivity. These emotional accomplishments met with responsive support from her father and brothers, giving her further impetus to maintain the developmental shift.

The third example is that of a mother who was withdrawn from her mate and consequently became envious of her daughter's developing sexuality. Here, the daughter needed to become aware of two factors: her mother's envy, cloaked in apparent concern for the daughter, and the father's actual availability as a male figure. The father's capacity to be emotionally responsive and his obvious interest in her development to genital maturity were the decisive factors in the girl's continued emotional growth.

The final example typifies the developmental sequence assumed in classic theory to be universal: the substitution of the boy baby for the missing penis. In our sample, this sequence occurred as a specific response to a "strong, phallic mother" who was disappointed in her "weak husband." There was fury towards the mother for not giving her daughter a penis. The girl experienced herself as weak and lacking because she did not possess the large, strong phallic organ so prized by her mother and felt that her mother had deliberately caused her an incurable narcissistic injury. This daughter did not engage in the reality testing observed in the other instances; her perception of her father as "weak" led to her inability to utilize him as a supportive figure to assist her in disidentifying with her mother. Instead, she discovered another way to "get" the desired penis, by fantasizing intercourse with male peers. This led to pregnancy fantasies and then to the birth fantasy: "The woman was walking down the road with a baby. From the waist down, the baby was a penis, and his head was pointed like a penis."

These four examples are not meant to describe all the possible developmental tasks encountered at this point, but rather to convey the complexity of the identificatory processes. Edgcumbe and Burgner (1975) state that sexual identity is largely dependent on the capacity to identify with the same sex parent; identification is defined as a modification of the self representation with the aim of acquiring *some* attributes of the object representation, a definition originating with Sandler and Rosenblatt. This subphase of development illustrates the importance of selective identifications (Jacobson, 1964), as the girl identifies with certain aspects of her mother's genital sexuality and discards or modifies other aspects.

One striking example of continued early identification with the mother is the element of rhythmicity. There are frequent references in this part of the subphase to shifts in time, periods of time, and to clocks, watches, and time pieces. The daughter focuses on the biological clock of the mother, which becomes a part of her female identity. As Blum (1976) states, "The body ego and biological role of the female indicate the metaphorical significance of both inner space and periodic time . . . Rhythmicity may be a special component of the feminine personality" (p. 184).

As she continues to develop her own identity as a sexual female the girl becomes aware of those aspects of her mother which are in direct opposition to her continued maturation. Elements in the mother may actually oppose the girl's development and seek to maintain the daughter in a dependent position in order to satisfy the mother's own dependency needs and to prevent the emergence of a rival.

The themes of destructive aggression emanating from the mother are not yet in the service of competition for the father, but are directed at the girl's maturational processes and genital interests per se. The "weapons" used are generally concerned with the nurturing processes necessary for survival. The talion principle is frequently evoked: "If you leave me (by your continued emotional growth and separation), I will die from the lack of your emotional sustenance; therefore, I will withhold nurturance from you or give you food which will destroy you." Thus, the girl may experience the mother as (symbolically) starving her when she notes the girl's developing interest in fecundity. "I was in an air shaft. There was a cat and its kitten, a rat and a baby rat, a dog and a puppy, all dead from malnutrition." Or she may stifle the girl: "I was helping take in a crop. We went into a glass house. The door was locked. We died of suffocation.'' She may threaten to poison her: "The can of food was about to explode. My father said I shouldn't eat it: I could get botulism.'' Or, the mother may vent her fury on the symbolized representations of future babies-in-the-womb: "The woman and her maid were scraping the babies off my plants with a knife."

The themes of death and dying at this moment in the subphase are frequent and primitive enough to suggest condensation of the daughter's separation anxiety along with the mother's retaliatory fury. There may be a projection onto the mother of the girl's terror at being alone and unnourished and/or a projection onto the mother of the anger which is necessary to propel the girl away from the temptation of prolonging the security of the attachment to the mother. Perhaps the dynamic is expressed in Kestenberg's (1976; this volume) finding that the little girl is very concerned with death and dying at this time, and seen in Frankel and Sherick's (1977) observation that the girl complains of the mother as rough and mean, particularly around the care of babies.

Another avenue used by the mother to maintain the daughter at a preoedipal emotional position is that of homosexual seduction. Her efforts at seducing the daughter are experienced by the girl as tempting but hostile: "You were stroking my breasts and saying, 'It's alright.' I was thinking, 'So you're coming on to me too.' '' There may be a regression to the helplessness of the oral stage: "A huge, gigantic, grotesque woman was eating me out; I had to reciprocate." But the ego regression to symbiosis is feared: "I was making love with a girl. It was good, but it wasn't good. The two of us turned into an undifferentiated sphere."

Torok (1970) discusses masturbation as forbidden by the mother in order to prohibit fantasies of having pleasure with the father's penis, thereby blocking the way to genital fulfillment. This is to assure the mother that the daughter, having no penis, will always be loyal to the mother and prevent the mother from lapsing into "bitterness and envy."

The girl makes use of both her mother's anger and her own response to propel her into the final portion of the third subphase, which deals with themes of differentiation and separation from the genital mother. The girl has become able to "claim her body as her own," as a female body which is differentiated from that of her mother and is therefore uniquely her own.

Barnett (1966) refers to the fact that gender identification is helped by identification with both parental objects. A certain portion of the separation from the mother is accomplished with the help of the identification with the father's phallus in its qualities of movement through space: "I was on a subway hurtling through space. I was a little nervous, but I thought if I don't do it now, I won't do it.'' More important, however, is the identification with the mother's femaleness, for instance in its relationship to the phenomenon of time: "To get out of the room, I had to throw pieces of garlic out of the window and see how they landed. I did that and got out into a gorgeous garden. Garlic is 'ail' in French, pronounced 'I'—and garlic exists through time."

Separation also creates anxiety connected with the awareness of time and rhythmicity: "I had a terrifying dream about getting old; time was divided into certain periods." Expectations of damage in retaliation for narcissistic injury to the mother accompany separation anxiety: "Hubris means standing alone. You are a good target, and you are doomed to destruction by the gods for your separateness." There is also the fear of regressing to the symbiotic relationship with the mother: "I climbed over a monument with holes. I wondered why people didn't fall in."

The father is seen as actively assisting the girl in her separation from the mother: "The man pulled down a square hole in the ceiling. There was another level with all kinds of furniture." There is a feeling of joy in her own femaleness and female genitalia. "I came on something like an excavation. The color was bright, cheerful red; I liked it." And there is the satisfaction of having accomplished another developmental step. "I did exercises. Then they took me into the forest: they had built a house for me. They gave me a celebration."

To summarize the third subphase, the girl is initially newly aware of her mother as a genitally sexual female. She especially notices the preoedipal genital aspects of her mother's femaleness and her mother's response to maleness and to her daughter's developing genital sexuality. The girl selectively identifies with particular attributes of the object representation of the mother in order to move to a clear genital sexual position. She then confronts the aspects of her mother which are opposed to her further development as a sexual or feminine being and deals with the mother's destructive impulses, such as starving, poisoning or physically damaging the girl or the symbolic babies-in-the-womb. The mother is experienced as discouraging the girl's interest in males through frightening the girl, demeaning her or seducing the daughter into a homosexual response.

The father has been experienced as an ally during this time of conflict with the mother. He is now used both directly and as an identificatory figure in the service of separation. The girl experiences herself as separate from the mother, yet female like the mother; there is a clearly developed self and body representation which encompasses both separateness and the possession of female genitalia. The girl is frightened by her own separation anxiety, as well as by her awareness of no longer being within the protective boundaries of her mother's strength. But the anxieties are compensated for by the pleasure of being able to "claim her body as her own."

Fourth Subphase

The last preoedipal genital subphase is the period descriptively closest to the traditional phallic phase. It is even more similar to Edgcumbe and Burgner's

(1975) "phallic narcissistic" phase; however, we prefer to use the term "genital narcissistic" to describe this subphase, as both phallic and inner-genital elements lead to narcissistic gratification. It is a developmental moment of great richness and complexity. Libidinally, the component instincts become organized into the mature genital drive. Phallic instinctual elements are neutralized and become the generative force behind competition and achievement; inner-genital instinctual elements are used in the service of fecundity and creativity. The major object of cathexis is no longer the representation of the father or the mother, as it was in the second and third subphases, but rather of the self. Father or mother, or both, are used in the service of supporting the development of a cohesive self that is both genital and feminine. In order to accomplish this, the girl must also become aware of and actively deal with the genital narcissistic needs of each parent.

In the first part of the subphase, the component instincts, exhibitionism, voyerism and sadism, are vividly expressed. During this time, the girl engages in competition in order to obtain narcissistic gratification. She competes indiscriminately with either male or female figures, including competition for her mother's sexual response. The usual object of cathexis is the girl's own body; when external objects are cathected, it is in order that they might be experienced as cathecting her. She begins to react to her own libidinal impulses with superego prohibitions, indicating an increasing degree of structuralization and of internalization of parental sanctions.

The little girl carefully delineates the areas of superiority and inferiority of the female and male genitalia, especially as to their functional value. In fantasy she combines and contrasts aspects of her identifications with both her mother and her father. She pretends to be a boy, or to be a child who is both girl and boy. With successful completion of the first part of the subphase she has firmly established her female identity, with an acceptance and feeling of worth about her total body, including her genitalia.

In view of its complexity, a schematic outline of the developments during the first portion of the subphase follows:

I. Shift in ego processes
    A. from inner to outer focus
    B. from passive to active stance re: genital narcissistic issues, with an accent on comparing the genital performance of females and males.

II. Shift in instinctual development
    A. heightening of component instincts
        1. exhibitioninsm
        2. scoptophilia
        3. genital sadism
    B. urethral eroticism as reflected especially in competition

III. Shift vis-à-vis the maternal and paternal objects
    A. identifications begun with the phallic father (2nd subphase) and the genital mother (3rd subphase) evidenced in
        1. beginning superego processes
        2. inner-genital and phallic themes related to exhibitionism and scoptophilia
        3. homosexual approaches to the mother
        4. playful alteration between the roles of female and male
    B. use of the mother and father to reflect and support narcissistic development towards a consolidated sense of self as whole, healthy and uniquely female

In the middle part of the subphase, there is further instinctual development as fusion and neutralization of the drives occur. Productivity, curiosity, "nesting" and exploration all become evidenced. Aggressive elements which are not neutralized are influenced by beginning superego elements and invade libidinal impulses to result in fantasies of commiting sexual suicide or murder. The girl sometimes expresses her identification with her father by externalization onto a male peer, who takes her into his own environment, away from her own; or she will instead bring him into her own inner world, to care for and comfort him.

During the last part of the subphase, just before the appearance of oedipal strivings, the girl returns again to an inner-genital focus and to inner-genital productivity. This inward focusing is quite different from that of the first subphase, as the girl is now quite object related and is concerned with the processes of pregnancy, giving birth and care of the neonate. Punitive superego elements can threaten the fantasied neonate's life; the girl struggles with the issue of preserving or killing the baby. If she allows its survival, she then protects it from the destructive impulses of the male and uses her creative strength to insure its health and well-being.

Having established her own sexual identity out of a melding of inner-genital and phallic identifications and on the basis of increasingly articulated ego and beginning superego processes, the little girl is ready to enter the emotional arena of the struggle with her mother for the favor of her father. The oedipal drama is about to unfold.

As the girl enters the subphase of genital narcissism, there is a resurgence of the sense of activity and outward focus that was displayed near the end of the second subphase, which focused on the phallic genitality of her father. As indicated during the description of the second subphase, we have concluded that when the girl shifts from an inner to an outer focus, the outward placement of inner-genital impulses is often confused with phallic elements.

Inner-genital processes are characterized by inwardness and receptiveness. In the active mode, in the outer world, they are characterized by qualities of empathic response, spirituality, wisdom based on intuition, creativity, and nurturance. Two portraits come to mind: the Mona Lisa by DaVinci and Botticelli's Venus. These paintings typify the placement outwards — to the face in one instance, to the entire body in the other — of the inner feminine world. The Greek goddess Demeter, goddess of the fruitful earth, expresses several of these qualities in her activity in the outer world.

Phallic processes, by contrast, are outwardly thrusting, penetrating, agile, and manifestly aggressive. Diana, the goddess of the chase, illustrates the "phallic female." In our material the identification with the phallus is usually expressed by aggressively competitive activity and by the body-moving-through-space — jumping, running, climbing and doing stunts.

A major theme of the first portion of the subphase is the attempt to achieve recognition and admiration. To attain this end the girl utilizes inner-genital processes which are outwardly placed: "A woman photographer was writing a poem on the wall of the room. I suggested she write it all around the frame of the house, which she did." She may also use phallic processes which invite admiration: "I could see girls doing fantastic stunts, very high flips in the air," or phallic and inner-genital impulses are interwoven: "I was running up some stairs to where this man and woman were in bed. I jumped into bed with them and said, 'Oh, these great things have happened to me!' " ("Running up stairs" and "jumped into bed" reflects identification with the phallus displaced to moving through space; "Great things have happened to me" is an outwardly placed inner-genital statement.)

While there is more use of phallic identifications and processes at this developmental moment than there is at other times, our data points to differences from Kestenberg's (1975) view that the girl closes up and denies her inner space during the "phallic" phase. While the theme of inner space does appear to be quiescent at this point, not to reappear until the closing part of the subphase, in our sample this is due to the gratification of narcissistic needs by outward-placement onto the entire body as the girl moves out into the world.

In agreement with Parens et al. (1976), we find that phallic processes are not the girl's major preoccupation even during the genital-narcissistic subphase of the preoedipal genital phase, being outweighed by outwardly-placed inner-genital processes. In addition, even these phallic elements do not seem to be an indication of masculinity in the little girl; instead, phallic identifications appear to be a necessary part of female experience and optimally are melded into the female self-representation to form a total sexual identity.

Edgcumbe and Burgner (1975) state: "In the preoedipal phallic phase, exhibitionism and scoptophilia are the most pronounced drive components" (p. 162). We also found this to be true in our material. In addition, we found that the expression of the instinctual impulse was followed by the theme that "the punishment always fits the crime." (Throughout this subphase early superego elements, based on parental identifications, are evidenced in themes of punishment for instinctual impulses, quite in contrast to earlier subphases where the impulse was linked to anxiety in regard to real or fantasied dangers from the outside world.)

Thus the impulse to display the body-moving-through-space "A girl was doing summersaults" is followed by the punishment of castration—"but you said 'cut that out!' '' The impulse to display the outwardly-placed inner-genital world—"I was shopping in Bloomingdale's with only my nightgown on," is followed by the punishment of harm to the entire body—"then I was in a hospital, being examined for something."

The girl's heightened scoptophilic impulses also lead to reactive punishment. "Fire was coming from where the television is. My mother was angry at me because my negligence had caused it." The "fire" is the out-of-control sexuality initiated by the girl's voyeurism. In another instance, both the girl and the object of her scoptophilic interest are punished. "A man was stealing candy and I was looking. The man was hit on the head by two boys [punishment of the object] and the boys put a piece of tape over my mouth to smother me [punishment of the self]." The punishment of the man is castration; that of the self is the closing of the vagina.[9]

Often the scoptophilic experience refers to a primal scene. The interest is preoedipal, focused on the sexual involvements of others rather than on jealousy of the person of the mother. "I saw a huge cat spring onto another cat and start humping her; I didn't know whether I was excited or frightened. Maybe both." Sometimes the primal scene is aurally experienced: "I heard a lot of noises in the middle of the night." Again the punishment fits the crime. "There was a driveway. On the porch was a big jar of ginger. The people were both blind and deaf."

Genital sadism (usually called phallic sadism) is the other component instinct seen in our sample. (Theoretically, masochism should also be heightened at this moment, but this was not evidenced in our small sample.) "The man was giving me a piggy back ride that allowed me to have an overview. He bent down with his finger tips on the ground and it hurt his fingers."[10] Or the man is punished by the inner-genital weapon of water for his participation in a primal scene: "I was watching a man trying to steal something in the basement. I turned

---

[9]The closing of the vagina, used defensively in earlier subphases, is now used in the service of punishment.

[10]William Steckel discusses this phenomenon from the male (victim's) point of view in "A Woman Is Being Carried" in Sadism and Masochism, Vol. 2, Liverright Publishing Corp., New York, 1929.

on all the faucets so the water filled the room; he slipped and drowned. The revenge felt good.''

Throughout most of the genital narcissistic subphase, the focus of the girl's libidinal interest is her own self and her own body-self. There is a very different quality from the narcissism of the earliest, inner-genital subphases. She now requires the active participation of both mother and father in responding to her own needs and interests. This necessitates her becoming aware of any narcissistic needs of theirs which interfere with their capacity to respond sensitively to her, for she then must deliberately make those needs secondary to her own. ''I went to visit the wise old lady. She started to talk and I said 'I'm not interested in that; there are a lot of things *I* want to talk about.' ''

Various and complex identificatory and ego processes are seen during this particular developmental sequence, which serve to help establish a highly individualistic, female identity. These include sexual role definition and comparisons of genital functioning. During the first portion of the genital narcissistic subphase, the little girl still playfully assumes various roles. (Jacobsen, 1964, p. 74). She plays at being a boy, or a girl who is also a boy, or a boy who looks like a girl. According to Frankel and Sherick (1977) at this time girls and boys envy each other's prerogatives, play opposite gender roles and engage in gender related play. As the subphase progresses, ''the child has to attempt to come to terms with the differences between the sexes in the physical formation of the genitals, the dominant erotogenic zone of the phallic phase . . . normal development requires a gradual divergence, in boys and girls, of drive derivative, fantasies, sexual identifications, and modes of relating to the object'' (Edgcumbe and Burgner, 1975, pp. 163–164).

The girl's fascination with body appearance and physiologic functioning leads to the questions of whether and how her body is superior or inferior to a boy's. As befits a narcissistic period, she is particularly concerned with questions of performance. (There remains some wonderment that she is not hermaphroditic, as had been expressed in earlier developmental subphases.) The functional superiority of the male body is especially evident when she watches boys direct their urinary stream. ''I had gone out to urinate. I spilled it all over myself and was embarrassed.'' Horney (1924) mentions the exhibitionistic advantage which the girl attributes to the male genital; in addition, the boy handles his penis during urination, which the girl interprets as permission to masturbate. Such a masturbation envy theme appears in, ''The man had a tool he wouldn't let the children play with.''[11]

---

[11]Traditionally, urethral erotism is thought to be the driving force behind competitive activity. In our material, the importance of the urethral performance is that it constitutes either a narcissistic triumph or a narcissistic blow. E.g.: ''I decided to go out on the lawn to pee. The man next to me was pissing—the wind blew it in my face—I didn't get a chance to piss.''

On the other hand, there are many themes of the functional inferiority of the masculine genitalia. A frequent one involves the realization that the male is incapable of giving birth: "A man was having a baby. He wasn't biologically set up for it. The baby was inside of a shape like a capsule with a transparent top (inside the penis?)." Due to the placement of his genitalia, the male is seen as particularly vulnerable to physical harm (castration): "I came naked out of the water. I met a man in the boat place with a yellow rain coat and a wooden leg." To be so genitally visible places him in jeopardy: "People killed him with a knife after he drank a luminous substance. They took his blood and dabbed it around his neck. If you turned off the light you could see it." Visibility also brings narcissistic injury: "There was a tall tower connected with sexuality. The tower was crumbling, losing its point." But there remains the wish to have it all: "I was on a hike with a man. I wanted to prove my dream was the same as his. It wasn't." "[T]he girl's sense of loss when she becomes aware that the boy has a penis and she does not . . . represent[s] . . . the girl's recognition that not all sex and gender possibilities are open to her . . . [There is] a demand for a lost experience of unlimited potential, a state of narcissistic completeness" (Fast, 1979, p. 447).

In addition to comparative themes, themes of competition appear. The identification with the phallic father begun during the second subphase is now used both for the discharge of component instinctual impulses and in experimentation with "masculine" roles, e.g., competition for the mother. The girl may compete with either a male or a female, so that we would not label this a negative oedipal phenomenon. Competition with a male: "I wanted to have sex with a girl. She meets my male friend; they talk about what to do for a dog that breaks its leg [punishment by castration]." Competition with another female: "I was pissed off at two women with their arms around each other."

If the complexities of libidinal and ego development during the initial portion of the fourth subphase have proceeded smoothly, the girl begins to experience a solid core of healthy self-esteem: "I had had contusions or blood clots on my face. By believing in my own worth, they had disappeared." As this occurs, there results a consolidated image of body-self which is a highly individualized expression of the girl's unique experience of herself as a female being. According to Mahler, (1975) the phallic phase has to be reached in order for the child "to receive the decisive impetus for integration of the gender-determined body-self image. This development is dependent on differentiation and integration of a cohesive gender-determined ego structure, which in turn is dependent on stratification and hierarchic organization of libidinal zonal cathexis and synthesis into a whole of the representations of parts of the mental images of the body-self" (p. 224).

One subject saw herself as a female figure of both outer beauty and inner knowledge and wisdom: "I was in a new place. I discovered a snake around my waist—long and thin and graceful like women in fashion magazines. Another snake was coming out of a book; it looked like me.'' Another described a concretization in the outer world of the inner-genital space: "I had a vision of a temple made of stuff I bought. It was incredibly beautiful.''

The other self-image in our sample was simply: "I was on the stage doing a talent show. My father came up to kiss me on the stomach.'' This is a statement reflecting ''narcissistic wholeness.'' The female takes pleasure in her own sexuality and in her sexual, fecund body, which receives the homage of the prototype male, her father.

During the middle part of the genital-narcissistic subphase neutralization and sublimation of both inner-genital and phallic-penetrating drive elements occurs. Themes include exploration, curiosity, nesting, productive achievement in the outer world, and creative achievement in the inner world. Aggressive impulses are often neutralized in these processes; when they are not, they are combined with libidinal impulses and used by the primitive superego for masochistic or sadistic fantasies of punishment by sexual suicide or murder.

Earlier, the identification with the penis-moving-through-space was seen as displaced to the body-moving-through-space. Now this process is expanded to include the fantasy of exploration of strange places: "A man wanted me to come to where he was: a very primitive place.'' The journey is seen as being in the company of a boy, as an excursion into territory which is identified as his. "I was with a black guy. We were going away together to Africa.'' The introjected father is projected onto the boy, leaving the girl in a stance of depending upon him for protection and leadership: "Sailing ships were going on a dangerous voyage. The captain's chair would stay level no matter what happened.'' The metaphor of a journey can also be experienced as an intellectual quest, with curiosity (neutralized scoptophilic drive components) leading to fascinating discoveries.

Alternately, the girl brings the father into her inner-genital world in symbolic fashion (neutralized exhibitionistic drive components). "I was to put my father's body to rest for the night. I wanted to protect his body from the outside world. All the windows were frosted. I made signs of trees and of nature to protect him.'' This is a typical statement of the ''nesting'' interests that now begin to be displayed; this is, perhaps, illustrated by the nursery school girls observed by Frankel and Sherick (1979) who at this point seek to bring boys into their games of playing house. The male is brought into ''her own inner space'' and the girl uses her own inner powers (nurturance, along with protection through special knowledge and mystical strength) to care for his needs. This is the first instance in the girl's development when she has used her own inner strength on behalf of the father.

Woven through these themes of neutralized libidinal and aggressive drive elements are again themes of punishment for the expression of instinctual impulses. Due to the increase of internalized, but still primitive, superego elements, the punishment themes are much harsher than they had been in earlier development. They generally have to do with sexual suicide or with murder of the object of the impulse; e.g., an inner-genital impulse of bringing the father into the girl's inner world is followed by the statement: "A girl was thinking of suicide by putting a sharp glass tube into herself through her vagina." The male object is also punished: "The man had died or I had murdered him out of self preservation. We put him in the garbage can." A phallic impulse of competing with boys for a prized achievement is followed by the statement: "I wanted to kill myself by plunging a knife into my throat." Thus, the mother introject punishes for inner-genital impulses, as with the glass tube; the father introject punishes for phallic impulses, as with the knife.

During the last part of the narcissistic genital subphase (the last part of the preoedipal genital phase) there is a return to the inward focus of the very beginning of the phase. There is no longer, however, the quality of withdrawal from the world. Rather, the inner world is seen as filled with external objects which are constantly involved in the inner proceedings.

Inner-genital productivity may be expressed through fantasies of pregnancy. The girl is not yet interested in bearing her father's child, nor does she connect the act of intercourse with pregnancy. These wishes and understandings will develop during the oedipal phase. At this moment in her development, the father is either not important or is seen as possibly dangerous to the babies-in-utero or the newborn.

The fantasized pregnancy is not necessarily caused by anything: "My body was pregnant. And pregnant was a very physical state." There is the fantasy of being filled with the growing fetus. "I was moving. All the boxes were packed." There is the fantasy of parthenogenesis. "I had a vision of a woman in another dimension who could multiply herself." References to the sun cast that ancient symbol in the role of impregnator. "I wanted to build a home under the ground with a glass roof for the sun." In our study, pregnancy seems to be the quintescence of the urge to produce combined with inner-genital strivings.

The relatively passive receptivity of impregnation changes to a beginning ego activity in relationship to the fantasized pregnancy: "A baby was crying in a house. I tracked down the noise. The baby was in the wall. I said 'we have to get the baby out.' " There remains, however, the surprised confusion as to how reproduction works: "I went to pick up a plant or to move it. As I began to, all these little tiny kittens began to fall out." Or perhaps she herself has reproduced: "This woman has little buttercups which she is planting."

The girl fantasizes the act of giving birth, using the identification with her mother and her own experience of defecation as bases for the fantasies. "There were huge, giant children in the mud of the beach right next to where the water broke. They were infants." There is the worry that the infant will disappear as do the feces: "I go to the toilet and see a giant turd. I look again and it isn't there. When I sit down, my wallet falls." There is the awareness of the efforts of labor: "I was pulling something up from the muddy bottom of the pond, clearing the water."

Finally there is the theme of the care and protection of the neonate, often symbolically played out by the care of the doll in doll play. The girl struggles with the impulse to destroy the "baby"; once again, superego punishment conflicts with the libidinal impulse. "The baby was formed in the fish tank. I was anxious that the mother might eat the children." She also may have a revenge fantasy against the "baby" for the pain that she has heard accompanies birthing: "I had a birth dream. I was in labor. It was a bloody show. The baby was black and white. I didn't know if I would keep it. A woman came to tell me to keep it and I did."

Sometimes it is the father introject that "destroys" the "neonate," usually out of jealousy. "He was throwing little baby kittens into the garbage bag. They were going to be alive, but starving to death." If she is successful in fighting these impulses to destroy that which she has created, the girl begins to manifest interest in protecting the "baby" and insuring its continued well-being. "Two women were holding a baby over the sink, painting designs on its back." The girl has thus begun to use her own inner-genital strength to nurture and care for the helpless neonate. Not until this time in her emotional development is the girl prepared to deal with the question of competition with one parent for the other.

To summarize the genital narcissistic subphase, when the girl enters this subphase, her component instincts are heightened. She becomes actively exhibitionistic in the service of her emerging genital narcissistic needs, and is actively scoptophilic in her quest to understand and actively relate to the narcissistic needs of her parents. Both inner-genital and phallic elements are evidenced in these impulses, although the inner-genital world is expressed through "outward-placement"onto the body-as-a-whole or to the body-as-focused-on by the outside world. The phallic elements, seen more frequently at this point than previously, now take on a feminine cast and are integrated into an emerging feminine identity.

The complex interweaving of themes includes an accent on the dimension of performance. The girl becomes fascinated with the ways in which the genitalia "work" and how well her own body "performs" in contrast to a boy's. She envys his possession of a phallic "tool" which can be used either in the service of exhibitionistic or sadistic impulses or for masturbatory pleasure. On the other hand, the girl sees her own body as superior, in identification with her mother's, because it is capable of bearing babies; she experiences her body as safer from harm and therefore better than the body of the boy who risks both physical castration and narcissistic insult due to the placement of his genitalia. She experiments with roles culturally appropriate to female and to male, playing at being one and then the other.

Other themes include shifts in her use of the identifications with her phallic father and her genital mother. Superego elements appear as the themes of instinctual gratification become linked to themes of punishment. The girl begins to sexually approach her mother, evidencing an active homosexual stance not seen in earlier moments. The girl integrates these many experiences of herself and her world into a consolidated sense of self that is unique and female.

The mid-part of the subphase is concerned with the fusion of genital libido with the aggressive drive and the neutralization of each. The girl is now intrigued with travel, exploration, new intellectual worlds, nesting, creative achievement, and competition. When the fused drive impulses are not neutralized we see fantasies of sexual suicide and murder. The identification with the phallic father is occasionally projected onto a boy peer, with fantasies of his taking the girl into "his territory."

During the closing part of the subphase, the girl turns her attention inwards, with fantasies of pregnancy, birthing and care of the neonate. The quality of inwardness is very different, however, from that of the beginning of the preoedipal genital phase; now there is constant reference to outer-world objects, with a feeling quality of the outer-world having been brought into the inner-genital world. The girl experiences "pregnancy" as a passive experience, without reference to a male figure. "Birthing," however, is experienced as an active endeavor. She is anxious lest the "neonate" be harmed (killed) by herself or by a male figure, but her inner-genital protective impulses emerge to protect the "newborn." With this emotional step, she has completed the developmental tasks necessary in order to move into the oedipal phase of development.

DISCUSSION

While pursuing our investigation of the vicissitudes and complexities of the preoedipal genital phase, we were particularly impressed with the urgency of the girl's need to consolidate a sexually differentiated feminine identity which included an anatomical body image, the mental representations of both parents and reality based conceptions of female roles and functions. At no point did we find that the girl had regarded herself as a boy. Even when she playfully assumed a male stance, or wondered why she did not possess male genitalia (and these were relatively minor motifs), she did so within the context of further scrutinizing and refining her own sense of femaleness. We would suggest that these data, so frequently interpreted as non-acceptance of female anatomy and function, are instead indications of attempts to define femininity. Her curiosity about male attributes, either as complementary to, or comparative with, her own attributes, can be seen as helping the girl further delimit her own boundaries. Our findings are consistent with the views of Kleeman (1976) and Stoller (1976) who regard the little girl as possessing elements of femininity before she enters the "phallic" phase, with Parens et al. (1976) who find the girl's "protogenital" phase to be an expression of her "dominantly feminine disposition" (p. 83), and with Frankel and Sherick (1979) who observed nursery school girls engaged in specifically feminine activities and fantasy play. Our findings are particularly congruent with Fast's (1979) "differentiation framework," which views the girl as developing from a relatively undifferentiated state of omnipotent expectation that she ought to have both male and female organs and characteristics, to a relatively articulated conceptualization of gender, with femininity attached to the self and masculinity to the reciprocal characteristics of the "other." Our findings are not consonant with the Freudian hypothesis that the little girl goes through a masculine stage of development, with penis envy and castration shock as primary organizers of female development. Again we would like to remind the reader that the present study is a retrospective one, based on the dreams of a sample of only six patients, with all the pitfalls and unconscious biases inherent therein. However, along with this caution we would hope that the richness of the material presented and its major congruences with data obtained by other investigators will render it useful in spite of its necessarily speculative nature.

Regarding penis envy, current criticisms and revisions of the concept seem to focus primarily on exploring and expanding its possible meanings. Alternate, but not necessarily mutually exclusive, explanations of penis envy have to do with separation anxiety and concerns around disloyalty to the mother (Torok, 1970; Lerner, 1976), with cultural attitudes which are disparaging of femininity (Menaker, 1979; Thompson, 1950), with narcissistic wounds and failed omnipotence (Grossman and Stewart, 1976), and with penis envy as a developmental step in terms of differentiation and consolidation of sexual identity (Lachmann, this volume; Edgcumbe and Burgner, 1975).

A number of the possible meanings attached to penis envy are demonstrated in our material. During the first and fourth preoedipal genital subphase, the girl's penis envy stems from her narcissistic orientation. During the first subphase, while her view is still relatively global, she expects that all people should have the genitalia of both sexes, and fears that she is damaged because she possesses only female organs. By the beginning of the fourth subphase, with the growth of her ability to differentiate, her expectation has become a wish, and she compares herself to boys, envying the penis which can direct urination and which has an exhibitionistic advantage (Horney, 1924). By the end of the preoedipal genital phase, when the girl has attained a consolidated sense of her sexual identity, this normative, narcissistic penis envy has been resolved and is no longer manifested. In our small sample, penis envy as an expression of separation anxiety and concern around disloyalty to the mother was seen only in one subject who experienced her lack of a penis as a narcissistic insult to her mother and therefore to herself; here, as in the classical literature, this narcissistic injury was resolved by fantasies of having a boy baby. Culturally determined penis envy was seen only in the single subject whose family structure consciously and overtly derogated women as part of a traditional pattern. These two subjects, who expressed the most intense and overriding degree of penis envy, had the greatest difficulty in integrating a female sexual representation. Their reactions, which indicated the least optimal developmental position, were closest to those described in classical literature, suggesting that the position of intense, all encompassing penis envy, traditionally presented as normative, is actually a pathological or culturally determined variant on normal, transitory penis envy.

The attention currently given to reformulations of the concept of penis envy has not been matched by explorations of reactions to the penis other than envy in the preoedipal genital phase girl. Horney (1933), Greenacre (1953) and Gillespie (1969) have respectively written about fear, awe and desire in relation to the penis, but all too frequently these and other reactions of the little girl have been considered displaced or symbolic expressions of penis envy. Our material revealed a wide variety of concerns and feelings relative to the phallus, including awe, fear, desire and contempt. These varied with the particular developmental moment and reflected comparative, complementary and/or identificatory processes. At the beginning of the second subphase, penis awe is the developmental reaction to the girl's awareness of the penis as a penetrating instrument; she is initially in a state of intense awe and generalized terror, experiencing the genital male and his phallus as huge, monstrous and foreign. Her attempts to devise ways to protect herself against physical injury by manipulating the male's phallic sexual aggressivity have frequently, we believe, been misinterpreted in the literature as intra-psychic defenses against penis envy.

A later reaction to the penis is that of welcoming it as a source of pleasure; the phallic father is seen as exciting and protective and a welcome complement to her feminine self. Still later during the preoedipal genital phase, the girl identifies with the phallic assertive qualities of her father in order to separate from her mother, especially by the displacement of the phallus-moving-through-space to the body-moving-through-space (another development which is frequently viewed as evidence of penis envy.) During the fourth subphase, when the girl is assessing the relative strengths and weakness of male and female genitalia, she regards the male genitals as inferior because they cannot give birth and because their greater accessibility and visibility may lead to castration or to narcissistic injury. On the basis of our data we would suggest that the girl's awareness of the phallus during the preoedipal genital phase evokes multiple reactions, of which penis envy is but one, whose meanings have all too frequently been obscured by the traditional assumption that they are substitutes for or defenses against penis envy, rather than developmental steps in their own right.

Like reactions to the penis, fears of genital mutilation in girls are complex phenomena, with many possible meanings; as we understand anxieties over genital damage, too often they have been misinterpreted as being symbolic of castration anxiety (i.e., fear that the penis has been, or will be, removed). In our small sample, castration anxiety per se was seen uniformly only in two instances: during the first subphase, when the girl inspects her genital body and expects to have both male and female organs, she questions whether she has been damaged by the removal of penis and testicles; later, on a symbolic level, the girl experiences castration anxiety as punishment, during those periods when she identifies with phallic aspects of her father. In our material the only instance of castration anxiety in the traditional mode accompanied penis envy in the traditional format; the same subject who experienced penis envy in identification with her mother's attitude also experienced the mother as having castrated the daughter and being castrated herself.

Fears of mutilation of female genital organs were far more pervasive than were castration fears, and rather than appearing displaced from concern about the missing penis, they seem to be primary developmental events. During the first subphase the girl inventories her body for damage, and is anxious in regard to possible injury to vagina, uterus, labia and clitoris; along with Kestenberg (this volume), we see evidence of the girl's anxiety that there may be damage to the potential fetus. Fears of damage to her female structures heighten during the second subphase, when the girl experiences penetration anxiety in response to male genitality, and fears of being mutilated should she refuse to respond. During the third subphase, the girl experiences fears of mutilation from the mother, whom she experiences as wanting to prevent the daughter leaving her and attaining genital maturity, a configuration similar to that proposed by Torok (1970).

According to Freudian theory, the clitoris is the cathected genital until the girl turns away from it when she recognizes its inferiority to the penis; she then is basically without an organ until she cathects the vagina at puberty. While contemporary theorists (Clower, 1975; Moore, 1976; Blum, 1976; Fraiberg, 1972) no longer consider the clitoris to be a masculine organ and recognize that masturbation, with feminine fantasies, continues throughout childhood, questions about the mental representation of the vagina are still unresolved. There is a lack of agreement on how differentiated a representation of the vagina a little girl possesses, and/or whether or not the vagina, having been discovered and valued during the inner-genital phase, is "closed" in favor of the clitoris during the "phallic" phase. (Kestenberg, 1968, 1976, this volume).

In our material, the vagina is quite frequently referred to in symbolic fashion, with the vaginal opening generally perceived as receptive and open. Themes vary from a passive receptivity in the earliest subphase to a later active, even demanding, receptivity. The vagina is generally presented as an orifice connected with genital pleasure ("a drive-way"), but it may also be used in the service of protection, aggression, or punishment. For example, in the emotional climate of the early inner-genital subphase, the girl "closes up" her vaginal cavity, with the help of the labia ("closing the curtains") in order to intensify the moment of turning inwards while keeping out the outer world. In the second subphase, when becoming aware of her father's frightening phallic sexuality, the girl may withdraw cathexis from her vagina as a protection against penetration anxiety. She may, on the other hand, make herself vaginally receptive in an effort to neutralize male phallic aggression ("I caught his bullets with my magic bracelet"). Or, if she feels frightened by her own beginning sexual response to her father as a phallic male, she may withdraw cathexis from the vagina and center it on the clitoris ("I went to the snack bar instead of the restaurant"). Thus we see a cathexis of the clitoris without accompanying vaginal cathexis only when the girl fears being overwhelmed by her own sexual responses, a finding which differs from Kestenberg's postulate of a closing of the "creative inside" in the service of phallic impulses.

Clearly our material indicates that there is a mental representation of the vagina throughout the preoedipal genital phase. However, we must remind the reader that our results are based on material from adult patients, which has been specifically criticized by Clower (1975) as being unable to capture, for the adult woman who has experienced puberty and intercourse, a time prior to vaginal cathexis. Even while noting this stricture, we cannot help being impressed by the clarity and particularity of the developmental sequences shown in our data on the growth of mental representations of all female organs. These follow so closely the patterns of differentiation and hierarchic integration intrinsic to all developmental schema, from the relatively hazy beginning of the preoedipal genital phase when female genitalia were not always distinguishable from the anal orifice and products and when a hermaphroditic body was considered normative, to the end of the phase when female structures were more or less firmly mentally represented, that we find it difficult to assume that these data are not expressions, on some level, of childhood experience.

A similar developmental progression is noted in the concepts of pregnancy and childbirth, from the earliest, inner-genital subphase, when there is the awareness of a place inside which will be used to carry a baby (e.g., "marsupial pouch," "bassinet of velvet"), to the end of the phase when the themes of pregnancy, birthing and care of the neonate predominate in the final moment before the oedipal triangle. Clearly these findings are not consistent with the Freudian hypothesis that the girl turns to her father for a baby as a substitute for the missing penis. In fact, in our material, even by the end of the preoedipal genital phase, the girl has not quite made the connection between the penis and impregnation; this must wait until the time of the oedipal situation. Rather, we would suggest that both the girl's feelings about her "baby place" and her fantasied neonate and her feelings about the penis become increasingly differentiated as she continues to define her sexual identity.

According to Freud, the phallic phase girl turns from her mother to her father since she blames her mother for her lack of a penis, she realizes that without a penis she will not be an adequate love object for her mother, and she hopes to obtain a penis from her father. However, recent observations (Abelin, 1975; Panel, 1976) indicate that the infant develops a specific attachment to her father well before the preoedipal genital phase; she relies upon him both for pleasurable excitement and for help in separating from her mother. In the sense that the father is a well-cathected object, there can be no total "change of object" during the preoedipal genital phase, although there is an extremely important change in the nature of the relationship to the father as the girl becomes aware of herself as a genital being both contrasting with and complementary to the male. Our material does not suggest that the girl turns to her father out of disillusionment or disappointment, either in the mother as a rejecting love object or in the girl's own deficient equipment, but rather in the service of "genital self-differentiation" (Abelin, 1975), in order to investigate his sexual aspects in relation to herself. In this enterprise, she appears to use her mother both as a stable, supportive figure while she experiences her father in a changing, surprising sexual manner, and as an identificatory figure whose coping processes she can utilize in dealing with her anxieties about the phallic father. Once the girl recognizes her father's approval and need of her as a female counterpart she actively demands his support for her growing sexuality, particularly in dealing with her mother, from whom she must separate sexually in order to claim her body as her own.

In terms of the relationship to the mother, our material does not indicate that the preoedipal genital phase girl goes through a negative oedipal period, in which she contends with her father for the love of her mother, much as the little boy in the positive oedipal phase would do. (At times the girl does identify with the power symbolic in the father's phallus, but this is not in order to win the mother for herself. For example, during the third subphase, the girl identifies with the powerful phallus and with her father as an aid in her struggle to sexually separate from her mother.) The girl goes through a period of competing with others for her mother's attention and admiration during the fourth subphase; this phenomenon has frequently been interpreted as a negative oedipal stance. However, our material, like that of Edgcumbe et al. (1976), does not confirm that interpretation, as the girl at that point will compete with anyone for her mother's attention rather than singling out her father as oedipal rival; in addition, we would speculate that this theme of searching for narcissistic gratification through winning a sexual competition for the mother is relatively minor, and is embedded within the context of integrating her experiences of relating the narcissistic needs of herself and her parents into a consolidated sense of self.

Earlier in this chapter, we presented Edgcumbe and Burgner's (1975) position, which questions the assumption that the phallic child is also an oedipal child and maintains that entering the phallic-drive phase is not simultaneously accompanied by attaining triangular oedipal object relationships, which are achieved only at the later portion of the phase; the earlier, dyadic, portion of the phallic phase is devoted to the acquisition of a sexual identity through concentration on narcissistic aspects of relationships with others. There is a high degree of congruence between Edgcumbe and Burgner's "phallic-narcissistic" phase and our fourth, "genital-narcissistic" subphase. Like Edgcumbe and Burgner, we find this subphase to be preoedipal, as the girl's sexual interest in either parent is not specifically tied to rivalry and hostility with the other; children in the genital-narcissistic subphase appear to compete with *anyone* for the attention of either of their parents, and are quite capable of enlisting the support of either parent in attaining sexual goals with the other. We also agree with Edgcumbe and Burgner and with Frankel and Sherick (1979) that the girl seems to be actively involved in comparing the genital performance of males and females and of using her mother and father to support her narcissistic development towards a consolidated female sense of self. Once the girl has established a relatively differentiated sexual identity, it is far easier for her to cope with the complex demands of the oedipal situation. As indicated in our study, the developmental sequence required for this maturational task is lengthy, dramatic and complex.

REFERENCES

Abelin, E. (1971). The role of the father in the separation-individuation process. In *Separation-Individuation*, ed. J.B. McDevitt and C.F. Settlage. New York: International Universities Press, pp. 229–252.

Barnett, M.C. (1966). Vaginal awareness in the infancy and childhood of girls. *J. Amer. Psychoanal. Assn.* 15:129–141.

Barglow, P., and Schaefer, M. (1976). A new female psychology? *J. Amer. Psychoanal. Assn. Supplement-Female Psychology* 24:305–350.

Benedek, T. (1970). The Psychobiology of Pregnancy. In *Parenthood*, ed. J. Anthony and T. Benedek. Boston: Little, Brown, pp. 137–151.

Blum, H. (1976). Masochism, the ego ideal, and the psychology of women. *J. Amer. Psychoanal. Assn. Supplement-Female Psychology*, 24:157–191.

Bonaparte, M. (1953). *Female Sexuality*. New York: International Universities Press.

Brunswick, R.M. (1940). The preoedipal phase of the libido development. *Psychoanal. Q.* 9:293–319.

Chasseguet-Smirgel, J. (1970). *Female Sexuality.* Ann Arbor: University of Michigan Press.

Clower, V. (1975). Significance of masturbation in female sexual development and function. In *Masturbation: From Infancy to Senescence*, ed. I. Marcus and J. Francis. New York: International Universities Press, pp. 107–143.

———(1976). Theoretical implication in current views of masturbation in latency girls. *J. Amer. Psychoanal. Assn. Supplement-Female Psychology* 24:109–125.

Deutsch, H. (1925). Psychology of women in relation to the functions of reproduction. *Int. J. Psychoanal.* 6:405–418.

———(1930). The significance of masochism in the mental life of women. In *The Psycho-Analytic Reader*, ed. R. Fliess, New York: International Universities Press, 1948, pp. 195–207.

———(1944–45). *The Psychology of Women*, vols. I and II. New York: Grune and Stratton.

Edgcumbe, R., in collaboration with S. Lundberg, R. Markowitz, and F. Salo, (1976). Some comments on the concept of the negative oedipal phase in girls. *The Psychoanalytic Study of the Child*. New Haven: Yale University Press, pp. 35–61.

Edgcumbe, R., and Burgner, M. (1975). The phallic-narcissistic phase. *The Psychoanalytic Study of the Child* 30:161–180. New Haven: Yale University Press.

Fast, I. (1979). Developments in gender identity: gender differentiation in girls. *Inter. J. Psycho-Anal.* 60:443–453.

Fraiberg, S. (1972), Genital arousal in latency girls. *The Psychoanalytic Study of the Child*. New Haven: Yale University Press, pp.439–475.

Frankel, S., and Sherick, I. (1977). Observations on the development of normal envy. *The Psychoanalytic Study of the Child*. New Haven: Yale University Press, pp. 257–281.

———(1979). Observations of the emerging sexual identity of three and four year old children: with emphasis on female sexual identity. *Int. Rev. Psycho-Anal.* 6:297–309.

Freud, S. (1925). Some psychological consequences of the anatomical distinction between the sexes. *Standard Edition* 19:243–258. London: Hogarth Press, 1961.

———(1931). Female sexuality. *Standard Edition* 21:225–243. London: Hogarth Press, 1961.

———(1933). New introductory lectures on psychoanalysis. *Standard Edition* 22:112–185, London: Hogarth Press, 1964.

Galenson, E., reporter (1976). Panel on the psychology of women: late adolescence and early adulthood. *J. Amer. Psychoanal. Assn.* 24:631–645.

———and Roiphe, H. (1976). Some suggested revisions concerning early female development. *J. Amer. Psychoanal. Assn. Supplement-Female Psychology* 24:29–57.

Gillespie, W.H. (1969). Concepts of vaginal orgasm. *Inter. J. Psychol-Anal.* 50:495–497.

Greenacre, P. (1948). Anatomical structure and superego development. In *Trauma, Growth & Personality*. New York: International Universities Press, 1952, pp. 149–164.

———(1950). Problems of early female sexual development. *The Psychoanalytic Study of the Child* 5:122–138. New York: International Universities Press.

———(1953). Penis awe and its relation to penis envy. In *Drives, Affects and Behavior*, ed. R. Lowenstein. New York: International Universities Press, pp. 176–190.

Grossman, W., and Stewart, W. (1976). Penis envy: from childhood wish to developmental metaphor. *J. Amer. Psychoanal. Assn. Supplement-Female Psychology* 24:193–212.

Horney, K. (1924). On the genesis of the castration complex in women. *Inter. J. Psychoanal.* 5:50–65.

———(1933). The denial of the vagina. *Inter. J. Psychoanal.* 14:1–33.

Jacobson, E. (1964). *The Self and the Object World.* New York: International Universities Press.

Jones, E. (1933). The phallic phase. *Inter. J. Psychoanal.* 14:1–33.

Kestenberg, J. (1968). Outside and inside, male and female. *J. Amer. Psychoanal. Assn.* 16:457–520.

———(1975). *Children and parents. Psychoanalytic Studies in Development.* New York: Jason Aronson.

Kleeman, J. (1975). Genital self-stimulation in infant and toddler girls. In *Masturbation: From Infancy to Senescence,* eds. I. Marcus and J. Francis. New York: International Universities Press, pp. 77–106.

———(1976). Freud's early views. *J. Amer. Psychoanal. Assn. Supplement-Female Psychology* 24:3–27.

Kramer, P. (1954). Early capacity for orgastic discharge and character formation. *The Psychoanalytic Study of the Child.* New York: International Universities Press.

Lampl-de Groot, J. (1928). The evolution of the oedipus complex in women. *Inter. J. Psychoanal.* 9:332–345.

LaPlanche, J., and Pontellis, J.B. (1973). *The Language of Psychoanalysis.* New York: Norton.

Mahler, M., Pine, F., and Bergman, A. (1975). *The Psychological Birth of The Human Infant.* New York: Basic Books.

Masters, W., and Johnson, V. (1966). *Human Sexual Response.* Boston: Little, Brown.

Menaker, E. (1979). Female identity in psycho-social perspective. Presented to the Council of Psychoanalytic Psychotherapists, October 1979.

Moore, B., (1976). Freud and female sexuality: a current view. *Int. J. Psychoanal* 57:287–300.

Parens, H., et al. (1976), On the girl's entry into the oedipus complex. *J. Amer. Psychoanal. Assn. Supplement-Female Psychology.* 24:79–107.

Schaefer, R. (1974). Problems in Freud's psychology of women. *J. Amer. Psychoanal. Assn.* 22:459–485.

Settlage, C.F. (1977). The psychoanalytic understanding of narcissistic borderline personality disorders: advances in developmental theory. *J. Amer. Psychoanal. Assn.* 25:805–833.

Stoller, R. (1976). Primary femininity. *J. Amer. Psychoanal. Assn. Supplement-Female Psychology* 24:3–27.

Stolorow, R.D. (1979) Psychosexuality and the representational world. *Inter. J. Psycho-Anal.* 60:39–45.

Thompson, C. (1950). Some effects of the derogatory attitude towards female sexuality. *Psychiatry* 13:349–354.

Torok, M. (1970). The significance of penis envy in women. In *Female Sexuality,* ed. J. Chassequet-Smirgel. Ann Arbor: University of Michigan Press, pp. 135–176.

APPENDIX A

The meaning of "clusters" of derivatives was ascertained through a complex and lengthy process. The following example of derivative analysis utilizes thirteen consecutive dreams from one of our patients, reflecting the initial part of the first subphase where there is a focus on the inner-genital world.

> *Dream 1*   12/21   Session #425   There was a *dam*. Like a *reservoir*. My friend Doris was somewhere around. Someone said the *dam had broken*. I remembered Doris was down there—*swept up in* the *water*. I got on a *horse* and *threw* her a *rope* and got her.

Dream 2 1/7 Session #429 I was with Bob, a *boyfriend* I used to go with. He was *trying to get into my house* — I guess my family was there. I saw him *coming up* the walk. I thought *everything is locked up*. I'm not sure what he wanted. He had *brought* someone like Orson *Welles*.

Dream 3 In another dream, Bill came to visit me, just to say hello. I met him. He came up on a *horse* — it was *exotic, red, gorgeous, different*. It seemed very calm and *gentle* and *sweet*.

Then I was *walking down the road*. A woman passed me in a car. She looked like a *gypsy*. Her face when she *saw my face* looked stunned. She stopped the car and asked me to get in the car. She said something about *beware* about some kind of *animal* — *someone might* try to *steal* some kind of *animal* — I thought she was referring to the horse Bill came on — that *in stealing* it, someone would *try to hurt me* — *like stealing my soul away*.

Dream 4 1/9 Session #430 We lived in a house in Connecticut. It was *burning*. I don't think I was in any *danger* but my sister — the *fire* started across the street. I yelled to my *sister* to come outside and she wouldn't come. She was *setting her hair*.

Dream 5 1/11 Session #431 My parents were taking me to dinner for my birthday. I was younger than I am. The waiter asked me *what* I'd *like*. I said a *screwdriver* with a *cherry*. The *waiter brought me cherries in whipped cream*. My parents said they had to go to him and *get it changed. I said no,* I didn't want to.

Dream 6 1/21 Session #435 I came home to an *old wooden house* on a hill — with *2 rooms* — like an *old house* that had been *turned into* a *vacation house*. My dog was there. *He came by the bed and lay beside me.* I felt very *content*, and *fell asleep* in the dream. *I woke up* and my *dog* was very *excited* about something. I went to the door between the 2 rooms and saw a *shadow hitting the window*. The *window opened* and a *man walked in*. I was a little frightened, not too much. He ended up being a friend.

There was something in the dream about *dancing in a big circle*.

Dream 7 Same session I was in a *motel/hotel*. It was a *big room with a terrace*. Next to the *hall door*, the *wall* was made up of something like *venetian blinds*. I was aware you could see into the room from the outside. I *fixed* the *blinds so you couldn't get in*. Then someone was out on the terrace, a *giant man, 8 feet tall*, very *large*. He came *thrashing* and *storming around the room like an ape*. I knew he wanted a woman, *so I fell down*. Then *he raped* me, but he wasn't *brutal*.

Dream 8   1/23   Session #436   I was *in a forest* — my *father* was around. We were *wading in the water*. I see a *snake* in the water — a rattlesnake, a small one. I *ask* my *father if he would carry me*, he says yes. When we get to the shore, there are *a lot of snakes*. I *get bitten* and *pass out*. It's like I'm in a *coma*. My *music teacher* is *tending me*.

Dream 9   1/28   Session #438   I am in a big department store fiilled with *interesting things* and having a *gay time*. At one point I *slide down* a *beautiful old mahogany banister*. *Bursting with energy*. I *knock over a table* and a *beautiful plate*. I think how awful. I went over to it. The *woman* there said she *could put it* back *together* again. The *plate turned into a plant*.

Dream 10   1/30   Session #439   The *buzzer* rang. I looked out the *peephole* and it was a young *man*. I was frightened and didn't answer — he kept *ringing* and then *banging at the lock with a broom handle*. *He got in*. I ran out *into a street* that is a *gay street*.

Dream 11   2/1   Session #440   There was a *baby* in a *big black hand bag*. Like if you go away, you put a *plastic bag over a plant* and *it will water itself*. I ripped off the bag. The baby was OK but weak. Its heart stopped beating. I beat its chest to start it again.

Dream 12   Same session   I was *in a play*. I had a number of *small parts*. The theme was not knowing my lines, not being prepared. It was different from the usual dream because I did forget some of my lines, but it was a *huge production*.

Dream 13   2/15   Session #444   My mother, sister, and self were going in a car *to see something*. My mother and I went up this *path* that lead *into a forest*. My sister said it was a *special day*, the day the *priests came down and opened up spectacular caves* where there were *magnificent paintings* — *natural caves*. I went in with my sister. It was just beautiful — modern designs but "natural". We were *going through* a *passage way-, came to some horses*. They were *giant red stallions* like *Viennese riding stallions* — except they were *giant*. My sister wasn't looking at the horse. She was wedged into a corner, looking at a *manuscript* encased in a *glass case*. Like she was in a *daze*. If she stepped back the *horses* would *hit* her.

The first step in the understanding of the primary themes in these dreams was accomplished by sifting out those words and phrases (italicized in the illustrative material) which seemed to "stand out," either because of their vividness, their visual symbolization, their meaning as a double entendre, and/or their unusualness in contrast to this patient's usual "dream language." Next, these words or phrases were scanned for possible repetitive use by the dreamer. Iterations were looked for in affect, in reference to physiologic state, in body image, in drive elements, and in reference to certain aspects of particular objects.

For example, in the preceding dreams physiologic state appears to be reflected in the following words: dam, like a reservoir (dream 1); everything is locked up (dream 2); house burning, fire (dream 4); pass out, in a coma (dream 8). Expressions of affect were closely related: content, excited, dancing in a circle (dream 6); interesting things and gay time, bursting with energy (dream 9); in a daze (dream 13). Two primary themes emerge: drawing back inside oneself and pleasurable excitement. The excitement is generated by the dreamer, hence apparently refers to her experience of her own drive impulses. The withdrawal is especially evident in dream 6 which seems reminiscent of the fairy tale about Sleeping Beauty, awakened by the Prince. A search through the dreams of the other patients at a parallel moment in treatment revealed consistently highlighted repetitions of similar words and phrases. It was therefore concluded that these experiences of affect and physiologic state were usual at this developmental moment.

In contrast, there are a number of references in this patient's dreams at this time to anxiety about being hurt by the phallic, genitally aggressive male: stealing my soul away (dream 3); a shadow hit the window, man walked in, I frightened (dream 6); giant man, 8 feet tall, thrashing and storming, raped me, brutal (dream 7); man banging at the lock with a broom handle (dream 10). Yet other patients' dreams at this moment in treatment did not include such images. It was therefore concluded that these were probably reflections of specific, atypical experiences in this particular patient's early life. These include an early traumatic experience when the patient was nearly raped and her perception of certain frightening aspects of her father at the point when she began to become aware of her own sexuality.

The symbolic representations of body image seen in the dream work appear to be genital in nature. Thus, one can understand "the dam had broken" (dream 1) as penetration of the hymen; "screwdriver with a cherry—cherries in whipped cream" (dream 5) as articulation of differences between the penis and the vagina; "old wooden house with two rooms" (dream 6) as representing the vagina and uterus: "motel/hotel—big room with terrace—venetian blinds" (dream 7) as the genital apparatus including especially the vagina, clitoris, and labia. Other words in this patient's dreams include: setting her hair, mahogany banister, buzzer, peephole, door lock, baby in a hand bag, small parts, spectacular caves, passage way, glass case. Similar images were seen ubiquitously throughout the other patient's dreams at this particular juncture.

The body image components in these dreams were sufficiently different from prior dream imagery to suggest a beginning libidinal focus on the genital apparatus. Ego activity, specifically emerging representations of the body self, was also implied in the keen perceptual awareness of parts of the body that are sexual and/or related to fecundity.

The next step in the process was the gathering together of similar images from *all* of our patients' dreams and grouping together similar representations of affect, physiologic state, body image components, etc. These groupings provided the basis for the conclusions appearing in our chapter on the early portion of the first subphase.

6

The Female Oedipus Complex: Its Antecedents and Evolution

MARIA V. BERGMANN

> . . . there has been a general refusal to recognize that psycho-analytic research
> could not, like a philosophical system, produce a complete and ready made
> theoretical structure, but had to find its way step by step along the path towards
> understanding the intricacies of the mind by making an analytic dissection of
> both normal and abnormal phenomena.
> —Sigmund Freud, 1923

In this work I will consider the female child from the viewpoint of her early relationship to her mother and to her father. I will discuss the decisive developments which influence the psychic experience of the girl's Oedipus complex from the standpoint of the developmental and structural factors which shape this universal constellation.

As the history of femininity begins before the child is born, the girl's emotional destiny is affected not only by her mother's attitude towards her own femininity, but by the reliving of the mother's relationship toward her own mother when she was a little girl. Awareness of gender identity thus provides an unconscious historical and dynamic generational link which is set in motion accompanying each birth, and the importance of this link sets a precedent for the girl for her later oedipal role.

For the first self and object representations to be firmly rooted in the psychic structure, the girl must feel welcomed into the world by a mother who accepts her child's femaleness without major psychic conflict. The child can then start her life with a primary acceptance of herself as a girl.

As the girl develops, the mother experiences certain reactions: maternal—fostering the child's capacity for identification; restitutional—representing the realization of an earlier wished-for self-image; or narcissistic, competitive, or clinging—oriented towards intrapsychic conflicts revived from her own childhood. The girl perceives how the mother experiences her *own* female body and whether she values it as a healthy and lovable narcissistic possession. If gender difference is established and accepted without too much hostility toward the mother, disillusionment and loss of self-esteem (during the phallic phase) will be more easily overcome, enabling the girl to reach the oedipal level. Under pathological conditions, however, fixation may result if earlier separation processes, particularly those of the rapprochement subphase, have not prepared the girl for her positive Oedipus complex, or if ambivalent feelings toward one or both parents prevented separation on the oedipal level.

FREUD'S VIEWS ON FEMALE SEXUALITY

For Freud, the Oedipus complex was the nuclear childhood event and the kernel of future neurosis. His concepts originally derived from reports from female patients of actual seductions by their fathers during childhood, although he soon discovered that these seductions were fantasies rather than facts.

In 1897, Freud wrote to Fliess that "sexual phantasy *invariably* seizes upon the theme of the parents" (italics mine, p. 260), and "I have found in my own case too, falling in love with the mother and jealousy of the father, and I now regard it as a universal event of early childhood" (p. 265). And in 1900 he wrote: "A girl's first affection is for her father and a boy's first childish desires are for his mother. Accordingly, the father becomes a disturbing rival to the boy and the mother to the girl" (p. 257). In 1900 Freud did not yet recognize the existence of a girl's affectionate relationship with her mother before or during the onset of her love for her father.

Freud's concepts were essentially phallocentric. He believed that boys and girls at a young age thought that all human beings have a penis, that girls believed the clitoris would grow into one, and that children of both sexes ignored the existence of the vagina until puberty. He believed that universal oedipal wishes in children (and later in adults) underwent repression and remained unconscious (1905), and that the origin of these repressions was both phylogenetic and ontogenetic. Freud focused on castration anxiety and the incest taboo as among the major determinants of the oedipal fantasy.

In 1931, his theoretical expansion included the preoedipal phase in which the mother was recognized as the first love object for both boys and girls. But whereas the boy is able to sustain an ambivalent relationship with father and keep mother as his primary love object into the oedipal phase, the girl proceeds along different developmental lines. For boys, the Oedipus complex was considered to be a primary formation, for girls, a secondary one. The achievement of the positive oedipal phase for girls could be reached only after completion of the negative phase, i.e., love for mother, hatred for father. Compared to the development of the boy who keeps the mother as his primary preoedipal love object, the girl's transfer of libido from mother to father constitutes an extra step.

Freud considered penis envy as the leading cause for the girl's shift from mother to father: "She has seen it and knows that she is without it and wants to have it" (1925). Penis envy and fantasies of castration propel her into the oedipal phase. The girl's desire for a penis is transformed into a desire to have a child (preferably a boy) from her father. Her mother not only becomes a rival, she is unconsciously reproached for the girl's lack of a penis as well as for having "seduced her" with loving care and attention. When the girl realizes that her desire for a baby from her father cannot be fulfilled, she abandons her wish (Freud, 1924a) and turns away from her father. Freud believed that for the girl to "grow out of" the Oedipus complex, she needed to give up clitoral masturbation at puberty. This in turn would enable her as a young adult to achieve a mature sexual state with a sexually cathected vagina, capable of true pleasure (1905).

Freud postulated that the girl is under less pressure than the boy to form her superego because she need not fear castration. This led Freud to consider her superego development deficient. He believed the demands of domesticity and motherhood limit the girl's life goals which in turn foster cultural approval of female dependency. The oedipal situation for the girl becomes a "haven of refuge" (1933) from her penis envy (from which she emerges only gradually). The boy's superego, by contrast, molded out of the need to achieve an oedipal victory over the father, has to overcome castration anxiety, unconscious guilt, and the need for punishment.

Although Freud later admitted the existence of early vaginal sensations, he observed that, "It is true that recently an increasing number of observers report that vaginal impulses are present even in these early years, . . . in women, . . . the main genital occurrences of childhood must take place in relation to the clitoris" (1931, p. 228). He did not include these impulses in his theory of female sexuality, or as part of the female Oedipus complex.

In Freud's views, the girl in reaching womanhood must effect a triple change in order to reach and resolve her oedipal conflict: from active to passive, from mother to father, and from the clitoris to the vagina as the primary locus of her feminine sexuality.

Freud continually strove for a clear distinction between biological and psychic phenomena and considered primary femininity a psychological issue. However, he was called a reductionist by some, because he believed that the ultimate answers to psychological problems of femininity would be resolved through discoveries in physiology and biochemistry.

Freud assumed that the child is born with a certain sexual identity and a bisexual potential. He wanted to discover how the child develops a *psychic* sexual identity. Freud considered this a psychological question which grew out of the active interplay of developmental processes, and not a biological, psychophysical, or cultural question. His inquiry centered on how the psychological experience becomes synthesized into a definite body and self image (1905). Although he constructed a purely psychological theory of feminine development, he conceded its tentativeness and candidly admitted that feminine sexuality continued to baffle him. Thus, in spite of Freud's awareness of the significance of his presentation, he continued to regard female sexuality as an unsolved psychological mystery.

Several of Freud's disciples took issue with his model of female sexuality. Melanie Klein (1928), Karen Horney (1926, 1932, 1933), and Ernest Jones (1935) did not regard penis envy as resulting from the girl's fear of castration or fear of something having been taken away or lost. They saw penis envy as related to hostile fantasies toward the parents, which were derived from conflict-laden experiences and interfered with later identifications with the parents. Fantasies of incorporation and destruction of the penis (actually, a part-object fantasy) may serve as an example. "The ultimate question is whether a woman is born or made" (Jones, 1933). Further, Jones (1935) put it thus: "In short, I do not see a woman . . . as 'un homme manqué,' a permanently disappointed creature struggling to console herself with secondary substitutes alien to her nature."

For Horney, primary femininity preceded the phallic phase and was based on biological and cultural factors; she believed that there was an innate sense of human femaleness and that the assumption that "half of humanity" thought of itself as anatomically inferior was ill-founded. Girls repress early vaginal sensations which exist before the phallic phase. "The undiscovered vagina is a vagina denied" (Horney, 1933): by boys, because of fear and hostile wishes projected upon the mother (or her body), and by girls, because of castration wishes toward the father, which turn into fears of internal bodily injury. These authors stressed that revenge fantasies result in bodily fears projected upon the parents by *children of either sex* and influence the child's capacity for identification.

DEVELOPMENTAL PRECURSORS INFLUENCING THE OEDIPUS COMPLEX

The first self is a body self. Body-image formation is dependent upon the child's successful completion and growing out of the symbiotic phase. During the subphase of differentiation, the body is gradually experienced as separate from that of the mother.

The integration of the body self, its differentiation from objects, and the capacity to distinguish inside from outside involve the mother's need-satisfying activity and regulation of pleasurable and painful affects. If the rhythm of need-satisfaction and frustration is disrupted, it will interfere with the development of reality testing, perceptual and cognitive development, motor activity, the beginnings of anticipation, and the signal function (Tolpin, 1971; Lichtenberg, 1978). Unless the child is traumatized, body awareness will remain constant, and body experiences will become autonomous even under stress (Hartmann, 1939). Loss of self-cohesion may arise from severe developmental disturbances which lead to fragmentation of the self-structure, and to disturbances in the differentiation of inner from outer reality.

As growth proceeds, and as inner body needs are perceived, the child learns to verbalize its needs and takes preventive and adaptive measures for self-protection. Identity formation begins at the time of psychic structure formation. A positive attitude on the part of the mother during the various psychosexual phases helps to ensure that feminine developmental determinants will not become involved in permanent intrapsychic conflict. If the girl experiences a "good enough" symbiotic period, she will reach and successfully pass through the subphase of differentiation with a gradually consolidating sense of gender identity. Libidinal and aggressive drive derivatives will tend toward fusion, leading to body enjoyment and exploration.

THE ORAL PHASE AS PRIMARY BODY CATHEXIS

For Freud the oral phase marked the dawning of psychic body experience: The mouth was the first erotogenic zone to be cathected and served as a model for affective experiences related to all other body openings later on (1905). Jones observed that the vagina derives its oral representation from the mouth and that all early stimulation relates to body openings. He related oral, anal, and vaginal sensations as dating from infancy: "The anus is evidently identified with the vagina to begin with, and the differentiation of the two is an extremely obscure process, more so perhaps than any other in female development . . . [and] . . . it takes place at an earlier age than is generally supposed" (1911). Hoffer (1949, 1950) described how infants use their mouths and hands to explore and cathect body surfaces with pleasure, and E. Kris (1951) observed that infants from loving homes cathect their bodies libidinally and experience auto-erotic pleasures much earlier than children from broken homes or institutions. In 1955, Spitz discussed the significance of the oral cavity in terms of its function as the first boundary between inside and outside.

Kestenberg stated that it was rare for the girl to cathect her genital as early as the boy, particularly "in the first two years of life . . . A cloacal concept of the genital pervades the girl's anal stage of development" (1956, 1968, p. 259). (See also Bonaparte, 1953.) It is thought that the cathexis of erotogenic zones may have a direct relationship to body image formation and to the nature of the child's identification with her mother (Greenacre, 1950).

The term "primary femininity" connotes pleasurable sexual sensations which constitute a "core feeling," or "anlage," including the beginnings of body-cathexis before there is an awareness of sexual differences. Early vaginal sensations affect body-schematization and differentiation of self from non-self on the earliest level of psychic-structure formation (Greenacre, 1950; Kleeman, 1976).

The hypothesis that self-stimulation of the vaginal introitus and labia is subject to primary repression (never having become conscious) of the vagina as an erotogenic zone was advanced by Barnett (1966). She suggested that voluntary muscular control over mouth and anus leads to a sense of mastery over these organs, as the child learns to control "what comes in and what goes out." The incapacity to experience control over the vaginal cavity, however, may threaten the developing body image of the girl and lead to early repression of vaginal sensations; clitoral hypercathexis emerges to assist vaginal repression.

Pleasurable sensations arise during the first year of life, with an increase in excitement between the fifteenth and twenty-seventh month involving penile erections in boys, and vaginal lubrication, self-stimulation of the lower vaginal canal, the clitoris, the labia, and introitus in girls (Kleeman, 1976). Vaginal sensations during infancy may also serve the purpose of discharging psychological stress (Greenacre, 1950; Kestenberg, 1956). The girl is capable of strong self-stimulation between the eighteenth and twenty-fourth month, but knows less about her genital than the boy.

It is unclear how vaginal sensations are registered before the psychic structure is sufficiently established. Baby girls enjoy masturbation, but the psychological role of such early sensations is difficult to assess before there is a psychic structure. It is difficult to visualize how these early sensations are registered and difficult to know whether they find their way into later feminine body-image formation. I believe that early sensations become significant only when they emerge from repression in a phase-specific context. When the parents enjoy the girl as a girl, the girl's sense of herself, her "core gender identity" (Stoller, 1968), will be facilitated. A dawning of the girl's pleasurable experience of her body in the first two years of life precedes penis envy as a developmental phase. Discovery of gender identity is later reinforced by cognitive developments and affective responses which confirm body cathexis and aid in the development of body narcissism.

Direct observations indicate that children become aware of their gender identity, from the fifteenth month on, long before the inception of penis envy in girls, which marks the beginnings of oedipal rivalry. Although girls before the age of two have been observed to experience a "low-keyed" (Mahler & McDevitt, 1968) emotional response upon discovery of the boy's penis, this did not appear to affect the girl's core gender identity unduly, nor her ability to cathect her exterior and interior genital representation (Roiphe and Galenson, 1971, 1973). Between the fifteenth and nineteenth month, perception of the missing genital becomes associated with fantasies of the mother's absence, and a sense of loss is experienced as part of the separation from the pleasure-giving mother.

Doll play provides a means for discharging and mastering vaginal tensions by projecting them to the outside (Kestenberg, 1968). Blum (1976) has pointed out that the doll helps the child during periods of fear of object loss and fears related to a lack of self-definition. Doll play is especially important between the ages of two and four, when the discovery of the vagina and the beginnings of genital masturbation normally take place. The doll represents various aspects of the self and helps the girl to consolidate her inner feminine core, and thereby to achieve a permanent cathexis of her vagina as a preparation for the development of her self-image (Kestenberg, 1971).

The role of the father is significant (Abelin, 1971) in both preoedipal and oedipal phases. Although parental attitudes vary with each child and each phase (Coleman, E. Kris, and Provence, 1953; Benedek, 1959), the ability of the father to complement the preoedipal developmental needs of the girl, should the mother fail in her maternal function, may save the girl from severe pathology. However, this may make the differentiation of the preoedipal from the oedipal father more difficult for her later.

Gender identity is based on a correct perception of self and others. If the child is exposed to anxiety-arousing interactions, the ego functions which promote play and speech may suffer distortions. Perceptual denial of gender differences interferes with symbolization and thinking processes (Galenson and Roiphe, 1971). There is a reciprocal relationship regarding gender identity, symbolization, and the development of thinking as an ego function. If mother-child interaction permits internalization, symbolization and thinking will be facilitated.

Thus, early vaginal sensations and preoedipal psychosexual experiences aid in the consolidation of preoedipal body cathexis and promote the development of body narcissism. Before the onset of the phallic phase, internalized parent-child interaction facilitates the development of those specific ego functions which prepare the girl for her oedipal experience.

THE IMPORTANCE OF THE RAPPROCHEMENT SUBPHASE FOR THE DEVELOPMENT OF THE FEMALE OEDIPUS COMPLEX

The rapprochement subphase marks a crisis of separation-individuation and is a critical period in the establishment of gender identity. Anxiety regarding object loss and loss of love emerges as the child follows a new spurt in attempting to separate from the mother. The first definite wishes to separate from, but not to lose, the mother emerge at this time. If the mother out of her own anxiety cannot permit the child to establish the independent space the child needs, or if she cannot tolerate the child's oscillation between independence and clinging, the rapprochement crisis will not be resolved.

This phase is also difficult for the mother, as she herself struggles with her own inner conflict to relinquish the dyad, and to give up the symbiotic tie to the child, a tie that represents the height of bliss to many women.

The child betrays an unconscious need to merge with the "good mother of symbiosis" and to avoid the "bad mother of re-engulfment." However, separation can be achieved only from the "good mother." If the mother cannot foster the successful completion of this phase because there is too much hostile interaction between her and her child, the child may resort to splitting the maternal representation into good and bad. It is not possible to separate effectively from an inner maternal representation that is split, or too ambivalently cathected.

The child who remains fixated at the level of the rapprochement crisis will manifest pervasive separation-anxiety and the rapprochement conflicts will not be resolved. There may be transient neurotic symptoms, or the beginnings of intrapsychic conflict, such as a phobia signifying unmastered separation anxiety (Freud, 1926; Mahler, 1975).

Manifest separation anxiety in the relationship between the girl and her mother will surface during the inception of the oedipal phase. Frequent fluctuations between the girl's positive oedipal feelings and regression to the negative oedipal conflict will make integration of the feminine self image more difficult, particularly the girl's acceptance of her penis envy without undue hatred of her mother. Under normal conditions, the resolution of the rapprochement crisis constitutes a preparation for the girl's capacity to reach the positive Oedipus complex (Mahler, 1966, 1975).

PENIS ENVY AND THE NEGATIVE OEDIPAL PHASE

Freud saw penis envy as the "bedrock" of feminine sexuality (1937, p. 252). The girl resents her mother for having "made her" a girl. Freud believed that penis envy (resulting from feelings of castration) could lead to certain characterological predispositions, such as female masochism, jealousy, frigidity, depression, and other symptoms referred to as the "masculinity complex" (1933). Freud believed that by giving up phallic wishes the girl preserves an essential aspect of her narcissism.

Girls sustain a "narcissistic blow" on becoming aware of anatomical differences. This narcissistic wound influences positive and negative oedipal wishes. I believe that if the girl has been able to develop feminine narcissistic body feelings, she will be able to value her genital and will not feel she must pretend or wish to be a boy. Bisexual elements will gradually be integrated into the character structure. Identification with the mother as a female person will make penis envy a transitory experience, phase-specific for the phallic period which precedes, or develops concomitantly with, the girl's positive Oedipus complex.

Anna Freud designated the early dyadic period of the phallic phase as the "phallic-narcissistic phase," and reserved the term "phallic-oedipal phase" for the later triangular segment of phallic oedipal relationships (Edgcumbe and Burgner, 1975). If, during the phallic-narcissistic phase, a girl becomes fixated on the penis as a part-object, she will experience feelings of rejection and unconsciously believe that she is not lovable because she is a girl. When the early relationship between mother and child has been excessively hostile, the girl will be unable to internalize a good image of her. A fantasy image will be formed to sustain the girl's inner representation of the "good mother" (Bergmann, M.V., 1980). The hostile interaction between the girl and her mother will be over-determined and the missing penis may become the issue upon which the mother-child relationship revolves. Possession of the penis will then symbolize the fantasized good relationship with the "good mother," which in reality has been lacking. Unconsciously, the part-object penis then stands for the whole-object relationship. The girl will fantasy that she might have been loved by the "good mother" if only she had been a boy.

During the phallic-oedipal phase, the girl's internalization processes may have led to the symbolization of feelings of deficiency, and penis envy may become a metaphor for other traumata. Penis envy may then have functioned as a screen or "shorthand" for childhood disappointments, and as an expression of unmet needs stemming from the mother-child dyad. (Grossman and Stewart, 1976). Unmet needs are conducive to narcissistic rage against the love-denying mother. Such unconscious fantasies against the mother can become transformed into penis envy. Clinically it is important to differentiate between women who demonstrate penis envy and those who wish to destroy the male genital. Only the unconsciously "castrating" woman wishes to destroy the man or his penis. The envious girl or woman does no more than envy; she is capable of object relationships and of symbolization. She wishes to feel "whole," but not to destroy. The unconsciously "castrating" woman wishes to destroy an object or body part.

Penis envy undergoes a transformation at different developmental phases; most likely it is reactive to object relationship problems in early development, and does not play a primary role in regard to feminine gender identity.

Clinical observations have not eliminated the ambiguities inherent in the concept of the negative Oedipus complex as it was originally conceived:

> No writer actually gives evidence . . . of a clearly negative oedipal phase in the girl in which she is active and masculine in her oedipal relationships with her parents, without awareness of her lack of a penis and without feelings of

being different from boys . . . They are more likely to formulate their material in terms of negative and positive aspects of oedipal development, if they use the concept at all. (Edgcumbe et al., 1976, p. 40).

During the phallic phase proper, the girl's psychic experience becomes increasingly object-directed. When envy toward her father develops, her unconscious masculine wishes are enhanced, which leads to a wish to "replace" him in order to achieve a new physical and loving closeness with the mother. The phallic phase thus culminates in the girl's reaching of her negative Oedipus complex and in a sharper more object-directed masturbation fantasy; this fantasy is, however, pregenital and preoedipal in its content.

The negative Oedipus complex is characterized by the girl's longing for the mother of the preoedipal period (sometimes leading to fixation and homosexuality in women). When the negative oedipal phase is not resolved, penis envy and breast envy may become unconsciously fused and substitute for each other. Exhibitionistic and scoptophilic activities may propel the girl into developing penis envy in rivalries with boys, feelings of castration, and dissatisfaction with her body. Lowered self-esteem may thus interfere with the development of feminine sexual identifications.

The girl may unconsciously substitute her body for the missing penis, and strive for a narcissistic identification with her father as a means of feeling closer to him. The wish to be like the father instead of having a baby by him is expressed in the body-phallus equation (Lewin, 1933) and substitutes for the loss of self-esteem in the girl. An identification with the father represents yet one more aspect of the negative oedipal conflict.

When identity formation has organized the boundaries of the self, early genital play paves the way for future acceptance of the vagina. However, if identification with the mother is disturbed, and the girl is disillusioned, there may be a loss of cathexis of the inside genital and a loss of self-esteem. The girl then may turn to the idealized father, unconsciously wishing to possess his penis. Revenge fantasies against both mother and father may result, leading to fixation on the negative Oedipus complex, with definite character traits similar to those of her father.

Clinical observation suggests that there is a constant oscillation between positive and negative oedipal feelings in children of both sexes; therefore, the negative oedipal phase cannot be viewed as a preoedipal phenomenon only. It undergoes developmental stages which include various adaptations to objects; not only from its inception and subsequent amalgamation into the phase proper, but also during later stages, negative oedipal feelings may be reawakened, as in puberty or adolescence.

Preoedipal fantasies may become so dangerous that there may be a precocious move toward oedipal fantasies as a defense. The term "oedipalization" (Kernberg, 1977) has been used to identify such seemingly oedipal conflicts which defend against more dangerous preoedipal conflicts which they cover. As will be demonstrated in my profile study, phallic-narcissistic object relations are usually pseudo-oedipal and differ radically from genuine oedipal conflicts.

The mastery of the negative oedipal phase leads to stable identification of the girl with her mother, in which libidinal feelings dominate over hostile ones and make penis envy an expression of a transitory self-representation of penislessness, rather than of femininity. Thus, the unconscious wishes of the negative Oedipus complex express a phase-specific step without which identification with the mother as a woman is impossible for the girl because it culminates in the acceptance of penislessness in both mother and child. These steps play a pivotal role in the development of the body image and help the girl to reach the positive oedipal phase.

Freud believed that the girl stops masturbating when she becomes disappointed in the performance of her clitoris; she feels inferior because she views her lack of a penis as a deficiency (1925). He also believed that girls would turn into frigid women unless they stopped masturbating before puberty. These views have not been clinically verified. It is now believed that the clitoris is the focal point of masturbation for girls from the oedipal period into maturity (Clower, 1977).

During the phallic-oedipal period, masturbation may express loneliness, ambivalent feelings, or destructive wishes towards the parents. The masturbation fantasy may comfort the child who has experienced narcissistic injury. A polarization between vaginal and clitoral impulses may develop, leading to difficulty in integrating body cathexis into a unified genital representation. The clitoris, possibly because of its accessibility, acquires an inner representation and body cathexis more easily than other parts of the female genital. A lack of harmony between clitoral and vaginal representations may lead to confusion in identity formation, reality testing and thinking.

The oedipal girl tends to masturbate actively and to have masturbation fantasies in which the clitoris functions as a fantasy penis. Both active and passive oedipal wishes remain unconscious. The fantasy phallus represented by the clitoris becomes the heir to previous unconscious communications with the mother; in such fantasies the phallus may represent the baby or the breast.

Girls generally experience greater masturbation guilt than boys. Hostility toward both parents, but particularly the mother, during phallic-oedipal development, is frequently based on the shattered hope that masturbation will produce a penis. Idealization of the penis frequently leads to depression, self-devaluation, and rage towards the mother. In adulthood the ability to integrate clitoris and vagina into a unified inner genital representation is the most important factor in genital maturation. If the mother forbids masturbation during the preoedipal or oedipal period, oedipal hatred may become intensified. In fact, for the girl to move from the preoedipal to the oedipal phase, her ambivalence conflict with her mother must be balanced; an excess of love or hatred may keep the girl fixated on the negative oedipal phase in the search for the good and active preoedipal mother (R. Brunswick, 1940). If this search for love from her mother leads to fixation, she will be unable to experience deeply passionate love feelings for her father during the oedipal period.

A CONTEMPORARY VIEW OF THE FEMALE OEDIPUS COMPLEX

We may ask: How is the Oedipus complex viewed today, and specifically, the female Oedipus complex? The oedipal stage is linked to developmental pregenital and genital psychic precursors. Psychic structure and function develop during ever-changing object relationships involving internal and environmental pressures affecting mother, father, and child. It appears that in psychoanalytic thought we have moved from Freud's hydraulic model of the psychic structure to one more closely resembling a Calder mobile, a tentacled structure balanced or unbalanced by the quality and weight of its parts.

Freud saw the Oedipus complex as a polarization of instinctual derivatives expressed in feelings of love and hatred toward the parents. Feelings of love tied to the parent of the opposite sex and feelings of hate toward the parent of the same sex are characteristic of the positive Oedipus complex. These conceptualizations are still considered valid today, but contemporary psychoanalytic thought sees these feelings as being in a state of flux and the Oedipus complex as an organizer of all psychic life before the latency period.

Freud regarded the Oedipus complex as the nucleus of neurosis. Neuroses were understood as failures in outgrowing or resolving the Oedipus complex. In his paper of 1924, Freud attempted to differentiate repression of the Oedipus complex from its dissolution. The word "Untergang" (literally, "to go under" in German) is traditionally associated with the setting sun, and is less final than the term "dissolution." Freud believed that the normal person resolves, or dissolves, the Oedipus complex, in contrast to the neurotic who only succeeds in repressing it. Thus, in later life the derivatives of the Oedipus complex can re-emerge from repression. The distinction between dissolution and repression appears less valid than Freud assumed, since a person who has truly "dissolved" his or her oedipal conflict would, in all probability, be incapable of developing a transference relationship, or of falling in love (M.S. Bergmann, 1971).

A number of authors have been concerned with the concept of "dissolution" and the fate of the oedipal fantasies. Loewald, for instance, suggested that repression narrows and limits man's choices. As an alternative to repression, he postulated a developmental process of internalization. Loewald's formulations suggest that repression is not the only psychic force at the disposal of the oedipal child. Ever-changing internalizations of the parental representations provide building blocks for an ever-changing psychic structure, keeping developmental avenues open. By contrast, repression by itself tends to freeze psychic structure. On the other hand, "internalization as a completed process implies emancipation and individuation from the object." (Loewald, 1973, p. 16).

In the 1930s, emphasis was placed on the events of the preoedipal period and their influence on the Oedipus complex. Lampl-De Groot (1952) states, "The central conflict [may] lie in the preoedipal relationship to the mother." As soon as the mother is recognized or loved as a separate person, there is the fear of losing her or of losing her love. Ambivalence and anxiety over hostile wishes toward her set in. The child's ambivalence is directed not only toward the "sexual" mother, but also to the survival of the preoedipal mother. In analysis, we often find that preoedipal problems need to be worked out before it is possible for a patient to experience oedipal wishes fully. The question has arisen whether pathology originates within the oedipal phase itself without preoedipal antecedents. There has been a controversy relating to the genetic origins of pathology regarding the fate of the Oedipus complex. The question is repeatedly raised whether "the psychic events of the preoedipal phase *influence* those of the oedipal phase . . . [but do not] . . . *determine* them (italics mine) (Brenner, 1979, p. 193)," or whether they determine the psychic structure within which the Oedipus complex is experienced.

Instead of a shift from mother to father (or vice versa), as Freud thought, we may conceptualize oedipal object relations as simultaneous identifications of varying strengths directed toward either parent, or of identificatory disturbances weighted with shifting valences at different periods of intrapsychic struggle and growth. At any given time, both the dyadic and triadic pressures determine oedipal object relationships from the phallic phase onward (on the model suggested by Anna Freud and discussed earlier in this paper). However, even during preponderantly "dyadic periods," triangulation plays a role.

The Oedipus complex has been described as an example "par excellence, of an individual's unconscious view of the world" (Shapiro, 1977, p. 563). As a universal human fantasy, it encompasses unconscious affect-laden ideas about parental objects related to good and bad, active and passive, male and female. The unconscious organization of the female Oedipus complex, although emanating from a combination of drive derivatives, environmental influences, and organizing functions of the ego, will probably be determined primarily by the fate of the girl's identification processes. At first, the girl will experience her own body in relation to her mother's. Later, in my view, a more encompassing identification with the mother will be the most important influence on the development of her psychic structure and her experience of herself first as a girl and later as a woman.

The oedipal phase is currently viewed in terms of ego functions and separation-individuation developments, as well as psychosexual phenomena and drive manifestations. The extent of separation-individuation achieved in the child will determine his or her capacity to fully reach and pass through the positive Oedipus complex. The need to revert to the negative oedipal phase may be viewed as an attempt on the part of the child to cling to a parent. Omnipotent fantasies sometimes going back to the practicing subphases may re-emerge during oedipal pressures which keep the child fixated on the negative oedipal level and do not permit separation.

The child's capacity to move from dyadic to triadic object relationships remains somewhat puzzling. In spite of the additional structural building blocks the child has acquired at the time of this transition, it is extremely difficult to construct, from the analysis of adults, the nature of internalizations during this crucial phase of childhood.

It would appear that if the girl can remain identified with her mother, both during oedipal rivalry and during experiences of the primal scene—the birth of siblings and other traumatic internal and external events which are unconsciously registered as being "the mother's fault"—she will be able to enter a triadic phase without fear of object loss. But if identification with mother is only partial, because the mental representation of her is vested with a predominance of hostile aggression rather than libido, a segment of the Oedipus complex will not be resolved; it will fall prey to fixation or regression. The girl's capacity to integrate her genitality depends not only on reaching the oedipal phase, but on its resolution.

Individuation from the parental representations comes gradually with the capacity for internalization, and it is at this time that the inner representations of parents and self begin to be consolidated in the ego and superego. This is possible only if channels for internalization are opened by new developmental spurts of separation and individuation and are not closed off by the intrusion of object relationship themes from earlier periods which have blocked development. As a mental organizer (Rangell, 1972; Mahler, 1975), the Oedipus complex represents a culmination or new synthesis of ongoing psychic processes. We think of the oedipal phase as one of transition, gradually reached and gradually resolved. Indeed, in the narrowest sense, the Oedipus complex may have no final resolution in either sex (Ticho, 1978). Phases of relative stability (and tranquillity) may alternate with revivals of oedipal conflicts later in life, requiring a new psychic integration. A woman's conflict concerning her femininity, her feminine ego ideal, or her autonomous strivings for self-realization, may continue throughout her lifetime (Blum, 1978).

Since the Oedipus complex is regarded as a structure of ongoing object relationships, its history and the manner and quality of its internalization are considered more crucial than isolated traumatic occurrences during childhood. Preverbal experiences, affective changes, and early ego functions have a direct bearing on later psychic organizers, which in turn are significant for oedipal development (A. Freud, 1971).

One of the most important clinical problems involves the question whether a patient has reached the Oedipus complex, or has reached it and retreated from it. The Oedipus complex is not merely an unconscious cluster of wish-fulfilling fantasies, nor do love and hate wishes within triangular relationships with either parent necessarily mean that structure formation has reached the oedipal level.

Clinically, the passionate love of the litle girl for her father is abandoned essentially for three reasons, or a combination of them: Mother won't allow it — a fear of the mother and her punishment — preoedipal reason; father doesn't respond — because he prefers the mother or other siblings — oedipal rejection proper; or the superego doesn't allow it. Only in relation to this last reason does the incest taboo play a central role. Patients differ with regard to which of these alternatives is the most crucial to psychic development.

Freud stated (1919) that the Oedipus complex, if not properly resolved, leaves a pervasive sense of inferiority throughout life. Its resolution and the building of self-regulating and autonomous structures depend on the capacity to cathect oedipal objects as separate. Ferenczi called the resolution of the Oedipus complex the most important experience of separation during childhood (quoted by Gedo and Goldberg, 1973). Only if objects are considered as separate and not as part of an earlier narcissistic self-structure is triangulation possible and only then can the oedipal experience become organized on a more mature level.

The Oedipus complex energizes all human activity. It is the source of both creativity and pathology. In creative persons bisexual wishes undergo a further transformation into creative activity itself. I believe that successful creative endeavor is achieved by the utilization of integrated bisexual wishes. Much of the creativity and richness of cultural life, including appreciation of the arts, but also much of the suffering imposed by neurotic illness, is derived from the Oedipus complex.

CONCURRENT DEVELOPMENTS INFLUENCED BY THE OEDIPUS COMPLEX

The positive Oedipus complex with its focus on triangulation, implies a new interest in the primal scene, with fantasies about sexual relations between the parents. The role of the child as an intruder leads to a high degree of sexual excitement, to fantasies of exposure, which contribute significantly to the shaping of the oedipal constellation.

Does a libidinal cathexis of motility and perception achieved within a primarily libidinal atmosphere with the *real* parents make primal scene experiences or fantasies easier to bear? Will looking, which becomes part of a libidinally cathected exploration leading to organized perception or motility—cathected with pleasure as the child seeks out the wonders of the environment—influence the extent to which parental lovemaking is tolerated by the girl during her phallic-oedipal phase? A less favorable environment may lead to a greater sense of isolation, or to narcissistic injury due to hostile fantasies connected to curtailed motility, distorted perception, and a sense of exclusion. These developing ego functions then influence the child's superego precursors.

In discussions of pavor nocturnus, the excessive overstimulation, sexual excitement, and infantile traumata of children have been noted where there has been close physical proximity during parental intercourse (Greenacre, 1967). Children whose parents have created a hostile atmosphere at home during the day fantasize a more sadistic version of intercourse and, as a result, are much more frightened. The child's ego resources and cognitive functions play a major role in fantasies and adaptive capacities related to primal scene experiences (Esman, 1973).

Freud was aware that masochism exists in both men and women: "[It] is easily verifiable . . . that . . . men often display a masochistic attitude—a state that amounts to bondage—towards women. What they reject is not passivity in general, but passivity towards a male" (1937). However, there is no biological or psychological evidence that boys or girls, or adults of either sex, wish to experience pain in conjunction with pleasure, unless they are suffering from a perversion. The position that a woman is not fulfilled in her self-feelings unless she has suffered the pain of childbirth has not been borne out by women patients.

The process of sexualization of pain seems to be an adaptive mechanism first mentioned by Freud (1924b), who called it "an economic problem" which may bind anxiety or hostility toward the object consciously or unconsciously held responsible for the pain, whether experienced as inflicted or fantasied by the child.

Freud spoke of a typical "female" masochism. He knew that masochism starting in childhood transcends gender differentiation and stems from excessive ambivalence toward introjected parental objects. Hostility not discharged against the object is turned against the self. Freud illustrated this clearly when he described the competitive and hostile feelings of children for siblings and parents in "A Child Is Being Beaten" (1919).

But the role of the mother as belonging to the fantasy of being beaten must now be added. Analysis provides abundant evidence that the girl in particular can experience pleasure only after she has rid herself of her guilt feelings toward her mother: the more hostile the relationship between mother and child, the more relentless and severe the beating fantasy will become.

Sadomasochistic fantasies from the preoedipal phase color the masturbation fantasies of the oedipal phase, and oedipal wishes in girls include a wished-for penetration, although the girl may consider this dangerous. Masochism has been observed to appear frequently when narcissistic rage is not properly discharged, as part of a syndrome related to yet unverbalizable traumatic events. The pain of surgery that has become sexualized in a girl's love for her surgeon would be an example.

SUPEREGO DEVELOPMENT

Freud postulated that the superego is formed through a "precipitate" of previous object choices, and that it represents a "gradient within the ego" which manifests itself after internalization of the parental figures following the oedipal phase (1923). When there have been difficulties in the internalization of parental representations, there will be a corresponding problem in impulse control. This will affect the nature of the oedipal experience. Sexual and hostile impulses and incestuous fantasies may then be acted out in adulthood affecting object choices. If the oedipal phase has been passed through normally, and internalization of oedipal conflicts has given way to more lasting identifications and character development, the superego will develop into a consolidated part of the psychic structure aiding in the selection of objects in adulthood.

We know that the beginnings of psychic structure formation are formed out of the capacity to delay gratification, whereupon the infant begins to internalize a loving maternal object. Although weaning, toilet training, separation problems, resolution of the rapprochement subphase, and the struggle to achieve object constancy all influence psychic structure formation and thereby the superego, it is the oedipal development, more than any other phase, that demands massive renunciation of unconscious sexual and hostile fantasies on the part of the growing child. Idealizing as well as critical attitudes toward parental objects help in forming the superego; they bind hostility, which would otherwise be turned against the self, and help to establish a firmer sense of identity in the child.

Although there are differences between boys and girls in the development of the superego, the evidence does not corroborate, as Freud maintained, that the female superego is more lenient or deficient, nor that superego development is primarily related to castration anxiety. In fact, the prevalence of depression in women, in part an outcome of frustrated ideals and aspirations, is considered to be an important indicator of the existence of a *severe* female superego (Jacobson, 1937). Referring to her 1937 article on the development of the superego under conditions of early disappointment, Jacobson (1964) stated: "I actually believe that because of the early onset of her castration conflict the little girl develops the nucleus of a true ego ideal even earlier than the little boy."

In the negative oedipal phase, there is an idealization of the mother and an identification with the father, whereas in the positive oedipal phase an idealization of the father and an identification with the mother takes place; both are instrumental in the formation of ego ideal and superego. As pointed out above, narcissistic injury and parental devaluation are likely to promote a serious narcissistic blow to the girl, heighten penis envy, and lead to identification with the father. Such a constellation often results in a fixation on the negative Oedipus complex. When objects are devalued, idealizations break down and lead to narcissistic character pathology (Chasseguet-Smirgel, 1970; Kernberg, 1975). If the ego ideal and superego have not yet been formed completely the child is unable to tolerate hostility-evoking experiences, and disillusionment and hostile devaluation of parents will cause her to suffer. Whether the female ego ideal will be part of a normal narcissistic self-structure depends on the girl's capacity to overcome her narcissistic injury, stemming from the "missing phallus phenomenon," on which other narcissistic problems have "landed." In narcissistic pathology a fantasy idealization of the mother will impede identification with the real mother on which an enduring object relationship could be based. If the girl succeeds in a stable identification with the mother, an integration of her bisexual needs will follow which will strengthen normal superego formation and will help in the formation of her oedipal and postoedipal internalizations.

The postoedipal superego loses some of the grandiosity and wishful fantasies of the preodipal and oedipal periods and becomes protective toward the self. Identifications are divested of the "preoedipal vicissitudes of aggression" (Hartmann et al., 1939). The superego helps the ego to control id derivatives and narcissistic strivings, and in general aids in impulse control. It also helps to build autonomous ego functions and reality testing (Stein, 1966). It is only after the superego has been formed that love, identification, or hostility can be directed toward one and the same object (Jacobson, 1964).

I shall conclude by presenting a profile study of several women patients who had been unable to achieve maternity. Difficulties in identification with both mother and father had prevented them from resolving oedipal conflicts in young adulthood. They had reached the oedipal level, but with a preponderance of unresolved preoedipal problems. The post-oedipal superego did not develop into a defensive structure adequate to deal with unresolved incestuous feelings, which remained characterologically active and later affected the choice of a mate.

The experience of motherhood, which consolidates individuation, depends on the girl's ability to loosen her preoedipal fixation to her mother. The struggle for liberation from the mother will fail if the split between good and bad has not healed. Blos pointed out recently (1980) that a girl may take flight into heterosexuality to cover her yearning for the preoedipal mother toward whom there has been too much ambivalence; hostility toward the mother may be deflected onto penis envy covered by an unconvincing heterosexuality. (This, incidentally, is a good example of "oedipalization" described earlier.)

My clinical profile demonstrates that oedipal development may remain partial and thereby create an internal conflict. Oedipal failure will consolidate during development when there is a shift from mother to father without sufficient previous identification with the mother. This takes place when hostile interaction between mother and girl dominates over the libidinal aspects of the relationship, or when an excessively maternal father causes confusion of parental roles and thereby influences subsequent identifications of the child.

The girl who is disappointed in her mother may identify with her as a sexual person ("the sexual vagina," Kestenberg, 1980), but be unable to identify with her maternal functions ("the non-sexual vagina," *ibid.*). The mother may appear as an independent, heterosexual woman loving the father (and with this the patient can identify, albeit as an excluded oedipal onlooker), or as having the characteristics of the threatening preoedipal mother "forcing" the patient into accepting an unwanted role.

Thus, if identifications with parents remain incomplete or confused, resulting in incomplete internalizations of the parents as a couple and of parent-child interactions, the oedipal experience will be fragmented. (Not only hostile but seductive behavior on the part of parents toward the child fragments identification processes.) Such experiences in childhood will influence the woman's choice of a mate and the strength of her wish to have a child. Failure in oedipal development may become manifest *at the point* when the young woman contemplating motherhood turns from a dyadic relationship with her mate toward a potentially triadic one including a child; conflicting identifications regarding parental and self-representations and a conflict between wishing to remain a child and having a child will influence her sense of feminine identity. On the conscious level this conflict may be expressed as a fear that having children will make intellectual or professional development impossible, or that professional success will increase the danger of not having a child.

The following character profile demonstrates that preoedipal and oedipal conflicts on various levels of identification with the parents stem from different developmental periods and coexist; conflicts from the negative and positive oedipal periods also exist simultaneously. These co-existing conflicts exert a lasting influence on the psychic reality of the girl. Oscillations of contradictory unconscious needs and wishes which affect her growth will reflect her later destiny as a young woman.

The group of women patients here described were between thirty and forty years old when they began to worry about their feminine destiny. They manifested differences in oedipal maturity and pathology in general. Many of them functioned well and without conflict in the external world, were ambitious and were thought of as achievers. They felt bewildered and distressed by the internal conflicts they encountered when they attempted to form a family and considered the prospect of having a child. Fantasies emanating from these conflicts were unconscious. There was a sense of personal failure associated with the danger of being unable to produce a child even while it was physiologically possible.*

These women had chosen lovers or mates whom they could not or did not wish to marry, or whom they did not consider suitable as potential fathers. (Sometimes the men had children from previous marriages, or, as it turned out, married and had children once their ties to these patients had ended.) The sudden realization by the women that they might not be able to have a child brought them to treatment.

From early childhood, these patients had been discouraged from expressing hostility toward parents or siblings. Without exception, they had become "little mothers," helping to take care of their own mothers' needs, as well as the needs of their younger siblings, at an age when children still experience being mothered as protective and pleasurable. Their mothers had been self-absorbed, sometimes worked, were frequently absent, and taught the eldest daughter how to care for the younger siblings, and how to relieve the mother of a great deal of responsibility. Sharing the maternal role tended to create a narcissistic alliance (Bergmann, M.V., 1980) which led to an incestuous closeness between mother and daughter. Separations in both rapprochement and oedipal phases were prevented by the narcissistic alliance (*Ibid*) and incestuous fantasies were ongoing, nurtured by the girl's role in her family.

Having shared the roles of mother and homemaker so intensely, the girl encountered greater difficulty during the oedipal phase in differentiating herself from the mother. As she narcissistically cathected her maternal role in the family, she felt oedipally "entitled" to replace either parent. A fixation on the preoedipal mother, kept alive by the girl's mothering role, also expressed itself in the wish to be a would-be wife to the father. Being thus enmeshed in an oedipal role toward each parent, phase-specific separation processes were curtailed.

The narcissistic bond with the mother and incestuous love for her oscillated with a virulent oedipal rivalry for the girl's father; an oedipal victory without struggle followed as these women experienced themselves as "exceptions" when they did not have to go through oedipal renunciation. Because of her intense emotional dependence on the child, the mother surrendered her role as the powerful oedipal rival whom the father loved and preferred. A strong wish to identify with the father and to take his place vis-à-vis the mother emerged as well, together with a growing hostility toward the younger siblings.

---

*Their fear of missing out on "having a child" as a most important experience in life appeared to be closely linked to social and psychological phenomena of our time. In the past these same women might have felt strong social pressure to marry and have children by a certain age, whether or not they felt emotionally prepared.

A precociously harsh superego helped repress rivalrous feelings toward the younger siblings, who, mothered by the parents *and* the eldest daughter, experienced a more carefree childhood than the patient. An overwhelming sense of guilt which drew its strength from the excessively strong incestuous ties of childhood resulted in failure to achieve autonomy and individuation.

As adults, these women revealed difficulties in differentiating their roles as prospective mothers from their experiences as children with their own mothers. Insufficient separation of the self from the mother in childhood led to the revival of infantile fantasies and fears of being "trapped" by motherhood. These were expressed by an anticipation that having a child would make marriage a new version of the "trap." There was an incapacity to visualize a life style in which professional and maternal life could be combined. Defensively some of the women identified with the phallic "forcing" mother and made life decisions for the men with whom they lived without consulting them. The phallic quest entered into a conflict with the women's ego ideal. Internalization of the "forcing" mother, sometimes on an oral or anal, but most frequently on a phallic, level, led to an organizing fantasy in which childbirth was perceived as "being forced," a state which would lead to a loss of autonomy. In treatment these women sometimes had the fantasy that having a child would "emasculate" them.

An external event, such as the marriage of a younger sibling or relative followed by the expectation of a first child, made these women seek analysis, often in a state of panic. An intensely conflict-laden sibling rivalry threatened to reach consciousness. There was a danger that preoedipal fixations and developmental arrests would surface in conflict with the wish to have a child. The patients reported "feeling stuck," and saw themselves in fantasy once more in the role of the outsider, the maiden aunt who would enviously witness the raising of a carefree and happy child. Typically, they identified with the new child, and not with the new parent. One patient put it thus: "I never realized that I didn't want a child for such a long time because I had not been mothered sufficiently myself."

The idea, "I want a child," was a narcissistic wish competing with the mother and excluding the father. Identification with the mother did not include the wish for a baby, but identification with the father did. It was therefore a restitutional wish in the service of overcoming a traumatic aspect of the preoedipal mother-child relationship which had interfered with subsequent oedipal identifications.

Mothers were accused of having burdened the patient with the responsibility of caring for the younger siblings in childhood, while at the same time having withheld permission to experience the pleasures of having a child. Idealized love feelings withdrawn from the disappointing mother appeared in transference as an idealized heterosexuality, which often covered disguised yearnings and love wishes toward the early preoedipal mother.

In the love relationship it initially appeared that the idealized mother had been "refound" in the sexual partner. He was idealized and unconsciously experienced as bisexual, a theme drawn from the preoedipal mother as well as from the maternal father. Anxiety and ambivalence stemming from the relationship with the preoedipal mother made it necessary to experience good mothering primarily from male lovers with strong maternal identifications. Good mothering was actively sought, but could be accepted only from members of the opposite sex who stood for a fused phallic parental representation, or for the idealized father with whom the patient identified.

Playing out the mother-child dyad with the lover, with a reversibility of roles in which the lover would become the child, made the relationship "very special" in view of the high degree of bisexuality and an unconscious living out of, and therefore an apparent disregard of, the incest taboo. Bisexual fantasies unresolved during the preoedipal and oedipal phases had surfaced again during adolescence or young adulthood. They appeared in analysis in the transference, in masturbation fantasies, or in the choice of unsuitable love-mates based on oedipal failure.

For a time, the adult heterosexual love relationship gave the partners the fantasy of triumph by symbolically circumventing the incest taboo. Forbidden oedipal incestuous wishes were lived out and experienced as a special "magic," often addictive in character; a fantasy of having an "exceptional relationship" nurtured the love tie. Being an "exception" made it possible to relive an aspect of the special narcissistic mother-child relationship and of the preoedipal tie toward the maternal father.

A mutual clinging, dyadic in nature (from the narcissistic phallic phase stemming from the early mother-child relationship), made it difficult for the lovers to remain apart and often strengthened resistance toward the expression of love themes in the transference. However, because of the tenuous link of the love relationship to reality, the prospect of realizing maternity remained a fantasy.

In these cases, a child was desired with only minimal participation of the prospective father. Since the child unconsciously represented the paternal phallus, as well as a link to the preoedipal tie to the mother, the fantasy of childbirth appeared as a threat of object loss as well as of castration. Frequently, the wish "to have a child" expressed itself by transitory maternal feelings toward the lover, sometimes by finding a mate decades younger or older. The wish to have a child even with an unsuitable mate relegated the father to an impermanent minor role.

A strong preoedipal tie to the father made sexual delineation more difficult, brought forth a greater tendency toward bisexual conflicts, and a need to maintain narcissistic omnipotent fantasies of merging with either parent. There was a stronger-than-usual unconscious wish that one could choose one's sex, or be mother, father, and child all at the same time.

The intensity of revenge feelings toward parents generated guilt feelings and overburdened these women's love relationships. Sometimes, revenge fantasies were displaced onto the would-be child.

The idealization of the love relationship had concealed hostile and incestuous fantasies forbidden by the superego. Thus, superego functions became linked to both building up and destroying the relationship. As soon as superego injunctions became projected upon the love partner, a third person was needed for the experience of the freedom to love, or the love relationship broke down and led to infantile regression and mourning. There was an incapacity of tolerating ambivalence within the "lover's dyad" because of the intensity of incestuous conflicts. Sometimes, the projection of hostility onto a third person involved in the triangle permitted displacement of envy and hostility for a certain period. The third person often represented the hated as well as envied mother. The relationship eventually broke down under this burden and the fantasy that had nurtured it had to be abandoned. Severe superego injunctions based on hostile wishes, ensuing guilt, and incestuous fixations prevented motherhood from becoming a reality. (No *real* child would be as satisfying as the "lover-child.") After passing the child-bearing age, these patients went into mourning, which sometimes represented a narcissistic regression, as the "lost child" represented the patient herself.

SUMMARY AND CONCLUSION

The evolution of a girl's feminine identity and of her Oedipus complex has been traced from "primary femininity," body-image formation, psychosexual phases, the subphases, and narcissistic and phallic strivings into a broader scheme of development. Sexual and aggressive drive derivatives and object relationships—developments crucial for the girl's maturation toward her Oedipus complex—were discussed. Identification with the mother in each crucial phase has been considered the most decisive feature for the development toward and resolution of the Oedipus complex of the girl.

Clinical work suggests that the girl has a more difficult task in overcoming her hostility toward her mother than has the boy, and that children of both sexes tend to experience greater hostility toward their mothers than their fathers. I suggested that "female" masochism is experienced by both boys and girls, and often appears in masturbation fantasies, particularly in the beating fantasies of children, in which a sado-masochistic object relationship between mother and child plays a prominent role.

A type of modern woman hitherto not described in analytic literature has emerged as someone who can identify with her mother's sexuality, but not with the mother's maternal role. A split identification, or high degree of ambivalence, and extensive bisexual conflicts too difficult to integrate into a coherent character structure were found to determine her internal conflicts. Crucial decisions related to the woman's adult role, her attitudes toward her career, her maternal role, and her future object choices were seen as determined by the nature of her preoedipal and oedipal identifications. An incapacity to move from dyadic to triangular object relationships prevented resolution of oedipal rivalry in adolescence. Thus, preparation and motivation toward motherhood were disturbed. There was often a strong oscillation between excessive closeness and wishes for merging with lovers, as well as separation anxiety and conflicts related to difficulties of individuation. The Oedipus complex thus did not appear as a permanent organization, and triangular relationships became revived and dissolved again.

REFERENCES

Abelin, E.L. (1971). The role of the father in the separation-individuation process. In *Separation-Individuation: Essays in Honor of Margaret S. Mahler*, eds. J.B. McDevitt and C.G. Settlage. New York: International Universities Press, pp. 229–252.

Arlow, J.A. (1969). Unconscious fantasy and disturbances of conscious experience. *Psychoanal. Q.* 38:1–27.

Barnett, M.C. (1966). Vaginal awareness in the infancy and childhood of girls. *J. Amer. Psychoanal. Assn.* 14:129–477.

Benedek, T. (1973). Parenthood as a developmental phase. *Psychoanalytic Investigations* New York: Quadrangle/The New York Times Book Co., pp. 378–407. Also presented in condensed form at the Fall Meeting of the American Psychoanalytic Association, Dec. 7, 1958, New York, and reprinted from the *J. Amer. Psychonanal. Assn.* III(3), July, 1959.

Blos, P. (1967). The second individuation process of adolescence. *The Psychoanalytic Study of the Child* 22:162.

———(1980). Modifications and Traditional Psychoanalytic Theory of Female Adolescent Development. Lecture delivered at the New York Psychoanalytic Institute, November, 11, 1980.

Bergmann, M.S. (1971). Psychoanalytic observations on the capacity to love. In *Separation: Individuation: Essays in Honor of Margaret S. Mahler*, eds. J.B. McDevitt and C.G. Settlage. New York: International Universities Press, pp.15–40.

Bergmann, M.V. (1980). On the genesis of narcissistic and phobic character formation in an adult patient: a developmental view. *Internat. J. of Psychoanal.* Vol. 61, 1980:535–546.

Blum, H. (1976). First Panel Report. The Psychology of Women. E.Galenson, reporter. *J. Amer. Psychoanal. Assn.* 24:105–108.

Bonaparte, M. (1953). Disturbing factors in feminine development. In *Female Sexuality*. New York: International Universities Press, pp. 46–61.

Brenner, C. (1979). Depressive affect, anxiety, and psychic conflict in the phallic-oedipal phase. *Psychoanal. Q.* 48(2):177–197.

Brunswick, R.M. (1940). The preoedipal phase of the libido development. In *The Psychoanalytic Reader*, ed. R. Fliess. New York: International Universities Press, 1948, pp. 261–284.

Byerly, L. (1976). First Panel Report. The Psychology of Women. E. Galenson, reporter. *J. Amer. Psychoanal. Assn.* 24:148–149.

Chasseguet-Smirgel, J. (1970). Feminine guilt and the oedipus complex. In *Female Sexuality, New Psychoanalytic Views*, by J. Chasseguet-Smirgel. Ann Arbor: University of Michigan Press, pp. 95–134.

———(1976a). Excerpts from Freud and female sexuality, the consideration of some blind spots in the exploration of the 'Dark Continent.' *Internat. J. Psycho-Anal.* 57-275.

———(1976b). Some thoughts on the ego ideal: a contribution to the study of the illness of ideality. *Psychoanal. Q.* 45:345–373.

Clower, V.L. (1977). Theoretical implications in current views of masturbation in latency girls. In *Female Psychology*, ed. H.P. Blum. New York: International Universities Press, pp. 109–127.

Coleman, R. Kris, E. and Provence, S. (1953). The study of variations of early parental attitudes: a preliminary report. *The Psychoanalytic Study of the Child* 8:20–47.

Edgcumbe, R. (1976), in collaboration with Sara Lundberg, Randi Markowitz and Frances Sale. Some comments on the concepts of the negative oedipal phase in girls. *The Psychoanalytic Study of the Child* 31:35–61.

Edgcumbe, R. and Burgner, M. (1975). The phallic-narcissistic phase: a differentiation between preoedipal and oedipal aspects of phallic development. *The Psychoanalytic Study of the Child* 30:161–180. New Haven: Yale University Press.

Esman, A. (1973). The primal scene: a review and a reconsideration. *The Psychoanalytic Study of the Child* 29:49–83. New Haven: Yale University Press.

Fenichel, O. (1945). *The Psychoanalytic Theory of Neurosis.* New York: W.W. Norton.

———(1953). Specific forms of the Oedipus complex. In *Collected Papers of Otto Fenichel.* First Services. New York: W.W. Norton, pp. 181–203.

Freud, A. (1971). The infantile neurosis: genetic and dynamic considerations. *The Psychoanalytic Study of the Child* 26:79–90.

———(1922). Beating fantasies and daydreams. In *The Writings of Anna Freud, Introduction to Psychoanalysis*, vol. I. New York: International Universities Press, 1974.

Freud, S. (1897). Extracts from the Fliess papers. *Standard Edition* 1:175–280.

———(1900). *Interpretation of Dreams*, part I, vol. V. London: Hogarth Press, 1953.

———(1905). Three essays on the theory of sexuality. *Standard Edition* 7:125–243.

———(1914). On narcissism. *Standard Edition* 14:67–102.

———(1919). "A child is being beaten." *Standard Edition* 17:177–204.

———(1920a). Beyond the pleasure principle. *Standard Edition* 18:7–67.

———(1920b). The psychogenesis of a case of homosexuality in a woman. *Standard Edition* 18:145–174.

———(1923). The ego and the id. *Standard Edition* 6:3–66.

———(1924a). The dissolution of the Oedipus complex. *Standard Edition* 19:173–179.

———(1924b). The economic problem of masochism. *Standard Edition* 19:157–170.

———(1925). Some psychical consequences of the anatomical distinction between the sexes. *Standard Edition* 19:243–258.

———(1926). Inhibitions, symptoms, and anxiety. *Standard Edition* 20:77–175.

———(1931). Female sexuality. *Standard Edition* 21:223–243.

———(1933). New introductory lectures on psycho-analysis. *Standard Edition* 22:3–182.

———(1937). Analysis, terminable and interminable. *Standard Edition* 23:209–254.

Galenson, E. (1976). First Panel Report. The Psychology of Women. E. Galenson, reporter. *J. Amer. Psychoanal. Assn.* 24:141–160.

———(1978). Second Panel Report. The Psychology of Women. E. Galenson, reporter. *J. Amer. Psychoanal. Assn.* 26:163–177.

Galenson, E., and Roiphe, H. (1971). The impact of early sexual discovery on mood, defensive organization, and symbolization. *The Psychoanalytic Study of the Child* 26:195–216.

Gedo, J., and Goldberg, A. (1973). *Models of the Mind.* Chicago and London: The University of Chicago Press.

Gitelson, M. (1951). Re-evaluation of the role of the Oedipus complex. *Internat. J. Psycho-Anal.* 33:351–354.

Greenacre, P. (1967). The influence of infantile trauma on genetic patterns. In *Emotional Growth.* New York: International Universities Press, 1971, pp. 260–299.

————(1953). Penis awe and its relation to penis envy. In *Drives, Affects, Behavior*, ed. R.M. Loewenstein. New York: International Universities Press, pp. 176–190.

Grossman, W. (1976). Freud and female sexuality. *Internat. J. Psycho-Anal*. 57:275–305.

Grossman, W., and Stewart W. (1976). Penis envy: from childhood wish to developmental metaphor. In *Female Psychology*, ed. H.P. Blum. New York: International Universities Press, pp. 193–212.

Hartmann, H. (1939). *Ego Psychology and The Problem of Adaptation*. New York: International Universities Press, 1958.

Hartmann, H., et al. (1949). Notes on the theory of aggression. *The Psychoanalytic Study of the Child* 3(4):9–36. New York: International Universities Press.

Hoffer, (1949). Mouth, hand, and ego-integration. *The Psychoanalytic Study of the Child* 3(4):49–56.

————(1950). Development of the body ego. *The Psychoanalytic Study of the Child* 5:18–24.

Horney, K. (1926). The flight from womanhood. *Internat. J. Psycho-Anal*. 7:324–339.

————(1932). The dread of women. *Internat. J. Psycho-Anal*. 13:348–360.

————(1933). The denial of the vagina. *Internat. J. Psycho-Anal*. 14:57–70.

Jacobson, E. (1937). The effect of disappointment on ego and superego formation in normal and depressive development. *Psychoanal. Rev*. 33:129–147 (1946).

————(1964). *The Self and the Object World*. New York: International Universities Press.

Jones, E. (1911). *Papers on Psycho-Analysis*. London: Bailliere, Tindall & Cox, 1948.

————(1933). The phallic phase. *Internat. J. Psycho-Anal*. 14:1–33.

————(1935). Early female sexuality. In *Papers on Psycho-Analysis*, pp. 485–495. London:

Kernberg, O. (1975). *Borderline Conditions and Pathological Narcissism*. New York: Jason Aronson.

Kernberg, O. (1977). Boundaries and structure in love relations. *J. Amer. Psychoanal. Assn*. 25:81–114.

Kestenberg, J. (1956). Vicissitudes of female sexuality. *J. Amer. Psychoanal. Assn*. 4:453–476.

————(1968). Outside and inside, male and female. *J. Amer. Psychoanal. Assn*. 16:457–520.

————(1971). From organ-object imagery to self and object representations. In *Separation-Individuation: Essays in Honor of Margaret S. Mahler*. New York: International Universities Press, pp. 75–99.

————(1980). The three faces of femininity. *The Psychoanal. Rev.*, vol. 67, no. 3, Fall 1980, pp. 313–335.

Kleeman, J. (1976). Freud's views on early female sexuality in the light of direct child observation. *Female Psychology*. New York: International Universities Press, pp. 3–28.

Klein, M. (1928). *The Psycho-Analysis of Children*. New York: Norton, 1932.

————(1949). Early stages of the oedipal conflict and of super-ego formation. In *Psychoanalysis of Children*. London: Hogarth Press, p. 179.

Kris, E. (1951). Some comments and observations on early autoerotic activities. *The Psychoanalytic Study of the Child* 6:9–17, 47.

Lampl-De Groot, J. (1952). *The Development of the Mind*, New York: International Universities Press, 1965.

Lewin, B. (1933). The body as phallus. *Psychoanal. Quart* 2:24–47.

Lichtenberg, J. (1978). The testing of reality from the standpoint of the body self. *J. Amer. Psychoanal. Assn*. 26(2):357–385.

Loewald, H. (1970). Psychoanalytic theory and the psychoanalytic process. In *The Psychoanalytic Study of the Child*, XXV. New York: International Universities Press, pp. 45–63.

————(1973). On internalization. *Internat. J. Psycho-Anal*. 54:9–17.

————(1979). The waning of the Oedipus complex *J. Amer. Psychoanal. Assn*. 27:751–775.

McDevitt, J. (1975). Separation-individuation and object constancy. *J. Amer. Psychoanal. Assn*. 23:713–739.

Mahler, M. (1958). In Panel: Problems of identity. D. Rubinfine, reporter. *J. Amer. Psychoanal. Assn.* 6:131–142.

——(1966). Notes on the development of basic moods: the depressive affect. In *Psychoanalysis—A General Psychology*, eds. R.M. Loewenstein et al. New York: International Universities Press.

——(1971). A study of the separation-individuation process: and its possible application to borderline phenomena in the psychoanalytic situation. *The Psychoanalytic Study of the Child* 26:403–424.

——(1975). On the current status of the infantile neurosis. *J. Amer. Psychoanal. Assn.* 23:323–333.

——, and Furer, M. (1968). *On Human Symbioses and the Vicissitudes of Individuation*. New York: International Universities Press.

——, and McDevitt, J. (1968). Observations on adaptation and defense *in statu nascendi*: developmental precursors in the first two years of life. *Psychoanal. Q.* 37:1–21.

Moore, B. (1976). Freud and female sexuality: a current view. *Internat. J. Psycho-Anal.* 57:287–300.

Muller, J. (1970). Psychoanalytic views on female sexuality: opposed to those of Freud. In *Female Sexuality, New Psychoanalytic Views.*, ed. J. Chasseguet-Smirgel. Ann Arbor: University of Michigan Press.

Rangell, L. (1972). Aggression, Oedipus and historical perspective. *Internat. J. Psycho-Anal.* 53:3–11.

Roiphe, H., and Galenson, E. (1973). The infantile fetish. *The Psychoanalytic Study of the Child* 28:147–168.

Shapiro, T. (1977). Oedipal distortions in severe character pathologies: developmental and theoretical considerations. *Psychoanal. Q.* 46:559–579.

Spitz, R. (1955). The primal cavity: a contribution to the genesis of perception and its role for psychoanalytic theory. *The Psychoanalytic Study of the Child* 10:215–240.

Stein, M. (1966). Self-observation, reality, and the superego. In *Psychoanalysis—A General Psychology*, eds. R.M. Loewenstein et al. New York: International Universities Press.

Stoller, R. (1968). *Sex and Gender*. New York: Science House.

——(1977). Primary femininity. *Female Psychology*. New York: International Universities Press, pp. 58–78.

Ticho, G. (1978). Female autonomy and young adult women. In *Female Psychology*, ed. H.P. Blum. New York: International Universities Press, pp. 139–156.

Tolpin, M. (1971). On the beginnings of a cohesive self. *The Psychoanalytic Study of the Child* 26:316–353.

Weil, A. (1970). The basic core. *The Psychoanalytic Study of the Child* 25:442–461.

7

The Latency Period

MARTIN A. SILVERMAN

The concept of a latency period in the development of children first appeared in a letter from Sigmund Freud to Wilhelm Fliess in 1896 (see Letter 46 in Bonaparte, A. Freud, and Kris, 1954). A number of years later, Freud put together an outline of psychosexual development (1905), in which he described latency as uniquely human and of considerable importance. He observed that the prolonged, relatively quiet period intercalated between the emotional storms of the first five or six years and the intense, adolescent turmoil that begins at age twelve or thirteen provides human beings with a significant developmental advantage. It affords an invaluable opportunity to build up and develop the defensive and intellectual apparatus with which we are able to regulate and transform our instinctual urges so as to be capable of leading a civilized, orderly existence as adults.

Freud's clinical researches indicated to him that the latency period's emergence is intimately connected with efforts to resolve the powerful, emotional struggles of which the Oedipus complex is comprised. It lasts until the influx of a powerful increment of increased drive tension at puberty overwhelms the ego's resources and upsets the fortuitous balance of psychological forces that prevails during the period of latency.

Since 1905, psychoanalytic research has greatly expanded our understanding of the latency period, both in general and as it is traversed differently by children of either sex. We know, for example, that the Oedipus complex is far from being fully resolved by six years of age. Its apparent disappearance at that time actually results from a combination of partial resolution, and, perhaps even more important, the utilization of multiple defense mechanisms to suppress, disguise, and divert its expression into acceptable, derivative forms so that it is rendered much less accessible to view, either by the child or by outside observers. In other words, the struggle to contain and resolve the powerful, mutually conflicting urges that make up the Oedipus complex continues throughout the latency period, although much more covertly than before its advent.

It is not clear whether there is an actual diminution of drive pressures during this time of life or if the picture that obtains results entirely from ego activities carried out by the psychological structures that have been developing before and during that time of life. One possibility is that there is a qualitative rather than a quantitative change in the nature of the demands placed upon the ego during latency. Yazmajian (1965) has offered an hypothesis, for example, in which he emphasizes that waves of reorganization of sexual and aggressive drive tensions, each of which imposes a new set of strains upon the individual's defensive and executive apparatus, tax the ego's resources severely during the prelatency years. By the time latency begins, however, the process of maturational unfolding that has been responsible for this reorganizational sequence has more or less spun itself out, so that the ego is no longer presented with new problems to be resolved. If this hypothesis is correct, the latency period is ushered in in part by an easing of the work required of the ego, since it no longer has to devise novel solutions for new dilemmas, but can concentrate upon reinforcing and improving the efficiency of the modes which it already has developed. The latter, of course, is much easier than the former.

Multiple defensive and executive modes are involved in the transition from the oedipal stage to that of latency. They include repression, regression, reaction-formation, avoidance, displacement, intellectualization, fantasy-formation, identification, self-control and abnegation (at times approaching altruistic surrender), and sublimation (see Blos, 1962; Bornstein, 1951; Fenichel, 1945; A. Freud, 1936; S. Freud, 1923b, 1924; Fries, 1958; Sarnoff, 1971, 1976). Ego development, in which defensive and conflict-free aspects are interwoven, is the central feature of latency as a developmental phenomenon. In this work, the development of girls during the latency period will be examined with regard to each of these various modalities of ego activity and the maturational and developmental problems to which they are applied.

REPRESSION

Repression plays a very prominent role among the defensive operations of the latency period. Oedipal interests are partly renounced by the average six year old, (along with partial desexualization of feelings toward one's parents and heightening of tender, affectionate attitudes toward them). In large part, however, the sexual interests are merely excluded from consciousness. The capacity for repression at this time of life is heightened, as Sarnoff (1971) has emphasized, by the appearance between six and seven years of age of concrete operational thinking (see Piaget, 1947; Silverman, 1971).

With the shift from preoperational to operational thinking, as with any major advance in cognitive organization, memory is affected in the direction of suppression and transformation of memories organized according to the cognitive mode that has been given up in favor of a new one. Since the human psyche tends to make efficient use of phenomena for multiple purposes (Nunberg, 1930), this suppressive tendency is seized upon to effect a massive repression of the urges, yearnings, and events of the preoperational years. The widespread amnesia that results wipes the painful narcissistic defeats and insoluble dilemmas of the oedipal and preoedipal periods all but completely out of consciousness, leaving only a few screen memories as a link with the past. One dramatic effect of this amnesia is the almost total lack of recall experienced by second graders of the events and people known to them in nursery school only a couple of years earlier.

For several reasons, there is less urgency for latency age girls to relinquish or repress their oedipal interest in their fathers than there is for boys to suppress parallel feelings toward their mothers:

First there is both less danger from and less societal opposition to incestuous feelings by girls toward their fathers than there is in boys toward their mothers. This seems to derive in part from the lesser threat to personal integrity and autonomy associated with urges to unite and merge with the father than accompanies the yearning to reunite with the mother, who once was perceived as an undifferentiated, integral part of the self (see Jacobson, 1964; Kernberg, 1975; Kohut, 1971). The yearning to be intimately embraced by and united with the father offers the early latency girl a welcome pathway through which to obtain relief from the powerful pull she experiences toward her mother as her primary object. It also offers her the possibility of soothing narcissistic injuries associated with anatomical differences and with inability to compete with and for her mother as a valued, superiorly endowed object of her loving inclinations and narcissistic yearnings.

Second, the more advanced ego controls of the more precocious and capable girl, as compared with those of the fidgety, less well controlled boy of the same age, make the girl more confident that she will be able to control her urges. She does not need, therefore, to disavow them so thoroughly as does the boy.

Freud (1931, 1933), postulated that, since girls are not pursued by the terror of castration as a fantasied, violent punishment for their oedipal strivings, they are not so drastically impelled as boys to give them up. A number of early psychoanalytic investigators questioned this. Karen Horney (1933) observed terror of being torn apart and destroyed as she reconstructed this phase of life with her adult patients. Ernest Jones (1927) felt that there was evidence of intense fear of punitive destruction of the genitals and of their potential for providing pleasure, which he considered to be comparable to the threat of castration in boys. Melanie Klein (1932) perceived evidence of terror in little girls of being attacked, devoured, mutilated, and destroyed by their mothers, which she traced to "projective identification" of their own aggressive, destructive urges toward their mothers.

The extent to which girls are motivated to give up their oedipal strivings partly out of fear of retaliative genital injury, parallelling the boy's terror of castration, remains a moot question to this day. It is clear, however, that a girl's Oedipus complex is more complicated than that of the boy, and that the girl's wish to obtain something from her father (a baby, his penis, and narcissistic supplies) pulls her toward him and keeps her positive oedipal strivings alive and active throughout latency. This contrasts sharply with the boy's need to suppress and repress his oedipal, sexual fantasies out of the terror of losing a highly prized and intensely cathected body part, as well as to ward off the humiliating, narcissistic injury of being unable to compete successfully with his bigger, more powerful, superiorly endowed father.

The girl's inability to give up her oedipal yearnings toward her father even though she cannot possibly hope to compete for his favors with her mother puts her in a very difficult position. She cannot give up the struggle, and at the same time she cannot hope to escape defeat. She is caught on the horns of a narcissistic dilemma in which she is drawn toward her father to repair the wounds she has suffered in her preoedipal relationship with her mother only to face defeat and failure once again. This is coupled with a poignant feeling of loss of the mother who had initially been the principal object of her love. This contributes to a striking difference between early latency boys and girls in the form taken by their predominant clinical symptomatology. Boys of five or six to eight years of age who are brought to child guidance clinics or to mental health professionals for assistance tend in general to be brought because of behavioral and learning problems, consonant with the difficulty they experience at that time of life in controlling and repressing their troublesome sexual and aggresive impulses. Girls of the same age, on the other hand, tend to be brought for assistance largely because of depressive manifestations, i.e., sadness, low self-esteem, and withdrawal. Normative observations of boys and girls of this age group point in the same direction. The problems presented to latency age girls by their feelings of narcissistic injury and defeat will be taken up at greater length later in this article.

Another related consequence of the persistence of positive oedipal strivings in early latency girls is the frequent presence of masochistic fantasies. This commonly takes the form of a phobic preoccupation with the idea of a robber entering the house and kidnapping her, killing her by stabbing her with a knife, or shooting her. When analyzed, either directly in latency or retrospectively in adult women, such fantasies are traceable to a combination of oedipal themes. One component is the wish to be penetrated, ripped open, and impregnated by her father's seemingly huge phallus, at the same time that phallic awe (see Greenacre, 1947) and the dread of sexual excitement (see Fraiberg, 1972) render the wish terrifying. A second set of themes consists of the guilty wish to be punished in kind for wanting to kill her mother and steal away her father and the sexual love and babies that he gives to her on the one hand, and on the other, wanting to castrate and kill her father and older brothers to punish them for rejecting her in favor of her mother. There are multiple variations of this core, female latency age fantasy, as is illustrated by the many forms in which it is expressed in such popular fairy tales as Cinderella, Beauty and the Beast, Rapunzel, and The Little Match Girl, to name but a few. Bluebeard is a prime example of its expression in the books and stories that are popular with school age girls. These fairy tales and stories contain masochistically organized, oedipal themes which stress the absence or loss of the loving, giving, protective mother of early childhood; deprivation, imposition of harsh tribulations, and primitive attack by a wicked stepmother or an evil, jealous witch; the shadowy presence of a helpless or ineffective father who is dominated and controlled by the wicked witch or stepmother; the struggle to finally be united with a rich and handsome prince; and/or an encounter with a frightening, ugly, or dangerously powerful animal who turns into a devoted prince once he is tamed by the girl's goodness and love. One or more of these elements can be present in a single tale, or they can be divided among several of them. They offer the latency age girl an opportunity to externalize her masochistic fantasies and to put them into an organized, controlled form in which their frightening horrible nature is mitigated by sharing them with other girls who are going through similar (and, therefore, presumably normal) preoccupations.

REGRESSION AND REACTION-FORMATION

Children of five or six are unable to fully renounce their oedipal desires or even to exclude them completely from consciousness, since they have not yet developed strong enough secondary process mechanisms to accomplish the task. Repression has to be supplemented, therefore, by additional mechanisms of defense. One of the most important of these is *regression* to a preoedipal drive organization in which the sadistic-anal component is the most prominent, although oral and phallic phase derivatives also can be observed. As will be discussed more fully later on, masturbatory impulses are warded off (and disguised when they are acted upon), and there is reversion to the total body activity accompanied by pleasurable kinesthetic sensations of the sadistic-anal period. The intellectual activity that is the hallmark of latency and the use of paints, crayons, and clay that is prominent at that time stem in part from regression to the interests of that earlier phase. The same can be said for the collecting of books, autographs, paper dolls, stamps, etc., that is a feature in the life of elementary school girls. Even the tendency of latency age children to turn away from their parents and to other people contains an element of defiance and refusal to acknowledge parental authority and importance.

Because of the regressive reactivation of sadistic primal scene fantasies that take place during latency, the observation of quarrels between parents provokes a great deal of excitement in children of this age. The fighting and squabbling that take place among latency age children appear in part to derive from regressively experienced erotic urges. In early latency, girls tend to cluster in small groups within which there are tendencies both to pair off as best friends with one other girl and to either intrude into a twosome to take away someone else's best friend or to maintain a vigilant watch lest one's own best friend be stolen away. Although the best friend is a treasured love object with whom shared secrets, intimacy, and sleepovers are cherished, there tend to be repeated quarrels and periodic discord that threaten to disrupt the relationship. Looking into this, one can see derivatives of oedipal, triangular rivalry (positive as well as negative) and of the possessiveness and the sadistic impulses to torture and hurt that characterize preoedipal relationships. In the latter part of latency, girls tend to congregate in larger groups and to victimize a few individuals via teasing, exclusion from membership in the group, or even physical attacks.

Anal interests at times are expressed directly, especially early in latency. They can take the form, for example, of refusal to bathe or of hiding dirty clothes (including fecally stained underpants) in the closet or under the bed. Oral impulses are expressed in gum chewing, thumb sucking and nail biting, or material acquisitiveness. Phallic or genital-urethral interests are demonstrated in a variety of ways, such as occasional enuresis, intense competitiveness, or exhibitionism, e.g., in academics, dramatics, and sports. (The narcissistic exhibitionism of the earlier sadistic-anal phase also contributes to the exhibitionism of latency.)

At least as prominent as the direct expression of these regressive urges are the *reaction-formations* that are developed against them. Especially in the first half of latency, there is an intense struggle not only against oedipal urges, but also against the preoedipal ones to which regressive flight has been taken. Pain is taken to acquire courtesy, fairness, generosity, and cleanliness. For several reasons, the struggle against preoedipal urges tends to be more successful in girls than in boys. There is a biological factor in their favor in that their smaller size and muscular power render sadistic and destructive urges less dangerous and easier to control. In general, girls are more regular in their rhythms and possess better intrinsic organization and control over impulses than do boys throughout prelatency and latency. Society also tends to tolerate much less aggressiveness in girls than in boys; it joins with and reinforces their inclinations to maintain order and control over their urges. Parents and society as a whole tend to expect better manners and behavior from girls and to condition them toward better self-regulation than it does with boys. In addition, a girl's identification with her mother, stemming from recognition of their membership in the same sex and the wish to be like her, directs her toward softer, gentler, more modulated and patterned behavior than that of her brother, who is expected and expects to be rougher, tougher, more impulsive, and more aggressive.

Another consequence of the regression to pregenitality is that masturbation fantasies contain strong sadomasochistic elements during latency. This contributes significantly to the aversion they feel toward masturbation and to the intensity with which they exert effort to suppress, disguise, and cover it up. Latency age children will use obsessional rituals to control and ward off masturbatory urges; bedtime rituals, in which the child must lie motionless on one particular side facing one particular direction and with the bedclothes arranged just so, are quite common among girls as well as boys. Obsessional doubting and mild compulsions, such as taking repeated showers or maintaining symmetry in a doing-undoing fashion, often appear. The connection with sadomasochistic impulses and the masturbatory urges with which they are associated are epitomized in the touching rituals (e.g., the compulsion to touch every slat in a picket fence) and avoidance rituals (e.g., stepping over cracks in the sidewalk—"step on a crack and break your mother's back"—and over the chalklines in hopscotch games) so common during latency.

The intense guilt that sadistic impulses engender contributes to a tendency to be kind and helpful to others or even to take up the plight of afflicted peoples, walk miles in a walkathon to raise money for the needy, root for the underdog, lavish tender care upon pets, etc. That these trends are reactive against opposing feelings is revealed in the intermittent outbreaks of sadistic behavior and fantasy expression that are quickly suppressed. Latency age children also demonstrate reaction-formations against phallic-exhibitionistic impulses, e.g., shame about nakedness.

AVOIDANCE AND DISPLACEMENT

One of the hallmarks of latency is movement away from parents, in part to avoid the dangerous temptations and narcissistic defeats associated with the oedipal pull toward them. Children begin to shift at the beginning of latency from devoted attachment to their parents to involvement with peers, siblings, teachers, and selected adults outside the immediate family. The same little girl who at four or five ran up to her daddy when he got home at night, squealing with excitement and expressing eagerness to climb on his lap or to wrestle with him, at six or seven tends to be much too busy with her friends to even notice his arrival.

An important aspect of the movement away from the parents that takes place during latency is that the parents are de-idealized, at least consciously. They cease being revered as seemingly omniscient, omnipotent beings, as teachers and other adults outside the family are idealized as new authority figures. This shift coincides with the crushes on older brothers, uncles, and TV and movie stars that replace girls' attachment to their fathers as they enter the latency period. A facet of the de-idealization of parents during latency to which Freud (1909) called attention many years ago is the so-called "family romance" fantasy in which children imagine themselves to have come from much more illustrious families than those of which they actually are a part. Dickens captured this fantasy in *Oliver Twist*, a book that is very popular with latency age children. The concern by very many school age children that they have been adopted stems in part from the family romance wish that they actually were born of aristocratic parents. The twin fantasies common among this age group owe their origin in part to this same source, as illustrated by Twain's *The Prince and the Pauper* and the Gilbert and Sullivan operetta *The H.M.S Pinafore*.

With the shift away from the parents, peer relations become more important. Not only does the actual time spent in activities with other children increase markedly, but the intensity of emotional ties to friends and schoolmates climbs sharply as well. The views and opinions of other children become very important, as do the clothes they wear and the possessions they acquire. After-school and weekend activities, visits and sleepovers with other children become extremely important during the latency years. Social relations assume increasing meaning and the insider-outsider dichotomy of the oedipal triangle is replaced by that established through the formation of social groups and cliques in which membership is limited. Leadership roles in these groups, which are even more prominent and more tightly defined and organized among girls than among boys, tend to be established as much as a result of boldness, confidence, and adroitness in relating to and managing people as they are out of intelligence, attractiveness, strength, and/or athletic prowess. More often than not, girls take the lead in initiating, organizing, and maintaining order in the boy-girl games and activities that take place during latency. This is consonant with the more precociously and more well developed intellectual, integrative, and social capacities which they possess during the prelatency and latency years. The lead which girls show in this regard appears to be derived from a combination of differences in inherent disposition, greater societal expectation and encouragement, and the need for girls to rely more upon wile and intellectual skill than upon brute force in their relationships with boys.

The sexes tend to be carefully separated from one another, not only socially, but in general. Boys tend to express disdain for girls at this age and girls look down on boys as wild, unruly, immature roughnecks. That these conscious attitudes are defensive in nature is reflected in the periodic breakthrough of a crush on a boy or even of the brief, short-lived acquisition of a boyfriend. The usual picture that prevails includes intense repression, displacement, avoidance, and disavowal of interest in the opposite sex, punctuated only by brief, self-limited expressions of such interest. Where there is, instead, ongoing, open interest in children of the opposite sex during latency, this is usually an indication of hyperstimulation and ego weakness. The latter is usually indicated as well by signs of nervousness, concentration and attention disturbances, underachievement in school, and behavioral problems. This was illustrated by an underachieving, borderline nine year old boy who stated: "I used to think I was different from other kids because I liked girls. But I'm beginning to see that I wasn't really so different from them as I thought. In second and third and fourth grade, all the boys like girls and all the girls like boys, but they can't show that they like them. They have to hide that they like each other. They even hide it from themselves. That's why it bothered them when I showed I liked girls. But I couldn't help myself."

The games in which school-age children engage when they do play with one another often reflect the sexual currents which they otherwise attempt to avoid. This is especially so in the early part of the latency period, when ego resources are not yet strong enough to consistently prevent impulses from escaping out of repression. When they play house or school the activity appears to be innocent enough; however, analytic investigation often traces the former to an interest in taking part in the more sensual aspects of married life (a variation in early latency, in fact, consists in acting out a wedding ceremony) and the latter to wishes to learn the sexual secrets possessed by adults. Playing doctor, with its focus upon bodily exploration and examination, reflects in less disguised form the sexual excitement and curiosity that largely motivate children to take part in these games. The insertion of a "thermometer" into body openings is an important feature of the doctor game. Games involving forfeits, such as the requirement that one kiss a child of the opposite sex or expose one's buttocks or genitals to others, are not rare, but they are not generally known to the adult world because they usually are carried out far from the gaze of disapproving adult eyes. Being *required* to carry out these acts circumvents superego opposition via the fiction that one is being forced to do so and by the provision of group sanction for them. The game aspect also provides the safety of rules, so that the danger of things getting out of control is greatly reduced.

Episodes of a boy and girl exposing their genitals to one another are often followed by pangs of remorse and anxiety over the sexual excitement that is experienced. At times, relief is obtained from the feelings of guilt and anxiety by one or the other managing to let their parents find out what they have done. Although the girl is frequently as much the active initiator of the activity as is the boy, more often than not it is the girl who reveals the "crime" and the boy who is blamed and punished for it. When a girl is led into genital exposure by another girl, which also occurs with relative frequency during latency, she rarely reports it to her parents. Analytic investigation indicates that when a girl reveals that she has engaged in mutual exhibitionistic activity with a boy and thereby gets him into trouble she usually is doing more than evading her feelings of guilt by blaming the activity on someone else. There also appears to be an element of vengeful retribution involved in her behavior, i.e., she is acting out the hurt and anger she feels toward her father and brother for rejecting her as a love object in favor of her mother; in addition, she resents their possessing the external genital organs which she lacks and which are associated with her mother's having turned to them instead of her as objects of her love.

Everything which has been stated above with regard to the latency age girl's relations with her peers also applies to her relationships with her siblings. Sibling relations are very important during this developmental period, both in their own right and in terms of the use of brothers and sisters as displacement figures to substitute for the oedipal parents. Since siblings are themselves subject to oedipal taboos, albeit less intensely than those which apply to parents, the order of displacement by and large is from the parents to the siblings and finally to the peer group.

An important aspect of a latency age girl's peer relations is her need for a best friend. Although a boy of the same age demonstrates a similar need, it is far more striking and urgent in a girl; the loss of a girl who was her best friend not infrequently is experienced as extremely traumatic and can be followed by long lasting depression or despair. Disruption of the best friend relationship by the two girls' respective families has even led in rare instances to a Romeo and Juliet-like joint suicide.

A latency age girl's relationship with her best friend is subject at times to jealous guarding against intrusion by a third girl that is reminiscent of the oedipal triangular relationship. It owes its intensity and urgency, in fact, to its evolution out of the Oedipus complex. The best friend relationship of the latency age girl derives partly from displacement of her positive oedipal yearnings toward her father, regressively reworked into a homosexual theme that affords relief from the bitter narcissistic injuries that his rejection of her as a love object entails. The intense relationship with the best friend provides a solution in which the post-oedipal girl can turn away not only from her father, but from all males, and instead love and be loved by a girl like herself. It is closely related to the twin fantasy that is very common among latency age girls, far more so than among boys of the same age group. The best friend also represents a displacement figure for the mother who was initially the primary love object in an intense preoedipal and early, negative oedipal relationship (see Brunswick, 1940). The latter was lost when her mother was experienced as having rejected her in favor of her father and brothers, when she rejected her mother as a love object out of hatred for her as a real and imagined source of multiple deprivations and of intense, positive oedipal rivalry. Usually the sexual and aggressive conflicts underlying the intensity of the best friend relationship are intensely repressed and sublimated, but its platonic nature often is intermittently punctuated by brief episodes of frankly homosexual activity (e.g., by one girl "teaching" the other to masturbate during a sleepover visit together) and by periodic quarrels and discord between them.

The latency period is a time of mushrooming ego development in which there is a mutually advantageous interweaving of defensive activity and primary autonomous functioning. This is especially apparent with regard to the cognitive advances that are made during this phase. As Piaget (Inhelder and Piaget, 1959) has demonstrated, the onset of latency coincides with a reorganizational leap from preoperational to concrete operational thinking that unfolds and expands throughout the school age years. This is a very significant step, both from the vantage point of its effect upon general ego development and from that of the specific shifts in the child's defensive armamentarium that takes place during latency.

Freud (1911) and Piaget (1940), proceeding through very different avenues of inquiry, each concluded that thought consists of trial action in which experimentation upon the symbolic, mental representations of things in the world provides an enormous increase in efficiency and mastery. Freud described emotional growth as resulting from the progressive advance from primary process functioning, characterized by peremptory discharge and immediate gratification, to the reflective delay and rational decision-making that characterizes the secondary process. Piaget's description of the development of operational thinking that takes place during the latency years, culminating in the emergence of truly hypothetico-deductive, abstract reasoning at the interface between latency and adolescence, closely corresponds to the progression from primary to secondary process to which Freud ascribed such great developmental importance (see Silverman, 1971, for a fuller explication). The spurt that takes place in cognitive development during latency is a measure of the extensive ego growth that takes place in general during the latency period, facilitating movement toward independence and self-sufficiency. The enormous time and energy expended in learning is not only invaluable for its own sake, but also contributes to the building up of general ego strength via the growth of logical thought.

The intellectual progression that takes place in latency does more than improve ego strength in general, however. It also is utilized specifically for the purpose of defense, as in the use of fantasy to deal with otherwise insoluble emotional conflicts. Sarnoff (1971, 1976), in fact, considers fantasy to be the central ego activity during the latency period. The latency child uses fantasy as a safe haven to which to withdraw from the losing battles and dangerous confrontations involved in the direct expression of conflicted urges in interaction with actual objects.

The fantasies begin essentially as masturbation fantasies, but they are split off from masturbatory activity and are progressively reworked and disguised so that their masturbatory roots are hidden. They are expressed in part in the form of daydreams, such as the kidnapping, adoption, twin, and movie star fantasies that are so common among latency age girls. In part, they are repressed and then permitted to re-enter consciousness by attaching them to the ready-made plots of stories, films, and TV cartoons. Another avenue through which they are given re-entry into consciousness is that of active participation in games, plays, and sports activities that can be woven together with the repressed fantasies which the conscious activities and interests approximate closely enough for them to serve as vehicles for their enactment.

Books with a romantic theme, often with a masochistic component, are popular among latency age girls because of the contact that is made with suppressed oedipal fantasies. The masochistic element that frequently is involved reflects the oedipal idea of being raped by the father and his huge phallus; the accumulation of repeated defeats and injuries that in part have been eroticized; the turning back upon the self of rage at those who are held responsible for her pain; thoughts about menstruation, defloration, and labor pains; the impact of the defensive modes of regression to sadistic-anal interests, self-sacrifice, and altruistic surrender. Stories about girls in pioneer families being kidnapped by Indians represent one variation of this, as do those about the hard life of a girl growing up, such as Laura Ingall Wilder's series beginning with *The Little House on the Prairie*.

Stories and cartoons in which figures who are smaller and weaker outwit, defeat, and humiliate their bigger and stronger adversaries tend to be popular, but less so than among boys of the same age. The intense interest which latency age girls have in the mysterious and wondrous forces within them that one day will transform them into sexually mature, menstruating, procreative women with breasts and curves is reflected in their attention to books and stories about remarkable women with fascinating, magical, witchlike powers which they use sparingly but wisely to help children and people beleaguered by forces of evil. *Mary Poppins, Mrs. Piggle Wiggle, Mrs. Pepperpot*, and the "white witches" in Margaret Storey's books exemplify this genre. At times, the difficulty in waiting for the dormant powers within them to finally emerge from their slumber is too agonizing, and fantasies are spun out in which limited magical powers express themselves in girls themselves.

The repeated narcissistic injuries endured by young girls, who lack the equipment with which to compete oedipally either with their mothers or with their fathers and brothers, contribute to the emergence of compensatory narcissistic-exhibitionistic and phallic-exhibitionistic fantasies that are acted out in a variety of ways. The generally superior intellectual and scholastic performance of school age girls derives from this source as well as from the advantages which they possess over boys at the beginning of latency because of their more advanced level of intellectual development. Their wishes to excel and to look good provide fuel to the thrust toward intellectual achievement that is generally observable in latency age girls. Girls' interests in music, dramatics, and dance stem from the same wellsprings. The same holds for the athletic activities of many latency age girls who tend to choose such activities as gymnastics and swimming, which provide an opportunity for exhibitionistic display not only of their athletic prowess, but also of their bodies.

SUPEREGO DEVELOPMENT

Superego development occupies a prominent part in the phenomena of the latency period. Freud (1923) defined the superego as a specialized portion of the ego that acquires the status of a semi-autonomous agency with major regulatory powers. It watches over the individual and renders judgments as to which acts, thoughts, and feelings it considers acceptable or even desirable and which it disapproves of or more or less proscribes. It enforces its decisions by rewarding the former with the comfortable feeling that one is good, worthwhile, and able to be proud of the way one has conducted oneself and by punishing the latter with painful feelings of guilt, shame, and aloneness.

The superego as a functional regulatory system crystallizes out of developmental progression during the prelatency period involving reality testing, self-object differentiation, self-esteem regulation, separation-individuation (Mahler, 1968), and the acquisition of self-control. As children come to appreciate that they are separate from their parents and that the latter possess the power to provide for their needs and to make them feel good, they are forced to relinquish their narcissistic fantasies of omnipotence and power and to curb the expression of their libidinal and aggressive impulses in accordance with environmental expectations. As they do so (in the course of a series of phase-specific, ambivalent struggles), they at first must lean upon their parents for the judgment and strength which they themselves lack. An important part of this consists in the evocation and recollection of their parents' visually, tactilely, and especially auditorally presented prohibitions and demands, which they incorporate into their mental representations of themselves and into their own behavioral attitudes.

The approving and disapproving parental looks, voices, and words are increasingly integrated into an organized system giving direction to the child as to what it should do, think, and feel in order for things to go well. It has qualities that at first make it seem in one sense like part of the self and in another sense like something external and foreign. This is because it is tied at first very closely to immediate experience (and, therefore, is most effective when reinforced by actual parental proximity) and to the child's ambivalence about restraining its impulses and about being separate or not from the mother. With increasing ego development, providing effective means with which to regulate drive impulses and to deal successfully with a realistically perceived external world, it will become possible for the child to remove itself more and more from restraining external forces and thereby achieve relative independence from them, but this is a slow process. Before it has progressed very far, the child finds itself immersed in the intense, conflicted jealousies and triangular rivalries of the Oedipus complex. The ambivalence conflicts of the oral and sadistic-anal period are relatively minor in comparison with the powerful, murderous impulses and incestuous fantasies which threaten dissolution of the separate identity for which the child has been striving, in addition to contributing to the danger of intense parental disapproval and retaliation, associated with the Oedipus complex.

The need to escape from the terrors associated with oedipal wishes provides a powerful impetus that sharply accelerates superego development at this point. An acute need is felt for the continual presence of someone to watch over and regulate thoughts and actions. There also is a powerful urge to be like one's parents in order to possess their power (and certain other attributes and capabilities which the child envies). These aims contribute to a wholesale introjection of and identification with parental prohibitions in the form of a stern voice of conscience that vigorously seeks the suppression and repression of oedipal inclinations. The superego crystallizes as a recognizable entity as the oedipal stage draws to a close, but in the first half of latency it does not carry out its functions very efficiently. It is harsh, yet relatively weak and ineffective, and it is not yet absorbed into the self as a smoothly functioning, integral part of it. The child is still battling against the supremacy and authority of the parents and this extends to their internalized representation within the superego (see Bornstein, 1951).

Superego admonitions are experienced early in latency as peremptory orders imposed by a tyrannical foreign invader whose exercise of control over unruly, internal elements is welcomed at the same time that it is resented and opposed. The child's terror of the intensity of its oedipal urges and of parental retaliation in response to them is projected into its relations with the superego, so that the child lives in fear of superego demands, but lacks confidence in its ability to carry them out. There is oscillation, therefore, between vigilant, at times obsessional attention to rules and regulations and breakthroughs of rebelliousness and gratification of forbidden impulses that often are followed by harsh self-reproaches. Since guilty feelings are not well tolerated, there is a tendency to externalize them, so that early latency children tend to become incensed at the transgressions of others and either punish them or report them to higher authorities while they allow themselves to commit the very same crimes almost simultaneously. Equally common (and somewhat more serious) is a tendency to project the guilt and to blame others for what one has done.

Rules are enormously important during latency. The games, school activities, clubs, organizations, and sports interests that are so enormously important in the life of school age children are all prominently regulated by rules of behavior that have to be followed if they are to be mastered successfully. At first, there is noisy alternation between efforts to learn and follow the rules and more or less blatant violation of them. Cheating, lying, and minor stealing are more or less universal in the first half of the latency period and are harbingers of serious trouble to come only if they are flagrant and unremitting. If all goes well, they gradually diminish as ego development proceeds and the child develops the strength to resist forbidden impulses, control his or her behavior, and function in a truly secondary process fashion.

Socialization plays an extremely important role in the gradual modulation of the superego's functioning and its integration into the self as an effective, reasonable, well-integrated agency within the individual's psyche. As the children distance themselves from their parents and move instead into relationships with their peers and, to a lesser extent, with certain, idealized adults outside their families, they are influenced more and more by peer pressures and by identification with the personal and social values presented to them by teachers and other significant extrafamilial adults. The character of the superego is continually modified and enriched by the accretion of new identifications that remove it increasingly from association with the parental images that formed its nucleus at the beginning of latency.

During latency intellectual development promotes the ability to think for oneself and progressive strengthening of the ego renders drive impulses far easier to contain and control than they had been earlier in childhood; therefore the superego becomes increasingly more realistic, reasonable, and effective in its functioning and its contents become more individualized until, by mid-latency, they are relatively comfortably integrated as a distinctive part of the unique self. By the latter half of latency, the child no longer needs either to fear or to struggle against the dictates of conscience. "Latency" of emotional conflict is much truer of the latter half of the latency period than the much more tumultuous, struggle-filled first half. This is reflected in the much greater ease shown by late latency children and their much greater resistance to analytic intrusion into their lives than early latency children, who by and large welcome assistance with their neurotic struggles.

The superego development of girls and of boys differs in various ways because of developmental differences affecting control of aggressive and libidinal impulses, the form and contents of the Oedipus complex, and the maintenance of narcissistic balance and self-esteem. From the very beginning, there are innate biological differences and differences in cultural attitudes toward boys and girls that affect their respective patterns of impulse control. Girl babies are more regular in their biological rhythms and are easier to manage than are boys. They are less impulsive, settle down more easily into reliable patterns of feeding, sleeping, and interacting, learn more quickly, and as a whole are less aggressive and more adaptable than are boys. They develop bladder and bowel control earlier and consequently are usually easier to toilet train. They are smaller than boys, are endowed with less muscular strength, and are less impulsive and volatile.

Complementing the intrinsic differences between boys and girls involving aggressivity and impulse control are the different behavioral expectations generally shown to them by their parents. Girls are not expected to be so impulsive and aggressive and parents are more stringent with them in requiring obedience and self-control. The cultural transmission of sex-related differences in behavioral expectations is reinforced by the little girl's recognition that she is of the same gender as her mother. Unlike the little boy, who pushes away from his mother and rebels against her behavioral demands and expectations in the course of separation-individuation, the little girl identifies with and incorporates her mother's conscious and unconscious values and attitudes about herself and her femininity and with the mother's role as the one who maintains order and control in the household routines and as the one who cares for and nurtures others. Not only is the little girl generally pressured by her parents to be neat, orderly, dependable, patient, and unaggressive, she is also indirectly guided by her identification with her mother's values and ideals involving girls and women.

There also are differences in the ways in which parents allow boys and girls to express aggression. Since girls are required to be more constrained and "unaggressive" than boys, the channels that are left open to them tend to be the indirect, subtle, less overt ones. They are much more likely to make use of their more precociously developed intellectual and verbal capacities to develop quietly effective means of asserting themselves and expressing their aggressive inclinations, using cleverness and social adroitness rather than striking out physically and violently. As reaction-formations develop against wishes and strivings which need to be suppressed in the interest of civilization, the character and functioning of the superego system that is built up reflects the pattern of discharge of and control over aggressive urges that develops during the preoedipal and oedipal years.

The differences in this regard, combined with the less intense and urgent pressure to abandon positive oedipal aims, the impact of a long, drawn out struggle to resolve the ambivalence conflicts involved in the relationship with the mother as the primary object, the lack of acute terror of retaliative castration for positive oedipal strivings (and of the castrative effect of a negative oedipal solution) that is present in boys, and the despair and resignation that comes from the girl's sense of defeat and deprivation tend to produce a picture of female superego functioning at the beginning of latency that is different from that observed in boys. The girl's superego operates with less dictatorial harshness and rigidity, less of a tendency to rule by terror and threat of retaliation, and less use of violent punishments to enforce its imperatives than does the boy's. It tends to function more smoothly, quietly, subtly, and effectively in its operation, but there is more of a tendency to masochism, over-control and abnegation, to the point at times of altruistic surrender (A. Freud, 1936). The female superego is not necessarily stronger or weaker than the male one, but it is different in its manner of functioning.

At the beginning of latency, the boy is impelled to suppress, repress, and renounce his oedipal strivings in order to escape the implied danger of retributive damage to or removal of his penis and testicles and to avoid the narcissistic mortification of rejection and defeat. The girl's situation appears to be more complex. Her feelings of rejection, humiliation, and inferior endowment are much greater than are the corresponding feelings of the boy of the same age. She feels spurned as a love object not by only one parent but by both of them. Whereas the boy compares himself unfavorably with his father as to the size of his genitals, he at least possesses similar, if smaller, readily observable and palpable genital organs, which need only grow in size. The little girl, in contrast, possesses neither the pubic hair, breasts, nor babies that objectively demonstrate her mother's possession of valuable sexual organs nor the observable organs with which her father and brothers are endowed. She is told that there are structures of value inside her, but she can neither see nor feel them, and she is told that some day she will grow breasts and give birth to babies, but she knows that she will have to wait for a long, long time before that ever happens. The little boy is distressed that what he has is too small, but the little girl feels that she has almost nothing at all.

She fears that what little she has (and the pleasurable sensations with which it provides her) will be taken away from her to punish her for her libidinal and aggressive oedipal fantasies, but we do not yet know enough about the fear of genital injury that is the female counterpart of male castration anxiety. We do have evidence that oedipal and early latency age girls at times view their interlabial cleft as a sign of genital injury which they associated with masturbation and exploratory sex play. Girls and women recalling childhood memories in analysis express anxiety over genital damage that often is displaced to intense feelings about dolls getting smashed or lost, kittens being killed or otherwise taken away from them, their hair being cut short, etc. Such recollections, in association with derivatives of oedipal guilt and anxiety, at times appear in the course of analysis when a woman is terrified by the threat of a possible hysterectomy or mastectomy.

The female superego that is observable during latency and thereafter seems to me to differ in a number of respects from that of the boy. Since their ego development in general is more advanced, and since they have been trained in general to restrain themselves and turn their aggressive inclinations back upon themselves rather than to discharge them outwardly, girls possess greater impulse control and a greater tendency to employ sublimatory, personally and societally more acceptable alternative channels of drive discharge. Superego pressures need not be so harsh and imperious, therefore, nor does the superego need to be so rigid and unyielding as it tends to be in boys.

It is my impression that there tends to be greater awareness of social nuances and of shades of gray between the extreme polarities of behavioral acceptability versus intolerability in the female superego's attitudes than that which is to be found in boys. Since girls are physically weaker, they are less terrified of their aggressive impulses and conjure up correspondingly less dreadful fantasies of retaliation and punishment. They tend to use intellectual and social skills to influence the people with whom they interact rather than employing brute force to realize their goals. The net affect is that girls appear less moralistic than boys, but it does not seem to me that they are by any means less moral. Although their superego functioning is less rigid and harsh, it probably is more effective than that of the latency boy in promoting impulse control and diverting primitive urges into more acceptable channels of discharge (such as intellectual activity). It strikes me that girls are not more "devious" than boys, but are less primitively harsh and moralistic in their superego attitudes, more roundabout in their channels of attainment of drive satisfaction, and more realistically pragmatic and worldly in the conduct of their lives.

THE STRUGGLE AGAINST MASTURBATION

A prominent feature of the latency period is an ongoing struggle to resist masturbatory urges. It is particularly intense in the first half of latency, with a partial relaxation of superego prohibition against masturbation later on (Bornstein, 1953). The fantasies that accompany masturbatory impulses are largely oedipal, exhibitionistic, and sadomasochistic in nature in girls. They tend to be repressed, desexualized, and split off from the masturbatory urges and acts with which they were originally associated, and then to be permitted re-entry into consciousness in disguised form as part of the content of stories, games, and dramatic play. This has been described in some detail in earlier sections of this discussion.

There are a number of sources that lead to the vigorous suppression of masturbation that takes place in girls during latency. One is the strong ego and superego opposition that acts against the gratification of oedipal and preoedipal desires, because of the anxieties, narcissistic injuries, and insoluble conflicts which they engender. Genital excitement is experienced by some girls as so overwhelming and frightening that it is warded off to the extent that genital anesthesia supervenes (Fraiberg, 1972). The capacity to obtain relief and at least partial, orgastic discharge through direct genital manipulation appears to be present at times (Sarnoff, 1972; Bernstein, 1974; Clower, 1976), but developmental immaturity usually prevents this from taking place. As one nine year old girl put it, "It's like climbing a tree for the first time; you can go higher and higher, but you can't get down, and you get scareder and scareder." Exhibitionistic fantasies lead to embarrassment and shame, and sadomasochistic fantasies produce guilt and disgust. The role of anal sensations and cloacal ideas in the little girl's struggle to define and comprehend her genital anatomy contributes to the disgust that is experienced. Dissatisfaction with fantasied genital inferiority is an additional motivation to abandon masturbation in girls who have developed intense penis envy. Societal prohibitions against masturbation, transmitted via parental admonitions, also serve as a powerful negative force that reinforces the girl's own opposition to masturbation.

Although some latency age girls do handle or otherwise directly manipulate their genitals in a masturbatory way, for a number of reasons this is far less common than in boys. The boy's protuberant genitals are exposed much more to tactile stimulation than are female genitalia, and reactive and spontaneous penile erections inescapably call his attention to genital sensations. The girl's vulva is much more safely removed from sources of casual stimulation, and the clitoral, vulval, and deep pelvic sensations that are produced with sexual excitement are more diffusely distributed and less observable than comparable genital sensations in the boy. The latter makes it easier for girls to stimulate their genitals indirectly, while they remain consciously unaware that they are doing so. Girls probably masturbate as much during latency as boys, although they appear to be masturbating less. In contrast to boys, who vigorously avoid touching their genitals, manually or otherwise, girls tend to use various methods of indirect and unobtrusive self-stimulation without their being aware that they are masturbating.

Latency age girls tend to engage in activities that contain a great deal of very active, often rhythmic, total body movement. These include jumping rope, roller skating, gymnastics, dancing, swinging on swings, and playing at hopping and running games. Such interests reflect not only a deflection of sublimated excitement and competitive, exhibitionistic urges from the genitals to the total body—which is typical in both sexes during latency—but the active movement of the body through space also stimulates very pleasurable, at times thrilling, genital sensations. Girls can also manipulate their external genitalia by methods such as exerting thigh pressure, bicycle and horseback riding, and cleaning the perineum with a sponge or shower spray while bathing (the obverse side of the reaction-formation involved in the compulsive showering or bathing that is so much more common in latency age girls than it is in boys), all without conscious awareness that they are masturbating.

For example, a woman in analysis asserted that she did not recall ever having masturbated prior to adolescence. Her next association was that when she was a schoolgirl she had done something that still puzzled her: Although she always had rebelled against her mother's efforts to get her to do housework, she gladly and cheerfully did sewing for her mother. When I asked for details, she told me that they had had an old sewing machine with a low-placed, curved, flat metal handle that "turned the machine on" when she pressed against it with her upper thigh. When I pointed out that she had been using the sewing machine to masturbate in a disguised way, at first she insisted that what I had said was absurd. She had to laugh, however, when she then remembered that she had been so little that the handle that switched the sewing machine on would reach into her genitals if she "didn't sit right," and that once, when her brother had slapped her on the back while she was sewing, it had jabbed her so sharply in the genital region that she was sore for days.

Since the latency age girl can mask her masturbatory activity so effectively, even from herself, she can obtain physical satisfaction without necessarily being plagued by burdensome shame and guilt. In one sense, she thereby deceives herself and her parents. Looked at from another vantage point, however, she is making effective use of her innate resources and potentials to circumvent the excessively harsh restrictions placed upon her by (jealous?) adult authorities and to give outlet to her natural sexual urges in a well-regulated, controlled, and harmless manner.

NARCISSISTIC VULNERABILITY AND THE STRUGGLE FOR SELF-ESTEEM

The persistence of sub rosa masturbation and the repressed and rechanneled oedipal and exhibitionistic fantasies that are connected with it are a developmental necessity in latency age girls. They cannot give up their quest for recognition and appreciation from the oedipal father, which they pursue directly, by proxy, in fantasy, and via displaced, sublimated activity. Girls enter the latency period via a series of losing battles and painful narcissistic wounds that threaten to demoralize them if they give up.

They have come through an oral and sadistic-anal, separation-individuation crisis of ambivalence, in which they have had to fight against and lose their primary love objects and their idealized models for identification and secondary narcissistic fulfillment. In the phallic and early oedipal periods, they have found themselves unable to compete with their fathers and brothers to be first in their struggle for the love of the oedipal mother or to dispute their culturally reinforced assertion of dominance and power. With their largely internal, unobservable genitals, which with their preoperational intellectual organization they have difficulty comprehending and appreciating, and with their lack of the breasts, pubic hair, procreative ability, and know-how possessed by their mothers, they experience themselves as being currently inferiorly endowed physically, which constitutes a major narcissistic injury (Silverman, 1977). The reaction is inevitably one of hurt, pain, and rage (see Kohut, 1972).

This aspect of early female development is captured in the story of a pretty four-year-old girl who went to visit her glamorous, movie star aunt. After a day of shopping, movie set touring, and an elegant lunch and dinner which both enjoyed thoroughly, they capped the day by taking a bubble bath together before retiring to bed. The film star noticed, much to her surprise, that her niece looked downtrodden and very sad. "What's the matter?" she asked, "We've had such a lovely day together." "Oh aunty," the little girl replied, "why is it I'm so plain and you're so fancy?"

The net effect is that girls at the beginning of latency by and large have a depressed self-image, lowered self-esteem, and an exquisite sensitivity to what is reflected back to them about their parents' (especially their fathers') views of and feelings about them and about their parents' (especially their mothers') attitudes toward females in general (Silverman, 1977). During the latency period they have an opportunity to use their operational intelligence and the ongoing input from family members and from new objects to correct and improve their distorted, debased self-image and to restore their self-esteem via intellectual, athletic, and aesthetic achievements. The need to know and understand themselves and their place in a complex world and the superiority over boys which their greater self-control and intellectual lead afford them give importance to intellectual and scholastic achievement as a pathway to narcissistic and exhibitionistic accomplishment that bolsters self-esteem. This combines with the use of the motor sphere for exhibitionistic success to reinforce the thrust toward accomplishment that is provided by the spurt in autonomous ego development that takes place during latency. Both the intellectual and motor spheres are used, furthermore, to impress and capture the attention of boys and men. Learning how to be attractive and how to deal with males is one dimension of this.

The way in which societal, parental, and sibling attitudes impinge upon girls during latency is very important, since they are so keenly observant of and influenced by what the world around them reflects back to them about themselves, and since learning plays such a major role during this phase. They need successes in their attempt to obtain favorable impressions from others and external reinforcement of their improving self-image. Societal downgrading of females to inferior status and lesser opportunities and male denigration of and scorn for females (arising out of defense against phallic-oedipal castration anxiety and against the pull toward the powerful, preoedipal mother), if it is intense and unremitting, constitutes an obstacle that can seriously interfere with developmental progress. The attitudes toward females presented in textbooks and stories are similarly important. Fathers who favor their sons or shrink back in anxiety from closeness with their daughters present a special problem.

The female genitals, much more than male genitalia, are associated with generativity and productivity. A girl's attitudes and feelings about herself and about females in general become centered upon and fused with those about her genitals during the phallic or genital stage, so that a negative self-image can contribute to intense, unresolved rage and penis envy that during latency can be displaced upward so that it affects the use of brain power and intellectual achievement. All too often, a denigrated self-image, the fantasy of genital inferiority, reaction-formations against narcissistic rage, and oedipal shame and guilt lead in this manner to impaired ability to think and learn, to a view of oneself as stupid and to impaired achievement and productivity that can persist throughout life (Applegarth, 1976). This is less likely to occur where there is a healthy latency period in which there is ego growth, realistic self-discovery, and zestful relationships with people who appreciate and care for one another and who do not consistently exploit each other for personal, emotional gain. Such a latency will tend to promote the development of healthy self-esteem and a realistic self-image, with a potential for productivity and enjoyment of life.

CONCLUDING REMARKS

The latency period in one sense is a quiet, relatively peaceful respite between one raging developmental storm and another. On the other hand, it is not a time of emptiness, silence, or inactivity, as the name applied to it might imply. Because it is a phase dominated by repression, avoidance, disguise, and removal from the eyes and ears of the adult world, its bustling activity is not nearly so discernible as that of the noisy, tumultuous periods which precede and follow it. It is a time of vigorous ego growth, vitally important superego development, improving self-perception that is correlated with increasing independence and a growing capacity to make realistic judgments and appraisals, and the pursuit of drive satisfactions via the coordinated use of fantasy and interpersonal activities, in which central themes evolve and change and others crystallize into stable form. The hunger for new information and for new channels of expression, which are used to revamp and build the content and organization of the psychic structures which children bring with them when they enter latency, makes the quality of ongoing experience and environmental input a very important consideration. Children do not take a vacation from the developmental struggles of childhood during the latency period. The processes that go on during this phase, however, make the growing pains much less observable, but none the less real.

REFERENCES

Applegarth, A. (1976). Some observations on work inhibitions in women. *J. Amer. Psychoanal. Assn.* 24:251–268.

Bernstein, I. (1974). Panel on Psychology of Women: Latency and Early Adolescence. Presented at Meeting of American Psychoanalytic Association, Fall 1974. Reported by E. Galenson, *J. Amer. Psychoanal. Assn.* 24:141–160, 1976.

Blos, P. (1962). *On Adolescence*. New York: Free Press of Glencoe.

Bonaparte, M., Freud, A., and Kris, E. (1954). *The Origins of Psychoanalysis*. London: Imago, pp. 163– 167.

Bornstein, B. (1951). On latency. *The Psychoanalytic Study of the Child* 6:279– 285.

———(1953). Masturbation in the latency period. *The Psychoanalytic Study of the Child* 8:65– 78.

Brunswick, R.M. (1940). The preoedipal phase of the libido development. *Psychoanal. Q.* 9:293– 319.

Clower, V. (1976). Theoretical implications in current views of masturbation in latency girls. *J. Amer. Psychoanal. Assn., Supplement-Female Psychology*, 24 (no. 5):109– 126.

Fenichel, O. (1945). *The Psychoanalytic Theory of Neurosis*. New York: W.W. Norton.

Fraiberg, S. (1972). Some characteristics of genital arousal and discharge in latency girls. *The Psychoanalytic Study of the Child* 27:439– 475.

Freud, A. (1936). *The Ego and the Mechanisms of Defense*. New York: International Universities Press, pp. 132– 148.

Freud, S. (1905). Three essays on the theory of sexuality. *Standard Edition* 7:125– 243. London: Hogarth Press, 1953.

———(1909). Family romances. *Standard Edition* 9:235– 244. London Hogarth Press, 1959.

———(1911). Formulations on the two principles of mental functioning. *Standard Edition* 12:213– 226. London: Hogarth Press, 1958.

———(1923a). The ego and the id. *Standard Edition* 19:3068. London: Hogarth Press, 1961.

———(1923b).The infantile genital organization: an interpolation into the theory of sexuality. *Standard Edition* 19:141– 148. London: Hogarth Press, 1961.

———(1924). The dissolution of the oedipus complex. *Standard Edition* 19:173– 182. London: Hogarth Press, 1961.

———(1931). Female sexuality. *Standard Edition* 21:221– 243. London: Hogarth Press, 1961.

———(1933). Femininity. *Standard Edition* 22:112– 135. London: Hogarth Press, 1964.

Fries, M. (1958). A review of the literature on the latency period. *J. Hillside Hospital* 7:3– 16.

Greenacre, P. (1947). Penis awe and its relation to penis envy. In *Emotional Growth. Psychoanalytic Studies of the Gifted and a Great Variety of Other Individuals*, vol. 1. New York: International Universities Press, 1971, pp. 31– 49.

Hartmann, H. (1950). Comments on the psychoanalytic theory of the ego. *The Psychoanalytic Study of the Child*, 5:74– 96.

Horney, K. (1933). The denial of the vagina. *Internat. J. Psycho-Anal*. 14:57– 70.

Inhelder, B., and Piaget, J. (1959). *The Early Growth of Logic in the Child* . New York: The Norton Library, W.W. Norton, 1969.

Jacobson, E. (1964). *The Self and the Object World*. New York: International Universities Press.

Jones, E. (1927). The early development of female sexuality. *Internat. J. Psycho-Anal*. 8:459– 472.

Kernberg, O. (1975). *Borderline Conditions and Pathological Narcissism*. New York: Jason Aronson.

Klein, M. (1932). *The Psychoanalysis of Children*. New York: Grove Press, 1960.

Kohut, H. (1971). *The Analysis of the Self*. New York: International Universities Press.

———(1972). Thoughts on narcissism and narcissistic rage. *The Psychoanalytic Study of the Child* 27:360– 400.

Mahler, M. (1968). *On Human Symbiosis and the Vicissitudes of Individuation*. New York: International Universities Press.

Nunberg, H. (1930). The synthetic function of the ego. In *Practice and Theory of Psychoanalysis*. New York: International Universities Press, pp. 120– 136.

Piaget, J. (1947). *The Psychology of Intelligence*. Patterson: Littlefield, Adams, 1960.

Sarnoff, C. (1971). Ego structure in latency. *Psychoanal. Q*. 40:387– 412.

———(1972). The vicissitudes of projection during the analysis of a girl in late latency-early adolescence. *Internat. J. Psycho-Anal*. 53:515– 523.

——(1976). *Latency*. New York: Jason Aronson.

Silverman, M. (1971). The growth of logical thinking: Piaget's contribution to ego psychology. *Psychoanal. Q*. 40:317–341.

——(1977). Cognitive development and female psychology. Presented to the Regional Association of Greater New York Societies of the American Psychoanalytic Association, October 22, 1977, at Grossingers, New York.

Winnicott, D. (1953). Transitional objects and transitional phenomena. *Internat. J. Psycho-Anal*. 34:89–93.

Yazmajian, R. (1967). Biological aspects of infantile sexuality and the latency period. *Psychoanal. Quart*. 36:203–229.

8

Narcissistic Development

FRANK M. LACHMANN

Until recently, a discussion of the narcissistic development of the female child would have been subsumed within a discussion of the phases of psychosexual development. In 1971, Heinz Kohut postulated a separate line of development for "narcissistic libido," independent of "object libido," and thereby offered a radically new perspective from which to consider this psychological development. Narcissism has, however, been as controversial an issue in psychoanalysis as has the psychological development of the female. Furthermore, of the various studies of female psychological development, the role of narcissism has been subject to the most frequent and extensive revisions.

Freud's (1914) "introduction" of the concept of narcissism and his several discussions of female psychosexual development (e.g., Freud, 1908, 1925, 1931, 1933) have provided Deutsch (1944–45) and others (e.g., Bonaparte, 1953; Greenacre, 1969; Reich, 1973) with the framework upon which they elaborated. Later refinements of the theory of narcissism were proposed by Hartmann (1950), Jacobson (1964), and many others. Concurrently, a literature which was critical of Freud's view of psychosexual development of the young girl appeared. These contributions have been aptly summarized from a historical perspective by Fliegel (1973), and more recently, among others, by Barglow and Schaefer (1976). The concept of narcissism has also been subjected to a critical review (Kernberg, 1975, 1976; Kohut, 1971, 1977; Pulver, 1970; Stolorow and Lachmann, 1980). These analysts have suggested wide-ranging revisions in both theory and therapy, with specific reference to the place that narcissism occupies in psychological development.

Though differing in their origins, the critique of the theory of narcissism and the propositions of female development have converged. The present study is an attempt to explore the intersection of these critical thrusts. In the first part of this study the theory of narcissism with its various amendations and revisions will be reviewed, with specific emphasis on its role in female development. In the second part a consolidation of these contributions will be attempted, with special emphasis on the contributions of Kohut's self psychology. In the third part the implications of this synthesis will be drawn out.

HISTORICAL PERSPECTIVE

Though Freud used the term ''narcissism'' prior to 1914, it was then, in his formal introduction of the concept, that he brought together a number of — up to that moment—disparate psychological phenomena. He offered analysts a unique vantage point from which to gain a deeper understanding of psychosis (termed ''narcissistic neurosis'' by Freud), sleep, hypochondria, homosexuality, love relationships and, through the connection between narcissism and penis envy, a theory of female gender identity.

The difficulties with the concept of narcissism, in spite of the clinical illuminations it afforded, have made it a ''disturbing concept'' not only to Jones (1955) who so labeled it, but to more recent writers as well (Mahler, Pine and Bergman, 1975; Pulver, 1970; Stolorow and Lachmann, 1980). Freud used the term ''narcissism'' in both a developmental sense—as a libidinal stage between auto–erotism and object love (1914)—and in an economic sense—as the libidinal investment of the ego.

While the seesaw relationship between narcissistic libido and object libido was applicable to the development of both sexes, narcissism was said to make a singular contribution to the development of the little girl's feminine identity. The anatomical distinction between the sexes (Freud, 1925) left in the little girl the conviction that she had been castrated. The recognition of her penisless state was seen as constituting a specific ''genital trauma'' (Deutsch, 1944–45), a narcissistic injury. Here narcissism was equated with an unconscious fantasy of possessing a penis which, in turn, was equated with genital adequacy and intactness and self-esteem. Consequently, the girl's reactions of outrage, self-devaluation, shame and humiliation, as well as compensatory over-estimation of herself or others, could be understood as her response to injuries to self-esteem and, on a deeper level, symbolic of castration or exposure of the castrated genital.

The little girl's belief that her genital is ''mutilated'' was seen as a manifestation of the ''genital trauma,'' and this perceived inadequacy was blamed upon the mother. Eventually, through defensive displacements and reversals, self-esteem could be regained. The sense of genital inadequacy and humiliation might then be converted into ''vanity'' or pride in physical appearance, sometimes referred to as ''a narcissistic investment in the face and body.''

The little girl's ''vanity'' is thus understood as essentially compensatory and therefore quite vulnerable to fluctuations and depletions. As was indicated earlier, within this view the blame for the loss of the penis is attributed to the mother, but the injury felt due to the loss is eventually converted into a wish for a baby from the father. In this context, Freud (1917) posited that the development of the woman progresses from part object to whole object—a development which is subject to regressions. The development from part object to whole object included both turning from the wish for a penis to the wish for a man and turning from narcissism to object love. The two uses of the term narcissism coincide here.

To summarize at this point, the discovery of the differences between the sexes, the little girl's comparison between her "inadequate" clitoris and the male organ, served to explain her sense of inferiority and humiliation, the presence of penis envy, and hence, a compensatory investment in bodily appearance. The little girl's development thus veered from its supposed masculine origins (her belief that she had a penis) through disappointment and loss ("castration") to an acceptance of her penisless body and the wish for a child. The "genital trauma" which sets this developmental progression in motion was for Deutsch (1944–1945) the basis for feminine character formation in which passivity and masochism are prominent but kept in check through narcissistic investments.

It will be necessary to review Deutsch's contributions in more detail since they constitute the earliest comprehensive psychoanalytic statement of the role narcissism plays in female psychosexual development. Deutsch (1944–1945; see also Wimpfheimer and Schafer's (1977) excellent critique) remained within Freud's biologically rooted framework and ascribed narcissism, passivity and masochism to woman's essential nature. The crucial assumption for Deutsch was the universal traumatic reaction of the girl upon the discovery of sexual differences. In consequence, according to Deutsch, the girl then does not have an "adequate" organ to provide a focus for phallic phase genital urges. The presumed genital inadequacy then prompts the girl to inhibit her active (phallic phase) strivings and turn them upon herself. She thus becomes more passive and increases her masochistic tendencies. Deutsch further argued that sexualized suffering as manifested in feelings of pleasure in mental and interpersonal suffering constitute woman's masochistic, self-destructive tendency. Such tendencies are countered by narcissism. This interplay of masochism and narcissism (Deutsch, 1944–1945) describes the "erotic feminine" in woman.

Deutsch (1930) has summarized her understanding of the female child's progression into womanhood:

> . . . When does the female child begin to be a woman and when a mother? Analytic experience has yielded an answer: *Simultaneously,* in that phase when she turns toward masochism. . . . Then at the same time as she conceives the desire to be castrated and raped, she conceives also the fantasy of receiving a child from her father. From that time on, the fantasy of partuition becomes a

member of the masochistic triad and the gulf between the instinctual act and the reproductive tendencies is bridged by masochism. (pp. 205–206.)

The woman who serves to exemplify this progression, Deutsch's model of a particular kind of psychologically healthy woman, is then detailed by her.

> . . . There is a group of women who constitute the main body figuring in the statistics which give the largest percentage of frigidity. The women in question are psychically healthy, and their relation to the world and their libidinal objects positive and friendly. If questioned about the nature of their experience in coitus, they give answers which show that the conception of orgasm as something to be experienced by themselves is really and truly foreign to them. During intercourse what they feel is a happy and tender sense that they are giving keen pleasure and, if they do not come from a social environment where they have acquired a full sexual enlightenment, they are convinced that coitus as a sexual act is of importance only for the man. In it, as in other relations, the woman finds happiness in tender, maternal giving. (p. 206.)

This so-called psychologically healthy woman described by Deutsch might today, as Deutsch even prophesized in the article cited above, be diagnosed as having a masochistic character disorder. Pivotal for this change is our current, better understanding of the early mother-child relationship and the specific developmental tasks in emerging from symbiotic attachments through the various phases of separation and individuation (Mahler, Pine, and Bergman, 1975). In the light of our current understanding, it may be instructive to reconsider a dream from a case vignette presented by Deutsch in the paper which we have been discussing.

> Professor X and you (the analyst) were sitting together. I wanted him to notice me. He went past my chair and I looked up at him and he smiled at me. He began to ask me about my health, as a doctor asks his patient; I answered with reluctance. All of a sudden he had on a doctor's white coat and a pair of obstetrical forceps in his hand. He said to me: "Now we'll just have a look at the little angel." I clearly saw that they were obstetrical forceps, but I had the feeling that the instrument was to be used to force my legs apart and display the clitoris. I was very much frightened and struggled. A number of people, among them you and a trained nurse, were standing by and were indignant at my struggling. They thought that Professor X had specially chosen *me* for a kind of experiment, and that I ought to submit to it. As everyone was against me, I cried out in impotent fury: "No, I will not be operated on, you shall not operate on me." (pp. 200–201.)

Deutsch then discusses the dream as follows:

> Without examining the dream more closely here, we can see in its manifest content that castration is identified with rape and partuition, and the dream–wish which creates anxiety is as follows: "I want to be castrated (raped) by my father and to have a child"—a threefold wish of a plainly *masochistic character.*
>
> The first, infantile identification with the mother is always, independently of the complicated processes and reactions belonging to the sense of guilt, *masochistic,* and all the active birth-fantasies, whose roots lie in this identification, are of a bloody, painful character, which they retain throughout the subject's life. . . . I am indicating the purely libidinal origin of feminine masochism, as determined by the course of evolution. (p. 201.)

Based on psychoanalytic knowledge which has become clearer since the publication of this case, Martin Bergmann (1969) has offered a revision of the interpretation of this dream. According to Bergmann, this woman has reached the level of phallic phase drive organization as suggested by her imagery but without adequate separation from her mother. The story of the dream indicates that the mother ("trained nurse") has remained in control and "thought . . . that I ought to submit. . . ." She "stands by" while the father (Professor X) performs the castration and she thereby cooperates in it. Her indignation at the dreamer's reluctance and struggle indicates that she is depicted as being involved in the girl's sexuality. From the standpoint of the woman who dreamed this, there has not been sufficient separation from the mother who is being maintained as an object of power. So long as this dependent position vis-á-vis the mother is maintained and the mother is retained by the girl in a position of control and superiority, masochistically tinged sexuality is a most likely alternative. In such a case, the demands of the phallic strivings must be reconciled with the pre-oedipal dependent longings. An attempt to resolve this conflict along lines which also take into account passivity and masochism might be as follows: "I do not actively want sex; I do not want to threaten mother's superiority since I need her; however, I can accept sex as being forced upon me while I remain passive." Given the essentially pre-oedipal aspects of this conflict and its resolution (a regression from or disavowal of active sexual strivings within a feminine identity), defensive and compensatory narcissism can be understood as averting further regressions and self-devaluation. Thus, our better understanding of the dimensions of the early mother–child relationship has prompted a reformulation of the relationship between narcissism and femininity, and has resulted in a more comprehensive understanding of masochistic attachments and of the consequent, requisite narcissistic compensations.

The theoretical refinements of Hartmann (1964) and his co-workers anticipated some of the observations later reported by Mahler and her co-workers. Hartmann's postulation of an undifferentiated id-ego matrix, though on a conceptual level different from Mahler's "symbiotic phase," addresses a similar issue—the dawn of the child's development and the formation of psychic structure in the child. Furthermore, Hartmann also clarified some of the theoretical ambiguities that surrounded the psychoanalytic theory of infantile narcissism and the formative moments of the ego (Laplanche and Pontalis, 1973). Hartmann's redefinition of narcissism as the libidinal investment of the self (rather than of the ego) opened the door to crucial clinical and theoretical elaborations. Hartmann (1950; see also Jacobson, 1964) distinguished between the ego (a structural mental system), the self (the whole person of the individual, including his body and body parts as well as his psychic organization and its parts), and the self-representation (the unconscious, preconscious and conscious endopsychic representations of the bodily and mental self in the system ego). These distinctions aided Jacobson (1964) in reformulating the complex interplay of drive endowment, physical maturation, psychological development and environmental influences in the formation of a self and object world. Her understanding of infant development has prompted her to place considerable emphasis on the child's growing capacity to differentiate and discriminate among objects and on the individuation and separation from them. According to Jacobson, the goals to be achieved after adolescence include "a final liberation from the symbiotic bonds of the family" and of incestuous and hostile wishes toward them. Toward this end, "narcissistic strivings" make a contribution.

Some twenty years after the publication of Deutsch's work, Jacobson (1964) offered a description of the paths along which the little girl establishes her feminine identity. She avoided some of the pitfalls of previous writers and anticipated the observations of later ones. Jacobson placed "castration shock" (her term for "genital trauma") into a developmental sequence in which it was preceded by earlier reaction formations and by the establishment of an immature, maternal ego ideal of an unaggressive, clean, neat little girl who is determined to renounce sexual activities. In turn, this ideal contributes to the later importance for the girl of attaining physical attractiveness. Furthermore, Jacobson emphasizes the role of the father, first as a rival with whom the girl can identify in her separation from her mother. Second, she emphasizes the importance of the father's actual attitude toward the young girl as she resolves her conflicting wishes between her identification with her mother and her wish for her father's penis. Third, Jacobson emphasizes the father's importance in his ability to navigate phallic–oedipal development with his daughter—from her phallic identification with him to a true love relationship with him.

It will have become apparent from the foregoing discussion that "narcissism" has been used in several conceptually different ways. In a clarifying paper, Pulver (1970) offered a critique of the term and the concept of narcissism. He outlined the four different ways it had been used:

1. Clinically to denote a sexual perversion characterized by the treatment of one's own body as a sexual object.
2. Genetically, to denote a stage of development considered to be characterized by that libidinal state.
3. In terms of object relationship, to denote two different phenomena:
   a) A type of object choice in which the self in some way plays a more important part than the real aspects of the object.
   b) A mode of relating to the environment characterized by a relative lack of object relations.
4. To denote various aspects of the complex ego state of self esteem. (pp. 323– 324.)

These varied uses of the term narcissism presented no conceptual difficulties so long as sexual pathology, ego pathology and object relations pathology were as perfectly correlated as Abraham (quoted by Fliess, 1948) had suggested. This meant that the succession of psychosexual stages, the development from part objects to whole objects, the advance from a pre-ambivalent to a post-ambivalent attitude toward objects and the development of a sense of reality were believed to be totally interdependent. The inaccuracy of this view has already been detailed elsewhere (Lachmann, 1975; Ross, 1970), while the seesaw relationship between narcissism and object relations was challenged by Kohut (1971). It follows then that pathology of ego function cannot be inferred from the extent of sexual pathology or the reverse. Furthermore, while Abraham's framework offers only one developmental line, instinctual development as evidenced by the psychosexual phases, other developmental propositions have been offered. For Abraham, the ego could only respond to the demands of the id; for Hartmann, the ego possessed autonomous functions. Additional developmental propositions include: self-object separation and individuation (Mahler, Pine and Bergman, 1975), self-object-affect units (Kernberg, 1976) and the transformation of archaic self-object configurations (Kohut, 1971, 1977). A further discussion of the developmental and clinical implications of these contributions is considered elsewhere (Stolorow and Lachmann, 1980). Once the possibility of various coordinated, interdependent but not perfectly correlated lines of development is acknowledged, the question can be raised as to where to place "narcissism."

To the challenge posed by Pulver's critique, Stolorow (1975a) responded by offering a functional definition of narcissism: "Mental activity is narcissistic to the degree that its function is to maintain the structural cohesiveness, temporal stability and positive affective coloring of the self-representation'' (p. 179). Previously, Kohut (1971) had freed narcissistic development from its moorings in object love, and in his 1977 publication, he elaborated upon the functions of defensive and compensatory narcissistic structures. Understood from the standpoint of the function of mental activity, representational structuralization proceeds from archaic self-objects through differentiation to integration and consolidation of increasingly more affectively complex self- and object-representations. Any mental act may be used and may function to maintain the cohesion, stability and positive affective coloration of these representations or may compensate for or defend against vulnerabilities in the representations. In elaborating upon these issues, Stolorow (1975b) also reversed Deutsch's formulation that narcissistic investments serve to keep masochism in check. Masochism, as well as sexual perversions, for example, can be viewed as having a narcissistic function (see also Goldberg, 1975; Lachmann, 1978). These reformulations of narcissism have wide ranging clinical implications which have been discussed elsewhere (Stolorow and Lachmann, 1980). From these more recent formulations of narcissism, we may postulate a structural development with related compensatory or defensive mental activity which functions to maintain a cohesive, temporally stable and affectively positive self-representation. Having defined narcissism in these functional terms, we are on a level of conceptualization at which there are *no sexual differences*. That is, we cannot propose sex differences in structure formation, but we can note them in the *content* and *elaboration* of the self-representation and in defensive or compensatory styles. (Schaefer (1974) offers an interesting explanation for the association between masculinity and an obsessive-compulsive style and femininity and an hysteric style). This reformulation of narcissism also releases it from its special genetic role in the psychological development of the young girl.

This completes a review of some contributions toward our understanding of the role of narcissism in the development of the female child. The term narcissism is still used in the psychoanalytic literature by a variety of writers in a variety of ways. It is still used as a description of behavior, as an explanation for behavior, in a pejorative way, and as a character trait. The functional definition of narcissism offers a way out of the conceptual dilemma. It encourages a broader view of child development by inviting an explanation of the narcissistic function of any act.

Any mental act has, among its multiple functions (Waelder, 1936), a narcissistic one—the maintenance or restoration of vulnerable aspects of the self-representation (Stolorow and Lachmann, 1980). This self-structure is neither masculine nor feminine, though we would postulate a core gender identity (Stoller, 1976) to which masculine qualities or feminine qualities accrue as its contents. Indeed, examples of the narcissistic function can be found in those activities whose specific purpose is to shore up a precarious sense of gender identity.

Narcissistic pathology—either the narcissistic personality disorders or the narcissistic behavior disorders (Kohut, 1977)—is related to the degree of vulnerability of the self-representation, and the extent to which defensive mechanisms covered faulty structuralization or compensatory mechanisms were sought and established for this reason. The self-representation may also be sustained by sexual fantasy (rape fantasies, fantasies of a phallic ideal, penis envy, etc.) or perversions (masochistic or promiscuous sexual activity). Conversely, these fantasies and perversions require and reflect specific achievements in self-object differentiation and structuralization. From this standpoint, feelings of shame, humiliation, mortification or outrage, as well as vanity, conceit or aloofness, in the past solely understood as related to genital trauma or castration shock and its compensations, can now, instead and/or in addition, be understood as describing various facets of the vulnerability and development of the self-representation.

If we now turn to the task of defining and describing the narcissistic development of the female child, we would first suggest that what develops is the child's representational world (Stolorow and Atwood, 1979)—from its archaic beginnings of predominantly self objects to its maturer form, which includes a self-representation with independent initiative and an independent recipient of impressions, though with retention of self objects to some extent (Kohut and Wolf, 1979). With respect to the task of structuralization, sex differences play a minor role. They do become crucial with respect to the content of the self-representation and the defenses and compensations for structural vulnerabilities.

CONSOLIDATION

Two interrelated topics have been pursued: narcissism and female psychosexual development. The historical survey has led to a functional definition of narcissism which in turn demanded a reexamination of the relationship between narcissism and female psychosexual development.

Psychoanalytically informed criticism of Freud's (1931) theory of female psychosexual development emphasized the "gap" in that theory (Stoller, 1976), the underestimation of the early mother-child relationship, pre-oedipal factors, the time prior to the little girl's discovery of sexual differences. The discussion of Deutsch's vignette of a dream analysis has served to exemplify this. The role of the pre-oedipal years and of the establishment of a feminine identity prior to the genital trauma has already been described by Jacobson, as cited in the foregoing section. Stoller (1976) has added his voice to those who posited a primary femininity (cf. Horney, 1933; Jones, 1961). He has presented experimental data and infant observational data which suggest that a core gender identity'' develops first and is the central nexus around which masculinity and femininity gradually accrete'' (Stoller, 1976, p. 61).

Of the various recent psychoanalytic contributions to the study of narcissism, only the work of Kohut will be presented in detail. Kohut has been singled out because he offers the most radical departure from the traditional views and therefore requires the greatest explanation. Furthermore, his treatment approach, *in concert* with the conflict defense model, adds immeasurably to the understanding of narcissistic phenomena. Finally, Kernberg's recent presentations (1975, 1976) which consider narcissistic phenomena as defensive do not, per se, challenge the earlier assumptions of female psychosexual development. Kohut's view, however, demands a reexamination of the relationship between narcissism and female development.

Kohut's two major works (1971, 1977) offer somewhat different views on narcissistic development. However, what is common to both is that narcissism as a line of development relates to the evolution and maintenance of self structures and the cohesiveness of the self-representation.

The subsequent discussion will rely upon Stolorow's (1975) functional definition of narcissism and Kohut's (1977) more recent genetic and dynamic elaborations of the self—its bi-polar nature and the role of self objects.

According to Kohut's view, the developing child utilizes both parents as extensions of himself—usually the mother as a source of admiration and mirroring for exhibitionistic, grandiose fantasies and the father as a powerful ideal with whom to merge. The capacity of the mother to mirror empathically and the father to accept the idealization secures these two poles of the self-structure and enables the child eventually to convert the infantile grandiosity into functioning goals and ambitions and convert the infantile idealizations into functionally effective ideals. Relative failures in one pole, by one parent, may be compensated for by turning to the other parent as the requisite self object. Failures by both parents lead to vulnerabilities of the self-structure and defensive attempts to hide its weakness. In this case, self objects are predominant rather than occasional in mental life. In adulthood, failures of, disappointments in, or less than the required empathy from self objects expose the weakness of the self-structures, calling forth narcissistic mental activity in order to reestablish the structural cohesiveness, temporal stability and positive affective coloration of the self-representation. As Kohut (1977) indicated, ''in normal development, . . . self objects . . . are the precursors of psychological structures and transmuting internalizations of self objects leads gradually to the consolidation of the self'' (p. 83). As stated before, the structuralization process does not, per se, require a differentiation between male and female, but the content of the self that is to be maintained must eventually include a gender identity.

The "nuclear self" gains its content, its actions and the relationship between these two from an endowment which contributes a healthy assertion and joy and from requisite responses from self objects. Emphasis is placed on the bi-polar nature of the self, these poles being roughly coordinated with but not identical with the two parents.

When the child's healthy self-assertion fails to evoke a confirming mirroring response from (usually) the maternal self object, healthy exhibitionism is relinquished and a preoccupation with part objects (feces, penis, breast) takes place. Under these circumstances, nuclear grandiosity remains and is repressed, and its transformation to nuclear ambitions and goals is interfered with. On the other hand, adequate maternal ". . . mirroring acceptance confirms nuclear grandiosity; and holding and carrying allows merger experiences with the self object's idealized omnipotence" (Kohut, 1977, p. 179). The consolidation of nuclear ambitions is placed, by Kohut, between the second and the fourth year.

The transformation of nuclear grandiosity into ambitions is the same process through which the functions of the self object are transformed into a capacity for independent functioning. From the side of the child's environment, this involves optimal gratification and frustration of the child's narcissistic needs. Or, put differently, the child's maintenance of the self objects for self-cohesion requires phase appropriate support and phase appropriate disappointments which, in turn, results in the accretion of self-structuralization. This process is referred to as "transmuting internalizations" (Kohut, 1971; 1977; Tolpin, 1971).

The most common pathway through which the bi-polar self gains a firm foundation is from the mother as the mirror for the child's exhibitionistic grandiosity to the father as an ideal with whose greatness and power the child can merge. However, the reverse and the utilization of one parent for both functions are possibilities which do not, per se, lead to a vulnerability of self-esteem. The customary sequence in which the child turns from mother to father as principle self object would have vastly different connotations for the father-son relationship than for the father-daughter relationship. Kohut places this phase somewhere between the fourth and sixth year, so that it overlaps with phallic, oedipal, latency development. The psychosexual content around which these issues may coalesce may markedly influence their outcome. The boy who attempts to merge with the father as a powerful masculine ideal may encounter a response different from his sister, whose wishes for merger with the powerful father are erotically tinged and contained in wishes to be admired for her beauty. From the standpoint of the developmentally expectable sequence, Kohut thus places the father in a pivotal position.

In the present attempt to offer a consolidation of the narcissistic development of the female child there have been three issues which have been touched upon and require further elaboration: (1) The role of the pre-oedipal mother-daughter relationship, (2) the role of the psychosexual phases and "penis envy," (3) the role of the father as an "ideal" and idealization.

ELABORATIONS

The Role of the Preoedipal Mother-Daughter Relationship

The effect of the early mother-daughter relationship on subsequent narcissistic development has been considered from two viewpoints — through the discussion of Deutsch's case and Kohut's references. Kohut has emphasized the mother's empathic responsiveness, her mirroring, self-esteem enhancing acceptance of the child's grandiose, exhibitionistic strivings. This enables the child to retain the mother as a self object, gradually to be internalized, and transmuted as psychic structure into a sense of self-cohesion and self-esteem. According to Kohut (1977):

> The mother responds to the child as if he had already built up a cohesive self. Maternal responses anticipate the consolidation of the baby's self—the mother imagines it to be more consolidated than it actually is; or in different terms, the mother, by being ahead of the child's actual development, does experience the joy of furthering this development by her own expectations (pp. 26–27).

The summary of the literature on the psychology of the female by Barglow and Schaefer (1976) emphasizes the effect of genital differences on the mother's reactions and responsiveness. Considering developmental, maturational and biological factors, Barglow and Schaefer propose that the infant boy's greater physical aggressiveness, his tendency toward more movement in space, and his greater size may make him more difficult to soothe and might thus shorten his symbiosis, as compared to the infant girl. They further suggest that the girl is able to retain the mother-infant symbiosis longer than does the boy and that she benefits from the lesser strain she puts on the mother's empathic capacity. Highlighted here is the importance of the task of separating while retaining the benefits of having undergone a successful symbiotic phase. Deutsch's patient resolved this dilemma by sacrificing strivings for separation through her dependency and submissiveness.

The analysis of Judith, a recently treated thirty-year-old woman, revealed that her narcissistic vulnerability was based on a specific failure in separation from her mother. Clearly, for her, masochistic attachments had a narcissistic function in that they served to maintain a particular self-representation. Only this aspect of her treatment will be described.

Judith sought analytic therapy after having suffered through two marriages and two divorces and a number of similarly patterned masochistic relationships in which she was excessively submissive. Her father had been killed in an automobile accident when she was two years old, and her mother quickly returned to the home of her parents. These grandparents then supported both mother and daughter. Judith's mother never worked or cared for her daughter but essentially spent her time in bars. The grandmother cooked while the grandfather, a violent man, worked. Judith was verbally and physically abused by all three adults, and on many occasions she was threatened with abandonment in an orphanage.

Judith's persistent fear of abandonment as well as her rage at and disappointment in her mother interfered with the process of differentiation between her and her mother. Instead, Judith established a precocious independence from her mother. She left home after graduation from high school and, without family help, even against their advice, worked her way through college and a master's degree.

The nuclear pathology, a defect in the structure of the self-representation, was most evident in her inability to be alone and in her excessive submissiveness toward men. At times of stress, when she could not count on an ongoing relationship with a man, she was vulnerable to states of intense anxiety and depression with quasi-hallucinatory experiences in which the corners of her room appeared to be elongated. These distortions derived from a childhood fantasy of the "orphanage."

On the surface her relationships with men followed a similar pattern. She took care of them and nurtured them as she wished she had been taken care of. From the standpoint of identifications and object attachments, these relationships offered vicarious gratification (through identification with the cared for man) as well as clearly delineating a self-representation as "unlike" her mother. Her mother's derogation of men, her mother's vanity and inability to form any attachments were converted by Judith into an identity which required derogation of herself, idealization of men and a self-sacrificial stance toward them. Their needs were met with total acceptance, and she thus also found herself collaborating in ritualized, perverse sexual activity.

The analytic understanding of the perverse and masochistic trends as narcissistic attempts to bolster a vulnerable self-representation enabled Judith to relinquish the more blatant facets of her masochistic enactments.

While the masochism described in Deutsch's patient was essentially viewed as part of her feminine nature and was then reinterpreted as a compromise formation in an intrapsychic conflict, in the case of Judith, masochistic enactments were understood predominantly as serving a narcissistic function.

Judith's masochism was a consequence of a developmental arrest which left her self-representation insufficiently structured; through her masochistic submissiveness she maintained and consolidated a self-representation which was crucially different from the representation of her mother. Her precocious independence, and a life style that not only embodied her "non-need" for her mother but demonstrated her ability to be the mother to others, were built upon a self-representation embodying the "negative" of the qualities she saw in her mother. Self-esteem was thus vulnerably established but dependent upon and maintained by the utilization of needy men whose presence reassured her that she was "satisfying" and not "needy," self-sacrificing and not "vain," nurturing and not dependent.

In a further reinterpretation of the dream presented by Deutsch's patient, we might consider the narcissistic issues raised by the dream element, "I wanted him to notice me." We may question whether the dream was prompted by narcissistic injuries and if, as in the case of Judith, masochistic imagery may therefore be serving a restitutive, narcissistic function. Finally, we wish to emphasize that the masochistic pathology described and its narcissistic compensations are just that. Neither should be understood as part of the normal woman's femininity.

The Role of the Psychosexual Phases and "Penis Envy"

In discussing narcissistic development, we have suggested that what evolves is the child's representational world (Stolorow and Atwood, 1979)—from its archaic beginnings in self-object ties to its maturer forms of self-structures. With respect to this task of structuralization, sex differences influence the responsivity of the parents, the content of the structures (sexual identity) and the defenses and compensations for structural vulnerabilities.

When narcissism is viewed from the standpoint of the function that certain mental acts perform with respect to the maintenance, cohesion and affective coloration of the self-representation, then psychosexual development can be seen as contributing to the development of separated, articulated self and object representations. Conversely, the development of increasingly more articulated and complex self and object-representations can signal the attainment of psychosexual phases. This reciprocal interplay between psychosexual and representational development has been detailed elsewhere (Stolorow and Lachmann, 1980). For the present context, the utilization of psychosexual imagery, imagery derived from each of the psychosexual phases, and its relationship to representational development will be summarized.

Experiences and fantasies along the dimensions of orality can serve, on the one hand, to gratify clinging, nurturant wishes but, on the other hand, enhance the structuralization of self and object-representations by distinguishing between the rudimentary self as a container and the non-self as that which can be appropriated and taken in.

The utilization of oral phase derivatives to support a vulnerable self-representation is described in a case reported by Goldberg (1978). The patient frequently recalled her mother's manner of talking *about her* as a child (rather than talking *to her*), overfeeding her and dressing her in an unsuitable manner. The analyst eventually understood these communications as reflecting failures in empathy on the mother's part which left unsatisfied the need for mirroring from the maternal self object. Traumatic tension states were evoked by this lack of empathy and required the development of self-soothing mechanisms by the young girl. These included thumb sucking and thumb rubbing, tongue sucking and "fiddling" with a piece of her blouse. The patient's analyst then explains:

> The patient's compulsive "orality" can be understood as sexualization of the deficit in the self-object relationship. She turned to her own body as a substitute for the cohesion-promoting experiences her mother could not provide. (Goldberg, 1978, p. 234.)

Exemplified here is the erotization of self-soothing, that is, using behavior that is usually understood as a fixation or regression to orality in psychosexual development as a sexualized substitute to support or consolidate a vulnerable self-representation.

With respect to anal phase derivatives, Greenacre (1969) has pointed out that, for the girl, anatomical proximity of anus and vagina may cause anal sensations rather than clitoral sensations to promote the discovery of and exploration of the vagina. Thus, for the attainment of a self-representation with female genital features, anal sensations may be said to make a contribution. Anal fantasies and experiences provide an affirmation of the pleasures in self-control and release. Finally, the inclusion of genital features in the self-representation, though there may have been precursors, attains its full force upon the discovery of sexual differences.

As was indicated at the start of this chapter, Freud, Deutsch, and others chained together female development and narcissism. The "genital trauma" and the consequent "penis envy" were crucial links in that chain. Clearly, however, we must distinguish between the observations of "penis envy" reported by analysts and the meanings ascribed to those observations, as well as the role given such constructs in the psychology of women. Observations and descriptions of the reactions of young girls to the discovery of sexual differences have been reported by Mahler, Pine and Bergman (1975) and by Galenson and Roiphe (1976). The various reactions noted in young girls when they discover the differences between the sexes include "penis envy" and the blaming of the mother for the "castration." These observations are a matter of record. However, to assume, as was done by numerous psychoanalysts, that penis envy was a rock bottom fact of female development—a truth that had to be accepted by every woman lest she remain in a constant struggle against her femininity through protests of masculinity—is no longer tenable. "Castration fears" and "penis envy" are better understood as developmental stepping stones. They serve as organizers of experience at many levels of psychic differentiation and integration. Conversely, they may also signal that certain representational structures have been consolidated. The role of penis envy as a developmental achievement has been illustrated elsewhere (Lachmann, 1978; Stolorow and Lachmann, 1980). Two patients were compared with respect to the meaning of penis envy as it occurred in their respective treatments. For one woman, images and associations reflecting penis envy emerged as a result of developmental advances. When she began treatment, her psychopathology was understood as reflecting a symbiosislike merger with a "phallic" mother. Later, she produced dreams and fantasies in which she, and not her mother, possessed a penis. Finally, she relinquished the penis to men, with anger, regret and envy, but with the newly developed recognition of sexual differences. For another woman, penis envy served as a condensation of both gratifications and defenses against oedipally tinged fantasies.

Penis envy, like any fantasy formation, is subject to analysis in a variety of ways. It can be understood as a developmental metaphor, as Grossman and Stewart (1976) have suggested, as a defense in oedipal conflict, and as a signal of advances in representational differentiation and integration. Grossman and Stewart (1976) and Kohut (1977) have described re-analyses of three woman who, in their previous treatments, had their penis envy interpreted as a "central issue" or as a "hopeless yearning to acquire a penis." One re-analysis provided clinical evidence that what was previously interpreted as an "immutable wish" could be better, more accurately understood as a reflection of a conflict involving the patient's importance and value—expressed chiefly in terms of being a woman. For a second patient, penis envy served as a defense against castration fears in that the penis embodied an identification with the father as aggressor. For a third patient, the wish for a penis (and penis envy) was a "healthy" attempt to extricate herself from her mother's influence.

We can no longer maintain that a genital trauma, per se, explains female development and that the narcissistic displacements to compensate for this trauma and its attendant penis envy are central to femininity. We must take into account the effects of the "genital trauma" in that, as castration shock, it plays a direct role in psychosexual development and (oedipal) object relations. As a narcissistic trauma it affects separation from the maternal (self-) object and archaic grandiosity. Finally, it also prompts the turning to the father as a self object whose power and phallic grandeur are more readily idealizable.

The Role of the Father as an "Ideal" and Idealization

The contribution of penis envy toward the girl's identification with her father can be observed with particular clarity in the analyses of women with work or achievement related conflicts. Often, such patients have retained their father as a love object in an intense oedipal attachment akin to phallic worship or awe. Competition and eventual identification with the father's phallic assertive qualities are thereby precluded (cf. Jacobson, 1964). Specifically, the oedipal attachment to the father is so forcefully maintained, his phallic qualities so idealized, that he remains too charismatic a figure in the daughter's psychological life. These phallic qualities are often described in terms of "an ability to make one's way through the world" and are attributed exclusively to the father, stamped indelibly with his identity. During the course of the analysis of these patients, penis envy imagery can be understood as a diminution of the awe or worship, of the pathological idealization of the father. The shift from penis awe (Greenacre, 1969) to penis envy suggests that a parity between father and daughter, hitherto absent, could now be imagined, considered, wished for or demanded. Competitive aspirations, especially as they appear in the context of a previously pervasive idealizing transference, can thus be understood as signalling an increase in self-estimation. The developmental advances from awe to envy signal an increasing identification with the father—not with his penis, per se, but utilizing phallic, psychosexual imagery as a metaphor. Qualities embodied in the phallic imagery, which had been seen as the property of the analyst (or other father images) had given rise to hopeless feelings of insufficiency, could later be eyed enviously and be envisioned by these patients as qualities they too might acquire.

The case of Jane (Lachmann and Stolorow, 1976; Stolorow and Lachmann, 1980) highlights two themes: retention of and dependence upon the mother as a self object, and interference in the attempts to share in or acquire the father's idealized qualities.

Jane sought psychoanalytic treatment because of her "writing block." She voiced a number of complaints (vulnerability to trancelike dream states, excessive need for approval and acceptance from others, etc.) which upon analysis reflected the vulnerability of her self-representation and overreliance upon self objects.

From early childhood on, the overt relationship with the mother underwent remarkably little change. An intense attachment remained whereby Jane sought her mother's blessings and advice. Events would become "real" for Jane only upon telling them to her mother. The mother's presence was needed to validate her experience.

Jane's father took pride in his role as the powerful, sole financial provider of the family. He implicitly, and at certain times, explicitly, conveyed his belief that Jane (and her younger brother and mother as well) lacked the equipment to deal with the competitive world.

> An event that became a focal point for Jane's psychopathology occurred at age seven when she was sent to ballet class to "cure" her of her "overweight" and to give her "grace." She returned home from the class one day in her leotards and looked forward to showing her father how delicately she could float across the living room. When her father returned home that evening she immediately performed for him. He let slip the comment, "Nothing helps."
>
> The impact of this experience was profound. It accelerated a social withdrawal with trancelike fantasy states used as a buffer against both realistic success and anticipated failure. Her exhibitionistic, narcissistic urges were depleted by the traumatic disappointment interfering with her self-esteem regulation, while grandiose expectations were repressed. The experience served to strengthen the regressive tie to the mother, while an implicit "contract" was made with the father: she would suppress all evidence of anger, disappointment, criticism, or general displeasure with him if he would refrain from verbalizing how disappointed he was with her appearance. (Lachmann and Stolorow, 1976, pp. 68–69).

As a result of this contract the father's idealized qualities were never to be challenged. Further, they were to remain his property. Jane's attachment to her mother embodied the need to maintain the mother as a self object, to retain a sense of self cohesion and self-esteem. Attempts to find a gleam in her father's eye which would signal an acceptance of her and offer a reparative alternative were met with rebuff. This led to a sense of hopelessness and futility about becoming a center of independent initiative and an independent recipient of impressions (Kohut, 1977). Archaic grandiose fantasies were left intact.

The establishment in the analysis of a specific narcissistic transference enabled Jane to work through a crucial aspect of her writing block. During this phase of the analysis

> . . . she described a vignette from her work as a teacher: interviews with two of her students, both of whom were personally very troubled about their poor academic work. Against the background of her complaints about the lack of help she was getting in her analysis, she described the help she was able to give her students in a half-hour interview with each one. The analyst's response here required an assessment of the extent to which a narcissistic transference still held sway, because an empathic failure by the analyst might repeat the

"ballet" trauma in the treatment situation. The analyst therefore reflected back to Jane the pride and pleasure she took at having helped her students—and stopped at that. At a later point in treatment she was able to return to this incident and deal with the implicit competitive aspects (Lachmann and Stolorow, 1976, pp. 573–574).

Jane could thus use the analyst as a mirroring self object and could share in his idealized qualities. These developments preceded the analysis of the psychosexual derivatives, for example, competition, also contained in this material. The transformation of the arrested narcissistic configurations both as they appeared in the transference and as they were noted throughout her life was most clearly in evidence in the changes that occurred in the ability to write.

The opportunity to share in the analyst's idealized qualities and the later acknowledgment of Jane's competitiveness with him led to a specific identification with the analyst. More and more, Jane was able to use the process of analysis as a model for work. Gradually, she was able to rely upon herself to validate and evaluate her own experience. These developments came about through the maintenance of a stable transference which encompassed the need for empathic mirroring, the non-interference in the sharing of the analyst's idealized qualities, and the acknowledgment of competitive strivings which signalled Jane's readiness to own heretofore idealized qualities of the analyst as a father-image.

SUMMARY

The theory of narcissism and the study of the psychological development of the female child have both been subjects of considerable controversy within psychoanalysis. Some issues central to these controversies have been discussed and evaluated with attention to the contributions made by advances in each area upon the other.

From a historical perspective, Freud's illuminating introduction of the concept of narcissism opened the door toward explaining a variety of puzzling clinical phenomena. Later, Deutsch elaborated upon Freud's contribution as well as upon his specific bias in her description of the psychology of women. Hartmann and Jacobson refined the definition of narcissism, and later, Jacobson addressed herself to a reformulation of then existing views of female psychological development.

Kohut's innovative clinical observations and Stolorow's functional definition of narcissism provided a unique vantage point from which to offer a critical restatement of narcissistic factors in the development of the female child. Specifically, narcissism was freed from its singular relationship to female development (the emphasis on "castration shock" and penis envy as rock bottom factors in female character formation) and related to structuralization of the representational world-self and object representations. Sexual differences can then be understood as most relevent for the content of these structures. In this context, the work of Stoller was cited.

Finally, three topics were considered with respect to the implications of the foregoing discussions: the role of the pre-oedipal mother–daughter relationship, the role of the psychosexual phases and an evaluation of "penis envy," and the role of the father as an "ideal" and idealization.

The reciprocal relationship between psychosexual development and the differentiation, integration and consolidation of self and object images has specific relevance for the manner in which femininity as the content of the self representation of the developing girl enhances and is enhanced by the structuralization of the representations. The unfolding of the psychosexual phases with their associated imagery can be viewed as the gradual unfolding of more complex, differentiated and articulated self and object representations. Conversely, the gradual separation, integration and consolidation of self and object representations makes possible the development of increasingly more advanced forms of psychosexual experiences. Thus, the original question of the relationship between narcissism and female development has led to much broader issues. Narcissism concerns the structuralization and maintenance of the self-representation. However, while narcissistic activities may promote structuralization, they may also serve to shore up a precarious sense of gender identity.

ACKNOWLEDGMENT

I am most indebted to Drs. Barbara Claster, James Fosshage, Lloyd Silverman, Robert D. Stolorow, and Ms. Phyllis Perrera for their critical reading of this chapter and for their helpful comments and suggestions.

REFERENCES

Barglow, P., and Schaefer, M. (1976). A new female psychology? *J. Amer. Psychoanal. Assn. Supplement–Female Psychology* 24:305–350.
Bergmann, M. (1969). Personal Communication.
Bonaparte, M. (1953). *Female Sexuality*. New York: International Universities Press.
Deutsch, H. (1930). The significance of masochism in the mental life of women. In *The Psycho-Analytic Reader*, ed. R. Fliess. New York: International Universities Press, 1948, pp. 195–207.
—— (1944–1945). *The Psychology of Women*, vols. I and II. New York: Grune and Stratton.

Fliegel, Z. (1973). Feminine psychosexual development in Freudian theory: A historical reconstruction. *Psychoanal. Q.* 42:385–408.

Fliess, R. (1948). An ontogenetic table. In *The Psycho-Analytic Reader,* ed. R. Fliess. New York: International Universities Press, pp. 254–255

Freud, S. (1908). On the sexual theories of children. *Standard Edition* 9:209–226. London: Hogarth Press, 1959.

―――― (1914). On narcissism: an introduction. *Standard Edition* 14:69–102. London: Hogarth Press, 1957.

―――― (1917). On the transformation of instincts, as exemplified in anal eroticism. *Standard Edition* 17:125–133. London: Hogarth Press, 1955.

―――― (1925). Some psychical consequences of the anatomical distinction between the sexes. *Standard Edition* 19:248–258. London: Hogarth Press, 1961.

―――― (1931). Female sexuality. *Standard Edition* 21:225–43. London: Hogarth Press, 1961.

―――― (1933). New introductory lectures on psycho-analysis. *Standard Edition* 22:7–182. London: Hogarth Press, 1964.

Galenson, E., and Roiphe, H. (1976). Some suggested revisions concerning early female development. *J. Amer. Psychoanal. Assn. Supplement–Female Psychology* 24:29–58.

Goldberg, A. (1975). A fresh look at perverse behavior. *Int. J. Psycho-Anal.* 56:335–342.

Goldberg, A., ed. (1978). *The Psychology of the Self: A Casebook.* New York: International Universities Press.

Greenacre, P. (1969). *Trauma, Growth, and Personality.* New York: International Universities Press.

Grossman, W., and Stewart, W. (1976). Penis envy: from childhood wish to developmental metaphor. *J. Amer. Psychoanal. Assn. Supplement-Female Psychology* 24:193–212.

Hartmann, H. (1950). Comments on the psychoanalytic theory of the ego. *The Psychoanalytic Study of the Child 5:74–96.* New York: International Universities Press.

―――― (1964). *Essays on Ego Psychology.* New York: International Universities Press.

Horney, K. (1933). The denial of the vagina. Contribution to the problem of the genital anxieties specific to women. *Int. J. Psycho-Anal.* 14:57–70.

Jacobson, E. (1964). *The Self and the Object World.* New York: International Universities Press.

Jones, E. (1955). *The Life and Work of Sigmund Freud,* vol. II. New York: Basic Books.

―――― (1961). *Papers on Psychoanalysis.* Boston: Beacon Press.

Kernberg, O. (1975). *Borderline Conditions and Pathological Narcissism.* New York: Aronson.

―――― (1976). *Object Relations Theory and Clinical Psychoanalysis.* New York: Aronson.

Kohut, H. (1971). *The Analysis of the Self.* New York: International Universities Press.

―――― (1977). *The Restoration of the Self.* New York: International Universities Press.

――――, and Wolf, E. (1978). The Disorders of the self and their treatment: an outline. *Int. J. Psycho-Anal.* 59:413–426.

Lachmann, F. (1975). Homosexuality: some diagnostic perspectives and dynamic considerations. *Amer. J. Psychotherapy* 29:254–260.

―――― (1978). Sexual fantasy and perverse activity: developmental considerations and treatment implications. Paper presented at meeting of Israel Psychoanalytic Society, April 1978, Tel-Aviv, Israel.

――――, and Stolorow, R. (1976). Idealization and grandiosity: developmental considerations and treatment implications. *Psychoanal. Q.* 45:565–587.

Laplanche, J., and Pontalis, J.-B. (1973), *The Language of Psycho-Analysis.* New York: Norton.

Mahler, M., Pine, F., and Bergman, A. (1975). *The Psychological Birth of the Human Infant.* New York: Basic Books.

Pulver, S. (1970). Narcissism: the term and the concept. *J. Amer. Psychoanal. Assn.* 18:319–441.

Reich, A. (1973). *Psychoanalytic Contributions.* New York: International Universities Press.

Ross, N. (1970). The primacy of genitality in the light of ego psychology. *J. Amer. Psychoanal. Assn.* 18:267–284.

Schafer, R. (1974). Problems in Freud's psychology of women. *J. Amer. Psychoanal. Assn.* 22:459–485.

Stoller, R. (1976). Primary femininity. *J. Amer. Psychoanal. Assn. Supplement-Female Psychology* 24:59–78.

Stolorow, R. (1975a). Toward a functional definition of narcissism. *Int. J. Psycho-Anal.* 56:179–185.

——— (1975b). The narcissistic function of masochism (and sadism). *Int. J. Psycho-Anal.* 56:441–448.

———, and Atwood, G. (1979). *Faces in a Cloud—Subjectivity in Personality Theory.* New York: Aronson.

———, and Lachmann, F. (1980). *The Psychoanalytic Theory and Therapy of Developmental Arrests.* New York: International Universities Press

Tolpin, M. (1971). On the beginnings of a cohesive self: an application of the concept of transmuting internalization to the study of the transitional object and signal anxiety. *The Psychoanalytic Study of the Child* 26:316–354. New Haven: Yale University Press.

Waelder, R. (1936). The principle of multiple function: observations on over-determination. *Psychoanal. Q.* 5:45–62.

Wimpfheimer, M., and Schafer, R. (1977). Psychoanalytic methodology in Helene Deutsch's *The Psychology of Women. Psychoanal. Q.* 46:287–318.

Index